CREED & CULTURE II

CREED & CULTURE II

A Touchstone *Reader*
1998 – 2011

EDITED BY
James M. Kushiner

ST. JAMES PRESS

CHICAGO, ILLINOIS

2022

Cataloging-in-Publication Data:

Creed & Culture II: A Touchstone Reader / edited by James M. Kushiner. —
    Chicago, Illinois : The Fellowship of St. James. c2022.

            p. ; cm.
    Essays originally published in Touchstone magazine.

    ISBN 978-0-578-25998-7
            1. Christianity. 2. Christian life. 3. Christian literature. 4. Essays.
    I. Kushiner, James M.   II. Creed & Culture 2.   III. Title: Touchstone

Published in the United States by:

    The Fellowship of St. James
    P. O. Box 410788
    Chicago, Illinois 60641

Dedicated to
Leon J. and Mary Elizabeth Podles

CONTENTS

Contents

JAMES M. KUSHINER

Creed & Culture II

Introduction

Our first volume of *Creed & Culture: A* Touchstone *Reader* was published in 2003 by ISI Books (Wilmington, Delaware). It was a harvest of first fruits, so to speak, comprising twenty-one essays selected by the senior editors as the best from *Touchstone's* first decade. For its first ten years, *Touchstone* was a small quarterly journal that had begun as a newsletter in 1986. During those formative years, it grew and matured, largely through the encouragement and generous support of friends and donors, but especially from the writers who so generously contributed articles to *Touchstone*. Many of these writers, whose essays were included in *Creed & Culture*, continued as senior editors.

Touchstone published its 30th volume in 2017, and it is well past time to publish *Creed & Culture II*. This new collection, unlike its predecessor, is not a compilation of "best essays," for that would have been too difficult to determine, given the much larger number of essays published since 1998, when *Touchstone* went from a quarterly to a bimonthly (six issues per year) publication, and for six years (2003–2009) produced ten issues per year. Instead, for this book, we selected eighteen representative essays from 1998 through 2011, the year *Touchstone* turned 25. All those who served as senior editors at some point during that period are represented in this volume, as are contributing editors Rod Dreher and William J. Tighe (who has since become a senior editor). Four essays by other authors round out the multicourse menu of *Creed & Culture II*.

Like each issue of *Touchstone*, this anthology has no single theme. Rather, it confirms the character of the journal, which is described on its masthead as "conservative in doctrine and eclectic in content, with editors and readers from each of the three great divisions of Christendom—Protestant, Catholic, and Orthodox." It is both ecumenical and eclectic.

But although there is no one theme to this collection, there is a shared conservative perspective, following *Touchstone*'s mission to provide "a place where Christians of various backgrounds can speak on the basis of shared belief in the fundamental doctrines of the faith as revealed in Holy Scripture and summarized in the ancient creeds of the Church." The editors view our world through the historical faith of the Church, and this volume presents their insights on a wide range of topics that are crucial for the Christian life today.

To highlight the fact that *Touchstone* often addresses contemporary issues from the perspective of Christian orthodoxy, in the spring of 2017 we added these words to our masthead: "To the confusion of voices in the world on matters of order in religious, social, and cultural life, it speaks with a unified voice of that which, manifest in creation and divine revelation, flows from the life of God himself." Our commitment is to a living orthodoxy that is, at the same time, faithful to tradition. Moreover, we believe the issues we take up are relevant to the life and unity of the Church today.

Touchstone's subtitle, *A Journal of Mere Christianity*, takes its cue, of course, from the work of C. S. Lewis, who wrote of the Church:

> It is at her centre, where her truest children dwell, that each communion is really closest to every other in spirit, if not in doctrine. And this suggests that at the centre of each there is a something, or a Someone, who against all divergences of belief, all differences of temperament, all memories of mutual persecution, speaks with the same voice.

That "Someone" is the source of our fellowship, and the Voice is that of Christ, the Good Shepherd. Lewis said as much again in 1947, when he wrote to a new Roman Catholic correspondent in Verona, Italy, Don Giovanni Calabria:

Common perils, common burdens, an almost universal hatred and contempt for the Flock of Christ can, by God's Grace, contribute much to the healing of our divisions. For those who suffer the same things from the same people for the same Person can scarcely not love each other. [English translation of the Latin original]

Lewis, who contended against rising secularism and deepening unbelief, would not be surprised by our current perils. He saw the unity of Christians even in his day as "sparks of hope in the darkness." *Touchstone* editors and readers heartily embrace, despite our differences, a love for the Lord that draws us together. I am assured that many *Touchstone* readers have found encouraging signs of such fellowship in its pages and have supported the journal as a welcome "spark of hope in the darkness."

May this volume of essays reflect such a hopeful fellowship and encourage readers in their Christian faith, as we all look together for the Lord's coming in everlasting glory.

—*James M. Kushiner*

ROBERT LOUIS WILKEN

Prayer & the Work of God

Reflections on the Daily Office & the Prayer of the Heart

I spent last spring living at Sant' Anselmo, a Benedictine house of stud-ies and monastery in Rome. It was not, as some of the younger monks from contemplative houses elsewhere reminded me, *un vero monastero,* a genuine monastery, because monks came from all over the world and would return to their home communities, and they were not under the discipline of the local abbot. But for this visitor from the United States it had enough of the rhythms of the monastic life and its practices (breakfast in silence, reading at the evening meal, praying the office in choir) to give me a feel for *un vero monastero.*

My reason for going was that I wanted to spend some time living, to use current sociological jargon, in a thicker Catholic culture than central Virginia. One thinks that in being received into full communion with the Catholic church one is being received into a large international fellowship extending to every corner of the earth. But what I discovered was that I had taken up residence in the diocese of Richmond—what a friend once called a missionary diocese. So you can perhaps appreciate why I felt a strong urge to spend some time in Rome. Though I am embarrassed to say that the second Sunday after I arrived I visited the local parish church in Testaccio, the neighborhood down the hill from Sant' Anselmo, and the first thing I heard on entering the church was the dispiriting sound of guitars warming up for the liturgy.

The chapel at Sant' Anselmo is a late nineteenth-century Byzantine revival building with a spacious choir for singing the office and a large semicircular domed apse. The monks allowed me to participate fully in their daily prayer and on cold winter mornings—there was no heat in the church; fortunately I had the prescience to pack long underwear—as I took my place in the choir stall I would look up at the apse mosaic. Christ was in the center and to the right stood St. Anselm and to the left St. Benedict, both bowing in adoration of the Risen Lord. Next to St. Benedict were written the words, "*Nihil operi Dei praeponatur,*" that is, "Let nothing take precedence over God's work."

The words come from Benedict's Rule and the work (*opus*) that is at the center of the monastic life is praying the divine office, the daily recitation of the psalms. It is this phrase, "*Nihil operi Dei praeponatur,*" that I would like to speak about for a few minutes this evening.

Work is not a term we are accustomed to use in referring to prayer, at least not in the non-monastic context. Perhaps obligation, responsibility, or from another perspective, "play." Liturgy is something we do for its own sake, for ends that are within the action itself, as in playing a game; liturgy is not instrumental. But the term *work* carries other connotations that are appropriate to the monastic context, and to daily prayer in the lives of the faithful outside the monastery. As the months passed and I contemplated Benedict's saying each day, I realized that here, as in many other things, St. Benedict had a profound insight into the Christian life.

One image can illustrate what I mean. Morning prayer was at 6:20 a.m. and a bell rang in the halls at 5:50. By 6:10 as I made my way to the church I would meet or pass monks scurrying to find their place in the choir or in one of the chapels in the cavernous building.

But before getting to my point perhaps I should say a bit about the daily schedule at Sant' Anselmo. The language of prayer in the house was Latin and the offices were sung in plainchant except for morning prayer. Pope Paul VI had charged the Benedictines with keeping alive the Latin office in Gregorian chant and Sant' Anselmo has taken on that responsibility as its own. But because the community of 120 monks is an international group, a few years back they decided to have daily morning prayer and weekday Mass in language groups (on Sundays they are in Latin). So each morning there is a Latin group, an Italian group, and French, German, and English groups for morning prayer and Mass.

The other offices are in Latin: midday prayer, which took place at 12:50 in the chapter room immediately before *pranzo* (which always began with pasta or risotto, meat or fish course, fruit—all accompanied by local white wine followed of course by a *riposo*); full sung vespers in the main chapel at 7:15, then *cena,* the evening meal with readings from the Rule and other books; and compline at 8:30 in the main church. I attended the Italian morning prayer and Mass in the church.

As the monks scurried about the building in the darkness of the early morning, thinking their own thoughts, I began to realize that "work" was the proper term to depict what they were about. They reminded me of workers walking silently in the cold morning darkness into a factory. The other image that comes to mind is that as the monks arrive in their stalls they busy themselves shuffling papers, opening books to the proper page, flattening out pages, putting in book marks—preparing, as it were, their tools for the task that is before them. The divine office requires a different kind of participation than the Mass, which can be done without a book in the hands of the faithful (something that has impressed me about Catholicism), and taking part requires preparation and organization.

But what made the deepest impression on me was the incessancy and regularity of the office. One of the monks there, Jeremy Driscoll (you may have seen his review of Aidan Nichols's *Looking at the Liturgy* in the May 1997 issue of *First Things*), is a poet. In one of his poems he speaks about his feelings as he stood in the chapel of his monastery (Mt. Angel in Oregon) on a hot August afternoon to pray the office all the while thinking of what others were doing to beat the heat:

> The monks chant their prayer in the hot church
> but their heart is not in it.
> Only their vows bring them here and keep them
> at the hot and useless task.
>
> Gone are the sweet first good days
> when prayer and singing came easy.
> Gone as well many brothers
> who used to stand here singing
>   the feasts with them.
> They know there are ways to beat this heat
> and that Americans everywhere are finding them
> but they beat instead the tones of psalms

and, by beating,
fall through the layers of heat
and the layers of prayer
and are standing there now
only with their sound
and their sweat
everything taken from them
except the way that this day in August has been.
(*Some Other Morning,* Brownsville, Oregon: Story Line Press, 1992)

It is easy to be romantic about monastic life until one sees it at close range. The permanence of it all is overwhelming to the mind. Day in and day out, week after week, month upon month, and year following year, the vocation of the monk is to be found at his place, organizing his books as he prepares his mind and heart for the work that is pleasing to God, the offering of himself in prayer.

At the beginning of the *Antiphonale,* the book of variable antiphons and hymns and prayers used at Sant' Anselmo, one can find a prayer to be recited before the office begins:

> *Aperi Domine os meum ad benedicendum nomen sanctum tuum: munda quoque cor meum ab omnibus vanis, perversis et alienis cogitationibus: intellectum illumina, affectum inflamma; ut digne, attente ac devote hoc officium recitare valeam, et exaudire merear ante conspectum divinae Majestastis tuae. Per Christum Dominum Nostrum qui vivit et regnat in unitate spiritus sancti per saecula saeculorum. Amen.*

> Open, Lord, my mouth to bless your holy name. Cleanse my heart from all idle, distorted, and unsuitable thoughts. Enlighten my intellect, set fire to my affections that worthily, attentively and faithfully I may be able to pray this office and that my prayer will be worthy of rising before your divine majesty. Through Jesus Christ. . . .

The phrases that stick in my mind are "*munda cor meum*" and "*affectum inflamma.*" Cleanse my heart from all distracting and foreign thought and kindle my affections, set fire to my heart. If the office is a work, one would perhaps expect the accent to be on "will" and the prayer to read, "strengthen my will for the task ahead," but it focuses on the heart and the mind.

On the first reading, "cleansing the heart" seems a far piece from "work," yet the work that St. Benedict was speaking about is prayer, and without the heart there can be no prayer pleasing to God. Some months back I began marking the verses in the psalms that mentioned the heart. Each day as I read the psalms appointed for that day I found myself underlining the term "heart" when it occurred. To my astonishment, "heart" occurs, I estimate, in fully half, maybe even two-thirds of the psalms. I have not done a statistical study, nor have I consulted a concordance. I wanted to find out the old-fashioned way, reading the psalms myself (so if there are any biblical scholars here you may be able to prove me wrong—but not by much). Here are a few examples chosen at random:

"My heart is firmly fixed, O God, my heart is fixed." (Ps. 57:7)

"I will give thanks to the Lord with my whole heart." (9:1)

"My heart shall rejoice in thy salvation." (13:5)

"I keep the Lord always before me. . . . Therefore my heart is glad, and my soul rejoices." (16:8–9)

"Let the words of my mouth and the meditation of my heart be acceptable in thy sight, O Lord, my rock and my redeemer." (19:14)

"Thou hast said, 'Seek ye my face.' My heart says to thee, 'Thy face, Lord, do I seek.'" (27:8)

"My heart became hot within me." (39:3)

"Create in me a clean heart, O God." (51:10)

"Blessed are the men whose strength is in thee, in whose heart are the highways to Zion." (84:5)

"Teach us to number our days that we may get a heart of wisdom." (90:12)

"I incline my heart to perform thy statutes." (119:112)

The activity of the heart even carries over into our sleep. "In the night my heart instructs me." (16:7) Some of you may know the compline hymn, "To thee before the close of day" in Latin: *Te Luci Ante Terminum*. Notice the beginning of the second stanza: *Te corda nostra somnient, te per soporem sentiant.* "Our hearts dream of you, they have you in mind while we sleep."

The heart is the organ of prayer, even when we are not conscious of what we are doing. Unlike the mind which is acquisitive, aggressive, critical, competitive, the distinctive mark of the heart is receptivity, openness, pliability—it is a place to be filled, a thing to be ignited. The mind receives on its own terms, always filtering, discriminating, judging, but the heart is patient; it waits, watches, listens, making space for what it is to receive. The heart thrives on stillness and quiet and delights not in its own cleverness but in the presence of the beloved.

Perhaps some of you know the little book by Caryll Houselander, *The Reed of God*. It was put in my hands by Robin Darling Young, my sponsor (in Italian, *la mia madrina*), when I was received into full communion. *The Reed of God* is a meditation on the Blessed Virgin Mary, specifically on her virginity. Virginity in the minds of many is associated with negative qualities, childlessness, barrenness, impotence, emptiness, but, says Houselander, virginity means an emptiness that is waiting to be filled. It is the emptiness of the Marian "fiat," "let it be done to me," of humility and obedience and patience. Mary's "fiat" is the voice of the heart. Houselander uses three images to speak of the heart that is waiting to be filled: the hollow in a reed whose narrow emptiness can have only one destiny, to receive the piper's breath and utter the song that is in his heart; the curve of the cup shaped to receive water or wine; the round warm ring of a bird's nest ready to receive the tiny egg.

Those who complain the loudest of the emptiness of their lives are often people whose lives are overcrowded and for whom "work" is the business of making admittedly laudable plans and carrying out the useful and necessary activities that occupy our days. What St. Benedict teaches us is that there is another work, far more important, far more enduring than what we call work: the quiet, patient, regular, repetitious, habitual work of cultivating the heart in prayer. St. Augustine says that the Christian life is a holy longing (*pium desiderium*), and just as a leather sack will stretch to make room for what we put in it, so the heart cultivated by the work of prayer stretches to make place for Christ's dwelling within us, or in the words of the first great Christian poet, Prudentius, the "privilege of entertaining the Holy Trinity" (*honorem Trinitatis hospitae*).

The work of prayer is tutoring the heart, a quite different work than training the mind or disciplining the will. The more one prays the psalms the more one realizes that one will not learn anything new. One knows the meaning of the words, the ideas are familiar, the historical allusions commonplace. Why then keep repeating them? We say them again and again so that their words can become our words, but more, that their feeling, their affections, their desires, can become our feelings, affections, and desires.

Prayer is an apprenticeship in keeping the first commandment, "You shall love the Lord your God with all your heart. . . ." It is a work without ending, as necessary to our inner life as the rhythm of breathing is for our physical life, and it occupies us for a lifetime and beyond.

St. Bernard comments on "I have hidden your words in my heart." "Keep God's words in this way. Let it enter into your very being, let it take possession of your desires and your life. Feed on goodness and your souls will delight in its richness. Remember to earn your bread in this way or your heart will wither away."

As for the Center for Catholic and Evangelical Theology, I can only remind you of the words of the great monastic writer, Evagrius: "A theologian is one who prays, and one who prays is a theologian." All our theological efforts, whether they be combating the forces of secularism in our society, or contesting apostasy within the church, will be in vain if we are not men and women of prayer, whose hearts are filled with yearning for the living God, and whose lives display the inner peace that comes from daily intercourse with the Father, Son, and Holy Spirit.

Reprinted from Touchstone: A Journal of Mere Christianity, *May/June 1998, Volume 11, Number 3. It was originally given as an address (titled "Opus Dei") by the author, June 2, 1997, for the Sixth Annual Banquet of the Center for Catholic and Evangelical Theology and was printed in* A Report from the Center, *Summer 1997.*

S. M. HUTCHENS

The Fairy-Tale God

Truth & Deceit in Children's Fiction

My girls are no longer young, but when they were, I paid some attention to the children's books they brought home from the library. Martha and Laura had orthodox tastes, and no interest in anything weirder than Dr. Seuss. Every now and then, however, they would bring home something that struck me as more than odd, but bad, and on rarer occasions more than bad, but genuinely evil. I began to keep my eyes open.

When I began to work as a librarian, cover art and titles of children's books that looked a bit "off" attracted my attention. So did the popular literature of professional librarianship, which indicated that there was deep moral sickness in the library world. Marian the Librarian, it turned out, was a very accurate stereotype of a person all too common in the libraries: the modestly educated libertine with a firm belief in her intellectual superiority and zeal to enlighten the local clodhoppers to the point where they can recognize it.

Marian has come into her own in our day, and she is going after the bourgeois prigs in River City with a vengeance. Exposing the village children to Rabelais and Balzac is no longer enough. She is now on to everything that Michael and Diane Medved have said, in *Saving Childhood*, corrupts the happiness of innocence. The American Library Association, Marian's political arm, in league with the ACLU and the like, is fighting and winning major court battles against a community's right to filter its public library's Internet connection, and thus is making everything imaginable, and some things that aren't, available to every patron who can operate a computer. Vigilant parents can protect young children from Internet pornography to approximately the same degree they could from dirty pictures that got handed around the playground in the old days, which is to say, some, but not completely. Such things have always been in the world, and innocence is still its own best protection. People don't get corrupted unless they wish to be.

I am concerned here with something more subtle, something that encourages despair more than lust, and is more difficult to detect and fend off. I refer to the numerous attempts by modern tellers of tales to impress into children's minds stories that are what Lewis's *hrossa* called "bent"—twisted accounts of what is and what should be—and to convince those who read them to children that these stories are just the things they ought to hear. Stories are images of reality that invite participation of the hearer's imagination. They have an attractive power that invites us to take part in them, to find our places in the story's world. Bent stories are bad places to wander into, for, made as they are from stolen bits of heaven, they hold out the promise of something good, but subject the imagination, once it is captured, to the philosophy of hell.

TALES FOR OUR TIME

Several months ago while browsing in the bookstore Half Price Books, I found an interesting collection of stories that I decided on the spot was indeed worth half price, and bought it, mostly on the basis of its fascinating title and cover illustration. On the cover of *The Outspoken Princess and the Gentle Knight* is a little girl with firmly planted feet, right arm akimbo, and in her left hand a golden sword. Bowing humbly at her feet is a king whose own sword has been placed on the ground. (This is one tough kid, who obviously never learned that only boys carry swords.) The editor, Jack Zipes, was at the time of publication a professor of German at the University of Minnesota, whose books include *Fairy Tales and the Art of Subversion* and *Don't Bet on the Prince: Contemporary Feminist Fairy Tales in North America and England*.

In the introduction, Professor Zipes tells us that there are problems with the magic of the traditional fairy-tale collections. We don't "pause to think that many of the tales that have become part of the classical canon like 'Snow White,' 'Sleeping Beauty,' and 'Cinderella' may have dubious messages when it comes to the depiction of gender roles, violence, and democracy."

"Since," he says, "we tend to internalize the values we were exposed to as children without seriously questioning them, there is a danger that we may perpetuate the cultural and political messages of traditional fairy tales rather than seek out tales more appropriate to the social temper of our times."

Up until relatively recently similar tales continued to "provide glimpses of happy heterosexual marriages, stable class systems, and successful heroes with wealth and power that may have been satisfactory for patriarchal world orders, but they offer very little hope for change in view of present day conditions and upheavals." In other words, what is both right and possible for the imagination changes with the times. Its life should mutate to reflect as much hope for happiness as the times permit, and in accordance with the wisdom of the new age. Fairy tales, says Professor Zipes, reflect utopia, a place we envision in our dreams. It constantly shifts its shape and meaning, depending on the real conditions of our society.

With an introduction so philosophically shallow and morally perverse (as though there were no perduring desires of the human heart, as though some utopias aren't dreams of terror, as though we must bow to "progress"), you can imagine what I expected to find in this book. What was actually there, however, surprised me, and brought me to wonder whether it is in fact very easy to "bend" a tale in accordance with the editor's belief that societal changes could and should affect what the imagination craves. If fathers are in short supply in the ghetto, and whole marriages are rare in the suburbs, does this mean that children, directed by radical scholars, can or should quit entertaining the imagination of strong kings who reign with their queens, who love them and destroy what threatens them? To be sure, there were what appeared to be a number of attempts to do that kind of thing here, and some got the message across quite clearly. But others didn't seem to work too well—and some of the tales selected by the editor, apparently on the basis that they were counter-cultural, drifted against the culture in very good ways. One expected an entirely bad show; what turned up in fact was a very mixed bag.

EVADING WOLVES

In *The Uses of Enchantment*, Bruno Bettelheim observes that "Little Red Riding Hood" has helped children, girls in particular, come to grips with their fears of danger in the real world, particularly that presented by the sexual predator who will certainly eat her up, as it were, if he is given the chance, and yet has given hope and comfort to even those who have been "eaten" that there is a redeemer—a huntsman—who has the power to slay the wolf and set them free. Here is, that is to say, an encapsulated story of sin and redemption of great sophistication and symbolic depth, combined with a valuable cautionary tale.

Witness in contrast Catherine Storr's contribution to the Zipes anthology, "Little Polly Riding Hood." Polly doesn't live in a forest. Hardly anybody does anymore, you know. She lives in the middle of a big city. There is a wolf there, and he is interested in having Polly for dinner, but he is an effete and bumbling anachronism. Polly regularly escapes him by such clever ploys as taking the bus, on which he can't follow her because he hasn't any money, or having her father drive her to grandma's. After numerous rebuffs to the wolf, the tale ends this way:

> "Bother, bother, bother, and *bother!*" said the wolf. "It hasn't worked out right this time either. And I did just what it said in the book. Why can't I ever get you, Polly, when that other wolf managed to get his little girl?" "Because this isn't a fairy story," said Polly, "and I'm not Little Red Riding Hood. I am Polly, and I can always escape from you, Wolf, however much you try to catch me." "Clever Polly," said Polly's grandma. And the Wolf went growling away.

And that's that.

So the child reading this story is assured that there are not any real wolves in big cities, but even if there were, they can be escaped with ease. And why? "Because I am Polly," says the child. Clever author. As for myself, I will confess that in my own perverse moments I have been tempted to commend "Little Polly Riding Hood" to whomever it interests, since any brat who finds the story appealing will be eliminated in due course by the wolves, and won't likely be missed.

THE GENTLE KNIGHT & THE FAITHFUL BULL

Richard Schickel's "The Gentle Knight" is about a nineties-kind-of-knight named Freddy who is more interested in reciting poetry than slaying dragons. Because of his station, however, he is expected by his people to do his draconicidal duty. A dragon is allegedly terrorizing the land, and Sir Freddy is dispatched to deal with it. He finds the dragon at the edge of a precipice, ready to leap over and end it all, since he is so lonely. The dragon, named Charley, is, as the reader fully expects by now, as harmless as the above-mentioned wolf, has never killed anyone, and breathes fire because of his irresistible craving for hot pepper seeds. He is a polite listener to Freddy's poetry, and turns out to be a good companion. No, it is not a gay tale, for Freddy eventually finds a princess and marries her. He and the dragon save her from a lowbrow creature called the Huff by outsmarting it—no violence is necessary. They and the dragon become traveling players who eventually end up in Freddy's old fiefdom, where the townspeople, who in Freddy's absence have undergone a conversion to a more liberal frame of mind, urge them to stay. They do, and live happily ever after.

Well, that's nice, isn't it? As in the case of Polly and her idiotic wolf, there is no real danger in the world for which the shedding of blood might be necessary. This is, of course, the anti-Christian aspect of stories written from the privileged standpoint of those who can't imagine anything serious enough to kill or be killed for. The redemption of the world is in Niceness, give peace a chance, and phooey, phooey, phooey, on anyone who thinks otherwise. Other than that, the story's main fault is that it is boring. I can't imagine any red-blooded boy who would want to hear this one twice, since he knows perfectly well that dragons are wicked and must die. Killing them is the most adventurous and satisfying work a man can do. Every normal boy—even the boy who likes poetry—wants to grow up to be a dragon-slayer, and will be, unless he is first captured and emasculated by his enemies.

Ernest Hemingway's "The Faithful Bull" is an odd but touching little story of a bull who, entirely in character for a bull—and for Hemingway— loved to fight. "Anything made him want to fight and he would fight with deadly seriousness exactly as some people read or go to church. . . . He was not a bully nor was he wicked, but he liked to fight as men might like to sing or be the King or the President. . . . Fighting was his obligation and his duty and his joy." His owner was a good man and wanted to keep this vigorous blood in his herd, so he did not sell the bull to the ring, but put him out to stud. Now here is the strange turn: the good bull, while remaining a fighting bull, becomes like a good man. He is not interested in serving the whole herd, but falls in love with a single cow and is faithful to her. This makes him useless to his owner, who reluctantly sells him to the ring, where he is killed. Hemingway has created a Christian knight—a Christ figure, in fact—who can be beloved of men and women. Perhaps he appears in this book because it is thought that in patriarchal literature the promiscuous man is glorified. Well, in some of it he is, but the Christian hero, like Hemingway's good bull, is chaste.

GENDER BENDERS

Sexual stereotyping—the wrongness of—is a major theme in these stories. I am not quick to write off stereotypes, for many of these are based on truths that the characterized find unpalatable. (When St. Paul called the Cretans lazy gluttons, he wisely defended it by a frank citation from one of their own poets.) What is known and admitted within a stereotyped group takes on another flavor when it comes from outside, but this does not eliminate whatever truth might lie behind the stereotype. The rules that stereotypes imply, however, have exceptions, and truth is served by pointing them out. Witness "The Wrestling Princess" by Judy Corbalis.

At first stop, it appears just another one of the I-Am-Woman-Hear-Me-Roar stories. The heroine is a princess, homely but strong, who isn't interested in girl-things, but likes to wrestle and work on forklift trucks. She is very good at both, and beats out all the men she faces in contests of skill and strength. OK, OK, one says to oneself, here is another feminist entertaining herself with luscious improbabilities—a woman who excels in physical strength and mechanical aptitude, two areas in which men in general are measurably superior to women in general. This doesn't rule out strong women mechanics, of course, for there are a few of them out there. But those with a better grip on the shape of reality know that in contests of the sort wrestling princesses favor, the woman will soon enough get beat by a man. And they might question the intelligence and kindness of those who encourage little women to beat men at their own games.

But lo, the wrestling princess meets her prince—a king's son, to be sure, but one who prefers being a helicopter mechanic to sitting around the court, and who adoringly says of her, "When I saw the Princess Ermyntrude, I fell instantly in love with her. She had axle grease on her neck and she was so big and strong. . . . Then when I saw her pulling faces and shouting insults and throwing princes on the ground, I knew she was the one person I could fall in love with." "Really?" said the princess. "Truly," said Prince Florizel. "Now, come and see my mechanical digger." To each his own. There are Ermyntrudes out there, and one would like to think there is a Florizel for each of them.

BENT TALES

Of the fifteen authors in this book, only two, I think, have been successful in producing truly bent stories. One is Dov Mir, who has managed to blend hatred of parental authority with feminism and socialism in his horrid but philosophically coherent tale "The Outspoken Princess." In fact, he is particularly successful, I think, in showing the connection between childhood rebellion, feminism, and socialist democracy. I am not going to go into detail on this one, but instead mention briefly the one other story here that successfully gives the patina of innocence to something evil— "Petronella," by Jay Williams.

This is a simple tale. Instead of the fairy tale's traditional third son who goes out questing in the world, a king was disappointed to have a daughter as his third child. She refused to stay at home like a proper princess and went adventuring in the world just like her two older brothers. By doing an act of kindness for an old man (the sort men never think of doing), she was told there was a prince to win from the grip of a sorcerer in the dark wood before her. Determined to liberate the prince, she faced the sorcerer, who gave her three tasks—to stay one whole night with his dogs, then another with his horses, then another with his hawks—all vicious creatures. She evaded death by acts of patience, kindness, and sensitivity. The prince she came to rescue turned out to be a spoiled, self-absorbed rich boy in whom the princess had no interest. The sorcerer, on the other hand, was the kind of man she wanted—evil and cruel, perhaps—but bright, accomplished, and interesting. She picked him, and off they rode into the sunset.

Of course the princess seeking the prince instead of the other way around is a reversal of the old order. Intensifying this and overturning to the highest degree, however, is the depiction of the prince as a worthless prize, and the sorcerer as the princess's true consort. In one deft and rather soft stroke, Williams has turned the world of enchantment upside down, substituting good for evil and evil for good. He could not *break* the story in that he could not come up with an entirely novel *dramatis personae*, nor could he alter its basic form. But within the form and the cast of characters, he overthrew its good and put evil in its place.

THE PRIMORDIAL STORY

If history, broadly defined, is all that has happened as it may concern man, then Scripture, even though it begins at the beginning and ends at the end, is not, strictly speaking, an account of history. From the standpoint of history, broadly defined, it is the chauvinistic account of the world as it concerns the Jews, whose peculiar gift is that they have been chosen to be the people at the world's defining center. All other histories are ancillary to this one, finding their ultimate meaning only in their relationship to the Jews. Zion is a hill that must draw all nations to itself, and those nations must bear tribute when they come. Part of that tribute is the confession that this nation is beloved above all, and that our own reconciliation to God can only come about through reconciliation with the Jews.

Christians believe that the Jews have given us *the* story, not just any story, but the canonical one, the defining one, the right one, the story told them about the world and about themselves by God, as God wants it understood. Whatever else we might find out about history we are expected to bring as tribute to this story, to receive its meaning from it. The story is that in the beginning, God made the world and all that is in it, including man, who was made good, but fell. He fell so far that God narrowed humanity to a single man and his family by killing the rest, and perfected that narrowing further by the calling of Abraham. In this calling was the non-calling of everyone else, and the necessity that the rest of the world seek its salvation through the Jew. Salvation is of the Jews, who themselves disappointed God by killing the prophets and stoning the righteous men who were sent to them. Finally God sent his own Son, and the man who was closest to him told his story in terms of creation:

> In the beginning was the Word, and the Word was with God, and the Word was God. The same was in the beginning with God. All things were made by him, and without him was not anything made that was made. In him was life, and the life was the light of men. And the light shone in the darkness and the darkness did not comprehend it. . . . He came to his own, and his own received him not, but as many as received him, to them gave he the power to become children of God, even to them

who believe on his name, who were begotten not of blood, nor of the will of the flesh, nor the will of man, but of God. (John 1:1–5,11–13)

There is another way to tell this same story:

> Once upon a time there was a handsome king's son who was in love with a beautiful princess. The princess, through her own foolishness, had been captured by a wicked sorcerer, cast into a drugged sleep, and imprisoned in his keep. The prince left his father's palace disguised as a commoner and set out to rescue her. The sorcerer was very strong and harmed the prince dreadfully, so that he was taken up for dead. But he was cured of his wounds by ancient magic against which the sorcerer had no power, and, subduing the sorcerer and his minions, he rescued the princess, whom he took back with him to his kingdom where they lived happily ever after.

There are many variations on this story, of course, and many other stories are coherent fragments of this one. It is a story that has been used mightily to awaken the imagination and stimulate holy desire in places where "religion" does not go. The principal point I am making here about it, though, is that it is not *a* story, but *The* Story. It is normative, the Zion of all stories, and draws all others to it. Because it has its foundations in the foundations of the world, it will not go away. It has made the world and will end it.

This means that the child in the ghetto can lawfully dream of her strong and loving king no matter what society does and no matter what smart people tell her about her prospects. It means the miserable and broken child of divorce may imagine in hope the faithful prince who, like the faithful bull, always loves his princess and no other, and that happily ever after means just that. It means the good fairy tales are good because God wrote them, and that the children are perfectly free to forget the ugly, stupid ones, since, quite contrary to what the wicked professors say, they aren't true.

Reprinted from Touchstone: A Journal of Mere Christianity, *November/December 1999, Volume 12, Number 6. "The Fairy-Tale God" was originally presented as a lecture sponsored by the Fellowship of St. James in Chicago on February 25, 1999.*

ROBERT P. GEORGE

Disinheriting the Wind

A Closer Look at the Scopes Trial

The widely misreported and misunderstood decision of the Kansas Board of Education not to require the teaching of the theory of evolution has, predictably, revived memories of the banning of such teaching in public schools by the state of Tennessee, leading to the infamous Scopes "monkey" trial of 1925. Whether or not the creation stories recorded in the Book of Genesis are best understood as myths, the account of the Scopes trial promoted by liberal social commentators and moviemakers is mostly mythical. The core of the myth is that Clarence Darrow, representing enlightenment, humanity, and intellectual freedom, made a monkey out of William Jennings Bryan and the other "boobs and bigots," as H. L. Mencken dubbed them, who sought to keep the children of Tennessee yoked to ignorance and superstition. The facts, as the self-designated enlightened are fond of saying in other contexts, are "more complicated."

TEXTBOOK EXAMPLES

In 1857, two years before Charles Darwin published *On the Origin of Species,* Professor Asa Gray of Harvard, one of America's foremost botanists, published a high-school textbook entitled *First Lessons in Botany.* He said, in that work, that "the Creator established a definite number of species at the beginning, which have continued by propagation, each after its kind." In that same year, however, Charles Darwin outlined his theory of evolution to Gray, soon making a convert of him. A few years later, Gray arranged for *On the Origin of Species* to be published in America and became one of the most influential defenders of Darwin's ideas. In 1887, when a new version of Gray's book was published under the title *Elements of Botany,* the role of the Creator was altered. Affirming "the tendency to variation which pervades all things," the text remarked that the "beautiful diversity of forms" was sufficient "to convince the thoughtful botanist that all are parts of one system, works of one hand, realizations in nature of the conception of one mind." As Edward J. Larson has observed in his 1997 book *Summer for the Gods: The Scopes Trial and America's Continuing Debate over Science and Religion,* "God still lies behind nature, but the secondary cause of evolution replaced his creative hand as the immediate instrument of speciation." (In what follows, I rely heavily on the account of the Scopes trial provided in Larson's splendid book.)

Gray's colleague at Harvard, Louis Agassiz, the leading American zoologist of his time, was unpersuaded by Darwin's arguments and never accepted his conclusions. While Agassiz also rejected biblical literalism, his textbook, *Principles of Zoology,* never revised its claim that "The records of the Bible, as well as human tradition, teach us that man and the animals associated with him were created by the word of God, and this truth is confirmed by the revelations of science, which unequivocally indicate the direct interventions of creative power."

By the 1880s, however, views like those held by Agassiz had gone the way of the dinosaurs, and textbooks like *Principles of Zoology* constituted nothing more than a kind of intellectual "fossil record" of the pre-Darwinian era. The generation of scientists trained after the publication of Darwin's ideas were committed evolutionists, and the textbooks they wrote for use in high schools and colleges fully reflected their commitment. While many of these scientists were Christians, their books tended to omit references to God or the Creator as the force behind evolution. Their accounts were fully "naturalistic" precisely in this sense.

These scientists did not shy away from teaching that man, too, was the product of evolution, having descended as a species from an ancestor common to all vertebrate animals by a process of natural selection, or "survival of the fittest." In a botany text published in 1903, Eliza F. Andrews taught that "the geological record shows that the simplest forms of life were the first to appear and from these all the higher forms were gradually evolved." The most influential biology text in the period leading up to the anti-evolutionist political agitation that reached a climax in the Scopes trial, George W. Hunter's *A Civic Biology,* published in 1918, cites the fossil record, spanning "millions of years," as evidence of the evolution of complex forms of life from simple forms, with man presented as the most complex form, and the Caucasian race as "finally, the highest type of all."

DARWINISM & PROGRESSIVE FUNDAMENTALISTS

Now, while Darwin was getting into, and soon dominating, the biological textbooks, some of his admirers were applying his theory to economic and other sociological issues. So-called social Darwinists defended more or less unregulated free-market ("laissez-faire") economics as the way to attain maximum productivity and efficiency. They invoked the notion of the survival of the fittest in opposing regulation of the terms and conditions of employment and other proposed social welfare policies. Industrialization was radically altering the social and economic conditions that had prevailed in America and was giving strong impetus to populist and progressive movements to bring government to bear to ameliorate the economic and social dislocations attendant upon rapid industrialization, and to protect the mass of unpropertied working people against exploitation.

These populist and progressive movements were strongly imbued with evangelical Christian religion. America's most notable progressive, a Nebraska politician named William Jennings Bryan, personified what one historian described as the "merger of Evangelicalism and progressivism." Born the year before the United States descended into Civil War, Bryan was deeply involved in a host of progressive causes before he became the leading national political figure in the conflict over teaching evolution. He fought for the national income tax, for example, as well as for women's suffrage and prohibition. According to William Allen White, Bryan "stood for as much of the idea of socialism as the American mind will confess to." At the same time, he shared the religious commitment and enthusiasm of his fellow progressive and anti-evolutionist, William Bell Riley, founder of the World's Christian Fundamentals Association (WCFA). Riley described Bryan as his "great co-laborer, the mightiest lay-leader associated with the fight against evolution."

In many respects, this fight was a classic progressive-era battle, pitting the interests, values, and beliefs of an elite against the interests, values, and beliefs, often religiously inspired or, at least, supported, of a populist movement. As Larson describes the pattern of progressive reform movements, they "first encourage others to bring their behavior voluntarily into line with some desired standard and then coerce laggards into conformity by force of law." According to historians of progressive reform Arthur Link and Richard McCormick, "a familiar scenario during the period was one in which progressives called upon public authorities to assume responsibility for interventions which voluntary organizations had begun." Drawing on the work of Link and McCormick, Larson concludes that "the anti-evolution crusade fits snugly into both the historical setting and the interventionist pattern outlined [by these scholars] for all progressive reform movements."

The idea that Bryan was a "liberal" for most of his life, and became a "conservative" later in the battle over evolution, does not hold water. Although Bryan, like many other evangelical progressives, became increasingly radicalized in the anti-evolution cause as more and more children became exposed to evolutionary ideas in classroom instruction, his "increasing preoccupation with Darwinism and evolution did not," according to biographer Lewis Koenig, "in any way curtail his promotion of political questions and reforms." In Larson's words, "the traditional picture painted by H. L. Mencken and Richard Hofstadter, of Bryan as a broken, seedy, and even reactionary figure during his anti-evolution years wilts under recent scholarship." Anti-evolutionism was of a piece with Bryan's progressivism, not in conflict with it.

What was true of Bryan was true of many other progressive activists, both clerical and lay. They loathed Darwinism, not merely because they believed that it contradicted sacred Scripture, but also, and not unrelatedly, because it threatened to unleash a social and economic philosophy that licensed cynicism, selfishness, exploitation, and abuse. In the midst of the battle against teaching evolution, John Roach Straton, speaking at the 1918 convention of the World's Christian Fundamentals Association—the original Fundamentalists—proclaimed that Christian ministers, such as himself, "are traitors to their trust unless they battle heroically against such evils as unjust wages, especially to women workers, child labor, and the hell-black social evil, lawlessness, and the shame and disgrace of the liquor traffic." Straton called explicitly for the redistribution of wealth through both welfare and the progressive income tax.

Between 1913 and 1920, progressives succeeded in amending the Constitution four times. The Sixteenth Amendment gave Congress the power to tax income without apportionment among the several states; the Seventeenth provided for the direct election of Senators; the Eighteenth prohibited intoxicating liquors; and the Nineteenth granted women the right to vote. William Jennings Bryan had been involved in all of these causes. He, and many of those progressives who shared his evangelical faith, were to turn their attention next to the teaching of human evolution, a teaching they found to be threatening to religion, morals, and social justice. And this turn would pit Bryan, and those Christians of like mind, against Christians of a more liberal view, as well as against more secularized Americans, including some who had been their allies in earlier reform movements.

PROTECTION AGAINST INDOCTRINATION

Bryan himself was not an early advocate of anti-evolution laws. His demand, as far as public schools were concerned, was a policy of what he called "real neutrality wherever neutrality in religion is desired." "If the Bible cannot be defended in [public] schools," he declared, "it should not be attacked, either directly or under the guise of philosophy or science." His preference, and the preference of many opponents of evolution at the time, was for a policy of silence in the public schools on the question of the origin of the human species. And he tirelessly promoted this view in speeches to religious and political meetings around the country.

Increasingly, Bryan and his supporters became convinced that legislative action in the states was needed to protect people from having their children indoctrinated with beliefs antithetical to their religion. As far as public education was concerned, he argued that "those who pay the taxes have a right to determine what is taught." As Bryan and others succeeded in focusing the attention of their constituents on the question of the teaching of evolution in the public schools, momentum began to build for legislation banning such teaching. Interestingly, the first state to enact such legislation was neither Tennessee nor any other state of the old Southern confederacy. It was, rather, Oklahoma early in 1923. In what was in those days an altogether unsurprising combination of anti-evolutionism and progressive support for public education, the ban went through the lower house of the legislature, dominated in those days by the Democratic party, as an amendment to a bill providing for free textbooks.

Although supporters of the ban frequently invoked Bryan's name, he had no idea that it was being proposed and did not learn about it until after its passage. As other states began to consider such a ban, Bryan warned more radical elements on his side against trying to enforce the ban by criminal sanctions. "I do not think there should be any penalty," he argued. "We are not dealing with a criminal class and mere declaration of the state's policy is enough." Moreover, Bryan maintained that a ban should apply only to teaching that claimed that human evolution was "true." "A book which merely mentions it as a hypothesis," he said, "can be considered as giving information as to views held, which is very different from teaching it as fact."

Here it is worth pausing to observe the similarities between Bryan's proposal for the treatment of evolutionary teaching in schools and contemporary liberal ideas about teaching religion. Just as many liberals today say that the place for teaching about religion is in the private setting of home, and not the public one of school where students of different religious affiliations are united in pursuit of common learning, Bryan argued that the place to teach about the sensitive question of human origins—a question with profound religious implications on anybody's account of the matter—is in the home and not in the public school. And just as some liberals today allow that schools should be able to teach about religion (to teach what in colleges is often called "comparative religions") without teaching a particular theological view as "true," Bryan allowed that evolution could be mentioned "as a hypothesis" in the context of teaching about "views held" so long as it was not put forward "as a fact." (As a matter of fact, in good liberal fashion, Bryan had attempted to persuade publishers of science textbooks to "publish books that present [both] side[s], so that students can read both sides and thus reach their own conclusions.")

BIGOTS & MODERNISTS

Oklahoma was followed by Florida, and Florida by solidly Democratic Tennessee. As the bill banning the teaching of evolution in public schools worked its way through the legislative process, proponents of evolution, including so-called modernist Christian ministers, began to organize in opposition. Their strategy, in a kind of anticipation of Mencken's famous coverage of the Scopes trial, was to depict the supporters of the ban as bigots and boobs. And often enough those supporters managed to make themselves fit these roles (though there was a certain amount of bigotry and boobism on the other side, too). Some opponents of the ban, particularly the "modernist ministers," argued that evolutionary teaching was no threat to religion in general or Christianity in particular, though it was inconsistent with a certain literalist interpretation of the creation account in the Book of Genesis.

Although it seemed important to opponents of the Tennessee ban to show that Darwinism could be squared with belief in a divine Creator and Judeo-Christian morality, many prominent evolutionists today (not to mention critics of evolutionary theory) say frankly, and confidently, that it can't be. Stephen Jay Gould, for example, says that "before Darwin, we believed that a benevolent God had created us." Now, though, we know that

> . . . no intervening spirit watches lovingly over the affairs of nature (though Newton's clock-winding god might have set up the machinery at the beginning of time and let it run). No vital forces propel evolutionary change. And whatever we think of God, his existence is not manifest in the products of nature.

William Provine of Cornell University goes still further:

> Modern science directly implies that the world is organized strictly in accordance with mechanistic principles. There are no purposive principles whatsoever in nature. There are no gods and no designing forces that are rationally detectable. . . . There are no inherent moral or ethical laws, no absolute guiding principles for human society . . . human beings are marvelously complex machines. The individual human becomes an ethical person by means of two primary mechanisms: heredity and environmental influences. That is all there is. . . . We must conclude that when we die, we die and that is the end of us. . . . Free will as it is traditionally conceived . . . simply does not exist. . . . There is no way that the evolutionary process as currently conceived can produce a being that is truly free to make choices.

Now, Provine's remarks could have been made by an opponent of evolution warning about its allegedly antitheistic and antimoral implications, or by a candid atheistic supporter. I should probably point out, therefore, that Provine is a candid atheistic supporter. His remarks, if they could have been transferred back in time, would have been very useful to supporters of the evolutionary ban in Tennessee both in the legislative debates and in the Scopes trial.

TESTING THE BAN

Bryan, the "Great Commoner," did not come to Tennessee to address the legislature or give public speeches in support of the prohibition of evolutionary teaching, as he had in several other states, though he did communicate with its leading supporters, urging them, for example, to drop the idea of a criminal penalty for teaching evolution. That advice was not taken. The same legislature that passed the ban, however, increased funding for public education and rejected proposals to forbid the employment of teachers who believed in atheism or evolution. The legislature's goal was to prevent the teaching of evolution, and only that teaching, lest the religious faith learned by students at home be imperiled by teachings they encountered in school.

The debate in Tennessee, and the enactment of its ban on teaching evolution, captured the attention of the nation. The American Civil Liberties Union, which had been active in supporting free speech for political radicals, labor activists, and conscientious objectors to the First World War, sought to challenge the ban with what Larson describes as "a secularized missionary zeal." Their cause hovered uncertainly between the desire to defend the freedom of expression of teachers, irrespective of their views, and the wish to promote the "progressive" cause of science, in the form of evolutionary doctrine, against the forces of what it perceived as superstition and reaction. In any case, the ACLU's first move was to advertise for a defendant to represent in a test case it wished to arrange. Its advertisement appeared in a Chattanooga newspaper on May 4, 1925.

We are looking for a Tennessee teacher who is willing to accept our services in testing the anti-evolution law in the courts. Our lawyers think a friendly test can be arranged without costing a teacher his or her job. Distinguished counsel have volunteered their services. All we need now is a willing client.

The idea of "setting up a test case," so familiar to us, was fairly novel in 1925, and it took supporters of the law by surprise. Governor Peay, who had resisted a good deal of pressure from scientists and liberal clergy in signing the bill, had assumed that it would be neither enforced strictly nor challenged. He was certainly surprised. The strategy made sense to the ACLU for a number of reasons. One possibility was that they could win. A more likely one was that, while losing in the law courts, they could win in the court of national public opinion. It was a chance to ring the alarm about what was, from the ACLU's viewpoint, a grave threat to freedom, sort of, but, in any event, progress.

Why do I say freedom, "sort of"? Because the ACLU's position as it developed in the course of the litigation was ambiguous about whether its attorneys wanted the court to hold that teachers could not be barred from teaching whatever they wanted to teach as a matter of free speech, or whether they could not be prohibited from teaching a doctrine, like evolution, which was believed by intelligent, progressive, right-thinking people, or, to use the sociological term, "elites." To put the issue graphically, does a biology teacher have a First Amendment freedom to teach that human beings were transported to earth by space creatures from Saturn? Or, for that matter, if freedom of speech is absolute, may teachers teach—in violation of William Jennings Bryan's doctrine of neutrality—the special creation of man as presented in Genesis?

In any event, the ACLU needed a defendant, and eventually one was provided. In Dayton, Tennessee, a businessman named George W. Rappleyea knew an opportunity when he saw it. He conceived the idea of arranging the test case in Dayton as a way of putting the town on the map and gaining for the local economy a nice infusion of cash from visiting partisans, journalists, and curiosity seekers. After reading the ad in the Chattanooga paper, he met with local businessmen, civic leaders, school officials, and lawyers to promote his idea. The group prevailed upon a young science teacher—though not a biology teacher—named John T. Scopes to volunteer to be the defendant. As it happened, Scopes had never taught evolution, so he hadn't actually broken the law. He had, however, helped students review for a biology examination and, in that connection, used material from the textbook *A Civic Biology*, which did, as you'll recall, confidently teach evolutionary doctrine. So, in the opinion of a prosecutor happy to accommodate influential local leaders, that was close enough.

DARROW & BRYAN STEP IN

So now we have Scopes in the case. How do we get Bryan and Darrow into it? Well, just as the ACLU wanted to publicize its idea of a threat to freedom, and the city fathers of Dayton wanted to publicize Dayton, the World's Christian Fundamentals Association wanted to publicize its idea of evolution as, to quote William Bell Riley, "an unscientific, anti-Christian, atheistic, anarchistic, pagan rationalistic . . . theory." As it happened, Riley's WCFA was holding its convention in Memphis while the Dayton leaders were cooking up their scheme. Bryan came to address the convention, where he praised the legislature for banning evolutionary teaching, while indicating his qualms about the criminal penalty and, interestingly, his opposition to teaching religion in the public schools.

Neither of these caveats lowered the Great Commoner in the esteem of the Fundamentalists. The leader of the WCFA pressed him to represent the association as interveners in the Scopes trial, and though he had not argued a case in many years, Bryan agreed to return to the courtroom to wage what he promised would be a "battle royal between the Christian people of Tennessee and the so-called scientists." (The "so-called," here, is important: Bryan never wavered from his belief that evolutionary theory—relying on inferences he believed to be unwarranted and philosophical premises he believed to be unverified and unverifiable—was, above all, bad science.) This event suited almost everybody, since just about everybody was interested in maximizing the publicity value of the case. Bryan was certainly the most famous anti-evolutionist and probably the most famous progressive political figure of the time. A case that was already bound to get attention was now bound to get even more.

On the other side, the ACLU's executive director, Roger Baldwin, chose Arthur Garfield Hays as the chief ACLU representative at the trial. It was apparently Hays's decision to conduct the case, not as a "facial" challenge to a law that restricted Scopes's freedom of speech—leaving the specific question of evolution out of it—as Baldwin had originally planned, but as a defense of evolution as such and an attack on the law as "conceived in bigotry and born of ignorance—ignorance of the Bible, of religion, of history, and of science." When Bryan stepped forward to accept the role of special prosecutor in the case, the famous defense lawyers Clarence Darrow and Dudley Field Malone volunteered to argue for the defense. As a defender of labor militants and others in sensational prosecutions, Darrow's stature and reputation were a match for Bryan's. Interestingly, like Bryan, Darrow was a supporter of workers' rights and an active Democrat. Indeed, he had supported Bryan for President more than once. On religion, though, they were radically opposed. Darrow saw the argument between agnosticism and atheism as a close call. He scoffed at Christianity, and was certain of the truth of purely materialistic evolution. (Malone, incidentally, was a lapsed Catholic and secularized liberal, who made his reputation in big money divorce cases. He, too, had supported Bryan's presidential campaigns.)

DARROW STRAITJACKETED

For their part, the press—or perhaps we should say the media, since radio and even newsreel coverage of the trial was extensive—certainly did not disappoint the Dayton civic leadership or any of the other publicity seekers associated with the case. Newsmen came from throughout the country as well as from Canada, Europe, and even Australia. They told the story of the great "conflict between religion and science." As Bryan and Darrow agreed, their readers, listeners, and watchers were the real jury in this case.

From a technical legal point of view, the lead prosecutor, Thomas Stewart, played it smart, in my view, by accepting the advice of Samuel Untermyer, a distinguished New York trial lawyer, and vice president of the American Jewish Congress, who had worked with the ACLU in a major free speech case. Untermyer, who himself rejected evolution, warned against attacking evolutionary teaching straight on, and suggested arguing instead that the state legislature has the right and duty to decide what will be taught in the public schools. Surely, that decision cannot be left to every individual teacher. Any manner of bizarre idea could find its way into the classroom that way. Remember the space creatures from Saturn? So, who is to decide? Obviously, curricular decisions are the province of the legislature that creates the public schools and finances them.

This strategy had the advantage of frustrating Darrow's desire to put on expert testimony as to the alleged reasonableness of evolutionism and the alleged unreasonableness of any alternative view of human origins. Bryan himself, though itching to take on evolutionism, began to see the wisdom of this strategy as it became clear that more impressive scientific witnesses were prepared to testify for evolution than against it. This, I suppose, is the fate of the populist courtroom warrior in a battle against elites. However that may be, the prosecution succeeded in frustrating Darrow's efforts to break out of what Larson calls "the fatal straitjacket" which Untermyer's advice to the prosecution had imposed on the defense.

Darrow's efforts were two-fold. The first was to attack the law as being so unreasonable as to be unjustifiable as an exercise of the police power of states. Patently unreasonable laws, the defense argued, violate the Fourteenth Amendment to the federal Constitution, at least when they limit liberties protected in that amendment or other constitutional provisions. Hays compared the evolution ban to a ban on teaching that the earth revolves around the sun: "Evolution," he argued, "is as much a scientific fact as is the Copernican theory, but the Copernican theory has been more fully accepted." That, he said, is "the only distinction." Thus, he argued, the defense was entitled to put on expert testimony to show the unreasonableness of views opposed to evolutionism. It was obvious, however, to Judge John T. Raulston that evolutionism was denied by reasonable people, whatever the dominant view among scientists, so he refused to rule expert testimony admissible on this ground.

Darrow's second line of attack was to take advantage of the imprudent drafting of the statute to place its meaning in question. The law, as written, banned evolutionary teaching as denying the "Story of the Divine Creation of man." He argued that this aspect of the statute invited expert testimony to show the compatibility of evolutionary teaching with "any interpretation of the Bible that intelligent men could possibly make." After all, if evolution is compatible with biblical theism, then teaching it, as such, would not violate the law and Scopes should be acquitted. (Of course, Darrow, in all probability, privately held in contempt efforts to render evolution compatible with Christianity.)

This strategy did manage to get one expert witness—a zoologist—onto the stand before the prosecution managed to block it. Judge Raulston ruled that the "ordinary, non-expert mind can comprehend the simple language of the statute." From this defeat, however, Darrow pulled his famous victory by calling Bryan to the stand as an expert on the Bible. Bryan certainly could have declined—and just as certainly should have. The astonished Judge Raulston said to Bryan, "Mr. Bryan, you are not objecting to going on the stand?" "Not at all," Bryan replied.

BRYAN'S FALL

As far as I can make out the psychology of the situation, Darrow shrewdly appealed to both weakness and conviction to lure Bryan onto the stand. The weakness was a certain vanity. Darrow had earlier insulted the intelligence of Bryan and of all disbelievers in the evolution of man. Bryan did not want to look as though he was unwilling to do intellectual combat with the noted agnostic or atheist on key points of religious faith. The conviction was a belief that the truth of his cause would show through and expose error, accompanied by the belief that Christians have an obligation to testify for the faith, even in the face of possible ridicule and embarrassment.

That a Christian apologist *could have* matched wits with Darrow or even bested him in a public disputation was made plain not long after when Darrow debated Darwinism with the equally intelligent and notably wittier British public philosopher and man of letters G. K. Chesterton in Canada. But Bryan was plainly not up to the task. Although he proclaimed a kind of literalism, Bryan was an "old earth creationist"—interpreting the "days" of creation in the Genesis account as ages in time. Moreover, he was forced to admit his bafflement about how Joshua lengthened the day by making the sun stand still, whether Noah's flood somehow killed fish too, and how the serpent moved before it was punished for tempting Eve by being made to crawl on its belly.

Bryan's humiliation became news and then legend. The jury, whose members were out of the courtroom at the time—expert testimony of this sort going to questions of law (for the judge) rather than fact (for the jury)— were probably the last to hear of it. In the end, everybody agreed that on the minimal evidence that had actually gone to the jury, they had no choice but to convict. Indeed, Darrow himself told them so in his closing argument.

As Darrow and the ACLU prepared their case for appeal, the Great Commoner died in his sleep in Dayton, the place of his final effort and his humiliation—a week after the trial ended. In the Tennessee Supreme Court, the defense raised its constitutional challenges to the trial judge's rulings, all of which were rejected. Darrow, conjuring up the trial of Socrates, argued that what was at stake in this case as in that was "nothing but the question of the intellectual freedom of man." The state, by contrast, depicted the matter as a question of whether we would have the anarchy of "every teacher his own legislature" in the public schools.

To have their constitutional claims rejected at this level was no special loss for Darrow and the ACLU. Their goal was the Supreme Court of the United States. And for that, all they needed was to have Scopes's conviction upheld. This, however, was ingeniously denied them by the justices of the state's highest tribunal. For they reversed the trial court's conviction of Scopes—not on lofty constitutional grounds, but on a technicality in sentencing (the judge, rather than the jury, imposed the $100 fine)—thus depriving Scopes (and his lawyers) of standing to take the matter any further. Scopes was free to go, though Tennessee could, of course, retry him. (The Tennessee Supreme Court had wisely requested that the prosecution drop the issue in the interest of "the peace and dignity of the state.") And thus the circus in Dayton ended.

DARWINISM STILL ON TRIAL

From there, the story of evolution and creation in the courtroom took a series of interesting twists. An uneasy truce lasted until the early 1960s when the Supreme Court of the United States began removing officially sanctioned religion from public schools. In 1967, the Court invalidated an Arkansas law against teaching evolution, not on free speech grounds, but as a violation of the no establishment of religion provision of the First Amendment. As the issue shifted to whether states could require equal time, or indeed, permit any time, for creationist alternatives to (or criticism of) evolution to be taught, the Court made clear its willingness to scrutinize legislative history and other data for evidence of impermissible religious motives for legislation. On this basis, equal-time statutes were struck down in the 1980s. And thus the teaching of creation, once mandated by legislatures, has been forbidden by the courts; and the teaching of evolution, once forbidden by legislatures, has been granted by the courts exclusive standing in the classroom.

It remains to be seen, however, whether evolutionary theory as traditionally taught will survive in the long run—with or without the special protection of the courts. Darwinian and even neo-Darwinian accounts of "evolution" are coming under attack as implausible and outmoded ways of thinking—ideological dogmas propped up by an entrenched and sometimes rather ruthless establishment bent on denying students and, to the extent possible, the public at large, access to ideas that challenge its hegemony. No longer is the threat merely the potential political power of believers in biblical literalism and "young earth" creationism. Secular thinkers such as David Berlinski, philosophers such as Alvin Plantinga, and even scientists such as Michael Behe have cast grave doubt on the methodological assumptions and many of the key inferences on the basis of which mainstream biology continues to embrace one or another species of Darwinism.

Increasingly, Darwinists are feeling the pressure to show that their belief in random mutation and unguided natural selection as the mechanisms driving "evolution" follows from the fossil record and other observable facts, rather than from philosophical assumptions derived from a decidedly nonscientific materialist (or "naturalist") view of the world and brought to the enterprise of science before the inquiries begin. The interesting question today is whether Darwin will follow the other two great secularist system builders of the nineteenth century, Marx and Freud, onto the ash heap of history. If, in the end, Darwinism proves unfit to survive, somewhere the Great Commoner will be enjoying the last laugh.

Reprinted from Touchstone: A Journal of Mere Christianity, *March 2000, Volume 13, Number 2.*

LEON J. PODLES

Missing Fathers of the Church

The Feminization of the Church & the Need for Christian Fatherhood

You may have noticed that, in general, men are not as interested in religion as women are. There are usually more women than men at Sunday mass, and there are far more women than men at devotions, retreats, and prayer groups. The men who do come are often there because wives or girlfriends have put pressure on them to attend. In fact, if men speak honestly, they will tell you that men have a general feeling that the Church is for women. They may add that women are more emotional than men are, or that religion is a crutch that a man doesn't need, as Jesse Ventura, the candidate of young white men, said in *Playboy*.

In my book, *The Church Impotent: The Feminization of Christianity*, I examine the lack of men in the Western churches, which only the unobservant doubt, and I look at the possible causes and results of the lack of men. My thought has continued to develop, and I have slightly revised my thesis. In what follows I will first summarize my thesis that men stay away from the Church because they regard it as a threat to their hard-won masculinity. Second, I will explore how the Church has become identified with femininity. Third, I will consider how this feminization has undermined fatherhood, and how the Church can reach men and help them to be Christians and Christian fathers.

I think the lack of men is self-evident, but the reactions to my book have shown me that some people have not noticed and that others choose to deny the obvious because of a feminist, or, what has surprised me, a traditionalist agenda. Sociologists have gathered statistics about both practice and opinion, and the studies confirm the popular impression: religion, especially of the Christian variety, is largely a feminine affair in Western society.

James H. Fichter asks, "Are males really less religious than females? Most of the studies made on the question seem to indicate that they are, and this appears to be true for all the Christian churches, denominations, and sects in western civilization."[1] Michael Argyle generalizes, "Women are more religious than men on all criteria, particularly for private prayer, also for membership, attendance, and attitude."[2] Gail Malmgreen points out the disparity between the gender of the clergy and the gender of the faithful: "In modern Western cultures, religion has been a predominantly female sphere. In nearly every sect and denomination of Christianity, though men monopolized the positions of authority, women had the superior numbers."[3] Christianity is a religion of and for women.

Nor do women simply join churches more than men do. They also are more active and loyal. Of Americans in the mid-1990s, George Barna writes that "women are twice as likely to attend a church service during any given week. Women are also 50 percent more likely than men to say they are 'religious' and to state that they are 'absolutely committed' to the Christian faith."[4] The differences seem to be increasing rapidly. In 1992, 43 percent of men attended church; in 1996, only 28 percent.[5] Patrick Arnold, a Jesuit of liberal theological leanings, claims that at churches he has visited, "it is not at all unusual to find a female-to-male ratio of 2:1 or 3:1. I have seen ratios in parish churches as high as 7:1." Women are more active in all activities of the church, both in public and social activities, such as peace and justice committees, and in spiritual activities, such as prayer and Bible study.

Church attendance in the United States is about 60 percent female and 40 percent male. The more liberal the denomination, the higher the percentage of females. Fundamentalists are almost evenly divided, but the only religions that sometimes show a majority of men are Eastern Orthodoxy, Orthodox Judaism, Islam, and Eastern religions such as Buddhism.

Men say they believe in God as much as women do, but the more Christian a practice or belief becomes, the fewer men will own up to it. Men go to church less than women do, they pray far less than women do, and they believe in the afterlife and heaven and hell far less than women do.

The difference is neither recent nor limited to North America. In seventeenth-century New England, Cotton Mather puzzled over why his congregations were overwhelmingly female. Nor is the United States the worst off. Latin men are notoriously resistant to going to church.[6] In one conservative Spanish village, for a man to be outstandingly religious is considered shameful. A man is humiliated, *pasar vergüenza,* if he is in debt, or "if he is seen in church holding a rosary, or sitting in the front benches in church."[7] A man can be a Catholic without disgrace, but to be outwardly religious is incompatible with masculinity. All over Europe the pattern is the same. In England, the difference has been growing: "the imbalance between the sexes is becoming more rather than less marked in contemporary society."[8] The difference can be traced back as far as there are statistics about church involvement—not only a difference in outward observance, but also in belief: far more women than men subscribe to basic Christian beliefs.[9]

In modern France the church is the domain of women. This was the situation after France had recovered from its bout of extreme anti-clericalism in the nineteenth century. The difference between men and women grew less in the mid-twentieth century, in part because more men were going to church, and in part because fewer women were going to church.[10]

The situation was even worse in the nineteenth century when anti-clericalism was in full rage. In 1858 the rector of Montpellier lamented that "religious duties are almost completely neglected by the men or practiced only for appearance's sake. Generally only women observe their duties."[11] He said this because only 15 percent of the men made their Easter duty. In 1877, in the western part of the diocese of Orléans, only 4.7 percent of the men made their Easter Communion, although 26 percent of the women did.[12]

The strategy of the French Church has been to maintain a presence in society through the influence of women.[13] This strategic decision even has affected doctrine. The Church had from time immemorial condemned contraception. But in France, peasants practiced coitus interruptus to limit the division of their inheritance. Acting on the advice of Alphonse de Ligouri, confessors decided that women were not guilty if their husbands practiced this form of contraception. This decision was based on a fear that rigorism would alienate women, and that the Church would thereby lose all influence in French society. In 1842 the Trappist (and doctor) Debryne argued against a rigorist position on the use of contraception: "One should give serious attention to this; that one should not alienate women through an imprudent rigor; the matter is one of immense importance. The coming generation is in the hands of women; the future belongs to her. If the woman gets away from us [the 'us' seems to be his priest readers], with her everything will disappear and vanish into the abyss of atheism—faith, morality, and our whole civilization."[14]

Wherever Western Christianity has spread, the Church has become feminized. Rosemary Reuther observes: "In Germany, France, Norway, and Ireland women are 60 to 65 percent of the active churchgoers. In Korea, India, and the Philippines, women are 65 to 70 percent of the active churchgoers."[15]

Anecdotal evidence indicates that this pattern of greater female piety goes back far before the Reformation. Even medieval preachers made reference to women as being more active in the church. Berthold von Regensburg noticed that more women than men attended church. He preaches to "you women, who are more merciful than men and go more willingly to church than men and say your prayers more willingly than men and go to sermons more willingly than men."[16]

A closer analysis of the sociological data shows that it is not exactly being male or female that makes the difference, but being masculine or feminine. That is, men who have feminine personality characteristics tend to go to church far more often than other men do. Women who have masculine personalities tend to go to church less than other women do.

MASCULINITY & THE CHURCH

Anthropologists and developmental psychologists who have studied masculinity have come up with a fairly widely agreed-upon topology of masculinity. I will begin with child development, because that is something almost all of us are familiar with.

A boy is born of a woman and has an intense and close relationship with a woman for the first years of his life. At first the child is not even aware of his mother as a separate being. He gradually realizes that his mother is a separate being, a separate person. He then starts realizing that his mother differs from him in an extremely important respect: she is what he cannot and should not become—a woman. The boy must break this intense, close relationship with his mother to establish his separate identity. The girl is separate, but she can become feminine by imitating her mother. The boy cannot become masculine by imitating his mother; he must turn from her to other models, usually his father.

Intense pressure is put on the boy to make this break. If he does not make the break, he is called a momma's boy, a girl, and much harsher things. He learns that at all costs he must become a man. A man has other responsibilities in life; he takes up the dangerous work of a society. He may work himself to death as a lawyer, or get shot in war, or anything in between. Even in the United States, men hold almost all the dangerous positions in our society, as measured by the chance of death or serious injury. Only after he earns his spurs as a man can the male reconnect to the world of women by marrying and becoming the father of a family. As a boy the male is protected and provided for; as a man he must protect and provide for others, even at the cost of his own life.

This pattern is almost universal. Societies in general have what anthropologist David Gilmore calls an *ideology of masculinity*. Boys all over the world are subject to initiations and trials to break their relationship with their mothers. Boys must learn to endure pain and suffer deprivation so that they will undertake the dangerous and destructive work that all societies have. The feminine world is (for a man) far safer: he doesn't have the hazard of childbirth. Therefore he must be constantly pressured to distance himself from the feminine world. He is given a higher status in return for assuming the masculine role, but he pays a price. Michael Levin says: "If sex roles are to be regarded as the outcome of bargaining in which men received dominance in exchange for the risk of violent death, it is hardly clear that they got the better deal."

Western Christianity has become part of the feminine world from which men feel they must distance themselves to attain masculinity. That is why men stay away from church, especially when they see that the men involved in church tend to be less masculine. The most religious denominations, those that have the most external display, have the worst reputation. Anglo-Catholics were lambasted in the Victorian press as unmanly because they devoted themselves to lace and plaster statues (in some cases, this criticism was justified). Psychological studies have detected a connection between femininity in men and interest in religion. There may even be a physical difference. Among men, football players and movie actors have the highest testosterone level, ministers, the lowest. Success and self-esteem can even change hormonal levels.

Why Is the Church "Feminine"?

Is there something innately feminine about Christianity? Many traditionalist Christians believe this. But God became incarnate as a man, and Jesus' life follows the classic masculine pattern of development. He even had to place some distance between himself and his mother: he left her as an early adolescent to teach in the temple, to do his Father's work; he left her to undertake his public ministry; and he had to leave her behind when he died.

The God of Judaism and the Father of Jesus Christ was masculine because he was a holy God, which meant he was separate from Creation. The Hebrew word for "holy" is *kadosh*, "separate." The Jews came to know the nature of God through his actions, which were actions of separating. He separated a people, the Jews, from the pagan nations; he separated light from darkness, the land from the sea. He created by separating, and his people were a separate people, set apart from the rest of the world.

Jesus' actions were those of God. He created a new people by separating them from the Jews. He came not to bring peace, but a sword that divides. He came to give the *Holy* Spirit, which *separated* out pagans and Jews from their old environments and brought them together into a new thing, the Church. As Christianity spread, it has provoked opposition, violence, persecution, and murder, from the Crucifixion to the contemporary Christians who are being crucified in the Sudan. This new people is called to be holy and separate from the world. In the Apocalypse, the angel commands the Church to come out, to separate, from Babylon.

The age of the martyrs and the Fathers, the first millennium, evinced no great signs that Christianity was especially for women or that it was a threat to masculinity, although there are some patristic precursors of later feminization. Christianity is not, as Nietzsche claimed, a religion of slaves and women, unfit for the hypermasculine Superman.

The feminization of Western Christianity can be dated rather exactly. Suddenly, in the thirteenth century, during the lifetimes of St. Dominic and St. Francis, women began to get involved in the Church to such an extent that both Francis and Dominic warned their followers not to spend all their time preaching to women and ignoring men. St. Francis of Assisi, in a somewhat uncharacteristic note, said (according to Thomas of Pavia), "The Lord has taken away wives from us, but the devil has given us sisters."[17] St. Dominic tried to keep his followers away from women. The earliest constitutions, written in 1220, before Dominic's death in 1221, prohibit Dominicans from undertaking the *cura monialum,* "the spiritual direction of women."[18] This prohibition seems not to be based on Dominic's fears about celibacy but on his fear that his followers would be overwhelmed by women and neglect their preaching to men.[19] This indeed happened. Within a century the Dominicans were devoting their time largely to women.

What happened in the medieval Church? In his immensely influential sermons on the Song of Songs, Bernard of Clairvaux taught that the relationship of the Christian soul to God was that of a bride to a Heavenly Bridegroom. In this he continued an allegorical exegesis that goes back to Origen, but his preaching fell on fertile ground, and was taken up by popular piety, which had undergone a mysterious transformation into what we might call affective, or sentimental, piety, although these words are not exact. Emotions and sentiments had always played a part in Christian life, but now for some reason the emotions were those of women.

Bernard's language expressing the union of the soul with God in erotic terms was highly congenial to women. Valerie M. Lagorio in her survey of mystical literature concludes: "In the works of the women visionaries, one notes the prevalence of *Brautmystik,* the love affair between Christ and the soul, leading to espousal and marriage."[20] Birgitta of Sweden usually referred to herself in the third person as "the bride."[21] After 1300 in Germany, "it was chiefly among women . . . that the *Brautmystik* was received with fervor."[22] Mechtilde had a vision of Gertrude of Helfta: "She [Mechtilde] saw the Lord Jesus as a Spouse, full of grace and vigor, fairer than a thousand angels. He was clad in green garments that seemed to be lined with gold. And she [Gertrude] for whom she [Mechtilde] had prayed was being tenderly enfolded by his right arm, so that her left side, where the heart is, was held close to the opening of the wound of love; she for her part was seen to be enfolding him in the embrace of her left arm."[23] Medieval eros, which delighted in bright colors and knights who had received wounds of love, is prominent here.

Christ had revealed himself to Gertrude as "a youth of about sixteen years of age, handsome and gracious. Young as I then was, the beauty of his form was all that I could have desired, entirely pleasing to the outward eye."[24]

The bridal union of the soul with Christ is not simply other and higher than earthly marriage; it replaces it, and takes on some of the physical eroticism of the missing sexual union. Margaret Ebner feels Jesus pierce her "with a swift shot (*sagitta acuta*) from His spear of love."[25] She feels her spouse's "wondrous powerful thrusts against my heart"[26] and she complains that "sometimes I could not endure it when the strong thrusts came against me for they harmed my insides so that I became greatly swollen like a woman great with child."[27] Jesus had spoken to her these words: "Your sweet love finds me, your inner desire compels me, your burning love binds me, your pure truth holds me, your fiery love keeps me near. I want to give you the kiss of love which is the delight of your soul, a sweet inner movement, a loving attachment."[28] She had learned of this kiss from Bernard: "I longed for and greatly desired to receive the kiss just as my lord St. Bernard had received it."[29]

This change in devotion found a justification in new Scholastic theories of the masculine and feminine. The Scholastics' reception of Aristotle in the High Middle Ages set the stage for the revaluation of women and provided a justification for the increasingly noticeable absence of men from the Church.

The Scholastics, as Prudence Allen has shown in *The Concept of Woman,* rediscovered and Christianized the Aristotelian analysis of the female. Aristotle followed Pythagoras in organizing reality into polar opposites. In the *Metaphysics,* Aristotle said that in a pair of contraries, one is the privation of the other.[30] Aristotle was especially interested in the contraries of form, and he placed the male on the side of form, the female on the side of matter: "the female always provided the material, the male, that which fashions it."[31] As the giver of form, man rules; as the matter that is given form, the woman obeys.

In the order of nature the woman is therefore inferior to the man. Nevertheless, in the order of grace, Christian Aristotelians taught, the woman is above the man, precisely because of her natural inferiority: "Mary herself became a kind of material for the formative power of God. Her perfect identity as nonresistant material for the working of the Holy Spirit led to her complete absorption of the wisdom of God. Therefore [for St. Albert the Great] it followed that Mary knew everything that God knew. She was the perfect philosopher, theologian, lawyer, physician, scientist, and so on."[32] What is true of Mary is true of women in general. Precisely because they are more like the raw material on which form is imposed, they are more open to the forming of the Holy Spirit. Men have a form already, a form that gets in the way of the shape of Christ that the Holy Spirit wishes to imprint on the human person. Women, relatively lacking form, are more open to receiving another form.

This analysis permeated all medieval discussion of gender. As Ann Astell says, "In the metaphysics of sexuality, every person, male and female, is more feminine than masculine in relation to God—because receptive, dependent, and small."[33] The philosophical and theological explanation for women's greater interest in Christianity was in place, and has continued to be the received wisdom.[34]

The explicit eroticism of the medieval mystics is still around, as anyone who has read *Mariette in Ecstasy* knows. Pseudo-mystics who have erotic fantasies about Jesus plague the Catholic Church. This is extreme, but much of popular devotion has a watered-down version of this eroticism.

Both Catholics and Evangelicals talk about a personal relationship with Jesus. Respondents to my book, *The Church Impotent,* have made it clear that what people understand by this language is a romantic relationship with Jesus, "falling in love with Jesus." Not only old hymns like "O How I Love Jesus" bear this mark. Frederica Mathewes-Green reports that there is a genre of Christian rock that Christianizes love songs by substituting the name of Jesus for the girlfriend. The Communion hymns used in Catholic churches in the 1950s used Victorian melodies and sang of "the Bridegroom of my soul"; the current melodies are frequently romantic ones suited to easy-listening love songs.

The devotion to the Infant Jesus that began in the Middle Ages and continues in full flower among Catholics today bears some traces of eroticism. But even when it is wholesome, it creates problems for men, who do not have strong maternal feelings. And is our relationship to Jesus that of caring for and protecting a helpless child?

I recently visited EWTN, where Mother Angelica does excellent work. But the young men who work on the TV programs sometimes feel like barking like seals and banging their heads against the iron fences, because the atmosphere is one of sentimental motherhood. In general, normal men stay away. They were far harsher than I have been in their appraisal of this atmosphere.

I think that even doctrine has been affected by the feminization of the Church. Femininity is characterized by themes of union, of integration, and of maintaining relationships. Universalism is the received wisdom in almost all churches today.

Universalism is the doctrine that all human beings (and some add even the fallen angels) will be saved in the end. Hell, if it exists, will be empty. Julian of Norwich heard Jesus say to her, "All shall be well." She questioned how, and was told only, "All shall be well." Other saints argued with God, asking how he could send even sinners to hell. This affects the highest levels. Hans Urs von Balthasar, a favorite of John Paul II, wrote *Dare We Hope That All Men Be Saved?* His answer was yes, and he clearly leans toward universalism. He was heavily influenced by a woman mystic, Adrienne von Speyr. While we all devoutly hope and pray that this will be so, Jesus gives us many harsh warnings about hell fire and the worm that dieth not. He will separate the sheep from the goats on the last day. Even in ordinary Christian life, judgment, damnation, and hell have vanished from the ordinary consciousness, as has the practice of confession. If we are all going to heaven why worry about repentance? If everyone is going to heaven, why do people need to become Christians? If Christianity is a mere verbal game, a decoration, men have better things to do with their time.

Men have sought their religious fulfillment outside Christianity. The Freemasons and similar organizations provided a confrontation with death and a rebirth as a new man. Sports became a new religion, as did war, nationalism, fascism, and Nazism. Men have sought and continue to seek the transcendent not in Christianity but in the new religions of masculinity. Men know the pattern of death and rebirth because they have all had to die to the boy and the safe maternal world so that they could be reborn as men. They know that to be fully masculine they must die and be reborn and they therefore seek this death and rebirth wherever they can find it. In seeking death, they may fall in love with it; they may become criminals and nihilists. Christianity is a religion of death and resurrection, but masculinity, separated from Christianity, too often provides an ersatz resurrection and a real death.

By driving men away from the Church, this feminization has undermined Christian fatherhood. A man cannot be a Christian father unless he is a Christian first, and even fatherhood has been undermined in the churches.

Medieval Catholicism weakened the family. In the Middle Ages, consanguinity, both natural and spiritual (that is, through the godparents) was grounds for annulment. Since almost everyone was related to everyone else, almost any marriage could be annulled. The Reformers, in denying that marriage was a sacrament, and taking it from the jurisdiction of the Church, were trying to strengthen it. The Counter-Reformation followed suit by forbidding secret marriages and reforming the laws on consanguinity.

Luther and Calvin, I suspect, reacted to the feminization of Christianity by stressing the patristic concept of the Christian life as a daily death and rebirth (Luther is especially moving on this), and by stressing the role of the natural family as the domestic church, the religious duties of the father within the family, and the spiritual nature of lay work. Luther did not want to see nuns mooning over religious dolls but mothers caring for real infants. The Catholic Church used the figure of St. Joseph to uphold the dignity of fatherhood and lay work. During the Middle Ages he was portrayed as a comic old man on the periphery of the story of Mary and Jesus; after the seventeenth century he became a young father, protecting and teaching the child Jesus.

In attempting to demonstrate to the feminists the importance of women in the Catholic Church, the current pope, for all his excellencies and orthodoxy, has undermined the role of men in the church. He states he cannot allow the ordination of women, but allows the presence of altar girls, who have replaced altar boys in many churches. He talks about mutual subordination, but has never mentioned the father as the head of the family. This doctrine has been repeated by every pope in modern times except John Paul II.

In parishes, fathers are ignored or denigrated. Priests boast that they became priests because of their mothers (don't they have fathers?), and I have been astounded at the personal revelations in sermons. One priest on *Father's Day* read his own poem about how his father used to come home and beat his mother and terrorize the children. I have sympathy for such men, but why are they allowed to function as pastors? The situation in the mainline churches is far worse. The seminaries have a female majority, and shortly the ministry will be a female occupation. One will have to say *male minister* as one now has to say *male nurse.*

Making Men into Christian Fathers

Men can be taught to be men only by other men, and all too many pastors are not real men. A pastor called me about my book. He had been ordained in the mainline Presbyterian Church. When he entered the seminary, he had to take a battery of psychological tests and talk to a psychiatrist. The psychiatrist looked over the tests, and the first question he asked the candidate was, "Are you a homosexual?" The candidate responded, "No, I'm not, and why do you ask?" The psychiatrist replied, "You have the psychological profile of a homosexual. But don't worry, *all the successful ministers in your denomination have this profile.*" The problem, as the minister realized after reading my book, is that pastors too often become pastors because they enjoy working in a feminine world, and they adopt the mental attitudes of women, who are their principal audience. In men, such a psychological profile is effeminate.

The pastor, in conjunction with the men of the church, should develop programs to help boys grow into men. Initiation into the mysteries of religion should be part of becoming a man, not something that leads away from masculinity. Boys and young men have a way of learning that differs from that of girls. Boys are far more physical, and for them, the usual Sunday school is but a continuation of the five-day torment of sitting still. Physical activity and training should be joined to religious training. The Scouts provide an excellent vehicle; they can easily incorporate initiatory rituals. One Lutheran Church in Baltimore has adopted the knightly initiation. The scouts pray all night in a darkened church, and in the morning receive a sword and their scouts uniform in a ceremony before the whole congregation.

Having accompanied the boy along the path to manhood, the Church can then help him become a father. Although obviously fatherhood is a fulfillment of manhood, it involves a reconnection with the feminine, domestic world that men may feel is a threat to their masculinity, or at least to that aspect of masculinity that they achieved by rejecting feminine safety and facing challenges and dangers. The role of protector or provider is also a challenge, and a deeper one, that young men must take on to avoid getting stuck in the stage of adolescent thrill-seeking. If the young man does not experience Christianity as a threat to his masculinity, he will more willingly accept its guidance in becoming a father of a Christian household.

Christian fathers should instruct their sons, primarily by example. Fathers should lead family prayers and read the Bible, and take the lead in getting the family to church. Fatherhood should be stressed in sermons as it is in the Bible. Much of the Old Testament is instruction in how to be a father, and the father is of key importance in the Christian household in the New Testament.

Preach the whole gospel, including the uncomfortable parts. Hell and damnation are realities, and it does no one any good to forget them. Christianity is a matter of infinite seriousness, far more serious than economics or politics. Christianity can give the true initiation into the mysteries of life and death, of heaven and hell, of spiritual warfare and the destiny of the human race. Men need training in spiritual discipline, and will think it worthwhile if they see the importance of Christianity. Although flawed, Mitch Finley's *For Men Only: Strategies for Living Catholic* has some good practical approaches.

Remember that the purpose of the Church is not to be a clinging mother. Pastors should not aim at bringing men in and getting them involved in all sorts of committees and devotions. Christian formation is necessary, but the role of the pastor should be a father, not a mother. The father's job is to separate his children from juvenile dependence and send them out prepared for the battle of life. The laity's role is out in the world, Christianizing our culture. Anyone who has tried to do this knows that it is a battle and that the Church needs more than just a few good men.

Reprinted from Touchstone: A Journal of Mere Christianity, *January/February 2001, Volume 14, Number 1.*

Notes:
1. James H. Fichter, "Why Aren't Males So Holy?" *Integrity* 9 (May 1955): p. 3.
2. Michael Argyle, *Religious Behaviour* (London: Routledge and Kegan Paul, 1958), p. 76.
3. Gail Malmgreen, "Domestic Discords: Women and the Family in East Cheshire Methodism, 1750–1830," in *Disciplines of Faith: Studies in Religion, Patriarchy and Politics* (London: Routledge and Kegan Paul, 1987), p. 56.
4. George Barna, *Index of Leading Spiritual Indicators* (Dallas: Word Publishing, 1996), p. 87.
5. George Barna, "The Battle for the Hearts of Men," *New Man*, vol. 4, no. 1 (January-February 1997): p. 42.

---

6. Carmela Lison-Tolosana, *Belmonte de los Cabelleros: A Sociological Study of a Spanish Town* (Princeton: Princeton University Press, 1983), p. 309.

7. Lison-Tolosana, *Belmonte*, p. 338.

8. Grace Davie, *Religion in Britain Since 1945: Believing Without Belonging* (Oxford: Blackwell Publishers, 1994), p. 118.

9. Davie, *Religion in Britain*, p. 119.

10. Femand Boulard writes (translated by Leon Podles): "The behavior of the sexes, very different during former periods, has distinctly changed in the direction of a similarity of rates. The Sunday census which covered the diocese of Versailles on November 23, 1975, made it clear that the rate of masculinity [the proportion of men in the assembly of practicing Catholics] has stabilized almost everywhere between 35 and 40% for those more than 25 years old; a little more weak among rural senior citizens, it attains an absolute parity of 50% among some urban senior citizens. In contrast, in 1907–1908 in the neighborhood of Versailles, the rate was 15.6%, and around 1880 for the whole diocese it did not reach 11%." (*Matérieux pour l'histoire religieuse du peuple français XIXe–XXe siècles* [Paris: Editions de L'Ecole des Hautes Etudes en Sciences Sociales, 1982], p. 19). However, the statistics in this book reveal a longstanding and massive difference in religious practice between French men and women.

11. Gerard Cholvy and Yves-Marie Hilaire, *Histoire religieuse de la France contemporaine*, vol. III (Toulouse: Bibliothecque histoire privat, 1985), p. 299.

12. Christianne Marcilhacy, *Le Diocèse d'Orléans sous l'episcopat de Mgr. Dupanloup* (Paris: Librarie Plon, 1962), p. 531.

13. The current situation in the Catholic Church, in which contraception is officially condemned but those who adhere to this doctrine are largely excluded from Catholic education and diocesan structures, may be due to the same strategy of not offending women.

14. Quoted by Langlois, Claude. "Féminisation du catholicisme," in *Histoire de la France religieuse*, vol. 3, *Du rois Très Chrétien à la laicité républicaine* (Paris: Editions du Seuil, 1991), ed. Jacques Le Goff, p. 303.

15. Rosemary Radford Reuther, "Christianity and Women in the Modern World," in *Today's Woman in World Religions,* ed. Arvind Sharrna (Albany: State University of New York Press, 1994), p. 285.

16. Berthold von Regensburg preached: "Ir frouwen, ir sît barmherzic unde gêt gerner zuo kirchen danne die man unde sprechet iuwer gebete gerner danne die man unde gêt zu predigen gerner danne die man" (*Predigten*, vol. 1, ed. Franz Pfeiffer [Vienna: Wilhelm Braumüller, 1862], p. 41). In another sermon, Berthold continues in the same vein, and says that women are "erbaumherziger, danne die man und betet gerner, mit venie, mit danne die man, mit kirchgengen, mit riuwe, mit ûf stên, mit salter lesen, mit vigilie. Mit maniger guottæte sît ir bezzer." (More merciful than men and more willing to pray with prostrations than men, with visits to church, with quiet, with standing, with reading the Psalter, with vigils. With many good deeds are you better.) (*Predigten*, vol. 2, p. 141).

17. "Dominus a nobis uxores abstuli, dyabolus autem nobis procurat sorores" (quoted by Herbert Grundmann, *Religiöse Bewegungen im Mittelalter* [Hildesheim: Georg Olms Verlagsbuchhandlung, 1961], p. 262, n. 149). Somehow this quote was omitted from the English translation, *Religious Movements in the Middle Ages,* trans. by Steven Rowan (Notre Dame: University of Notre Dame Press, 1995).

18. The decision reads "prohibemus ne aliquis fratrum nostrorum de cetero laboret vel procuret, ut cura vel custodia monialum seu quarumlibet aliarum mulierum nostris fratribus commitantur" (we prohibit either to labor or to seek out that the care or custody of nuns or of any other women be committed to our brothers) (quoted by Roger De Ganck, *Beatrice of Nazareth in her Context* [Kalamazoo: Cistercian Publications, 1991], p. 21, n. 89).

19. Grundmann says of Dominic: "On his deathbed, in his last conversations on the order, he pressingly warned his brethren against association with women, particularly with young women. Was he only warning against the moral attitude of individual friars? Is it possible that the founder, preoccupied with questions about the future of his order in these last utterances, had been discussing whether the order should incorporate further women's communities, placing friars to oversee and supply them, thus withdrawing from the order's primary duty of preaching?" (*Religious Movements*, pp. 94–95).

20. Valerie M. Lagorio, "The Continental Women Mystics of the Middle Ages: An Assessment," in *Roots of the Modern Christian Tradition*, p. 81. Leclercq et al. concur: "It was chiefly among women . . . that the Brautmystik was received with fervor" (Jean Leclercq, François Vandenbroucke, and Louis Bouyer, *The Spirituality of the Middle Ages*, trans. by the Benedictines of Holmes Eden Abbey [London: Burns and Oates, 1968], p. 373).

21. Birgitta explains: "One should know that this most humble handmaid of God never presumed to call herself or have herself called the bride of Christ, or his channel, because of vainglory or transitory honor or any temporal advantage, but at the instruction of Christ and of blessed Mary, his most worthy mother, who both called her so." (*Birgitta of Sweden: Life and Selected Revelations,* ed. Marguerite Tjader Harris, trans. Albert Ryle Kezel [New York: Paulist Press, 1990], p. 71).

22. Leclercq et al., *Spirituality,* p. 374.

23. Gertrude of Helfta, *The Herald of Divine Love,* trans. and ed. by Margaret Winckworth (New York: Paulist Press, 1993), p. 82.

24. Gertrude, *Herald,* p. 95.

25. Margaret Ebner, *Major Works,* trans. and ed. by Leonard P. Hindsley (New York: Paulist Press, 1993), p. 156.

26. Margaret Ebner, *Major Works,* p. 135.

27. Margaret Ebner, *Major Works,* p. 150.

28. Margaret Ebner, *Major Works,* p. 122.

29. Margaret Ebner, *Major Works,* p. 96.

30. Aristotle, *Metaphysics* 1055b, 25–29 in *The Complete Works of Aristotle,* vol. 1, ed. Jonathan Barnes (Princeton: Princeton University Press, 1984), p. 1667.

31. Aristotle, *Generation of Animals,* 738b in *The Complete Works of Aristotle,* vol. 1, ed. Jonathan Barnes (Princeton: Princeton University Press, l984), p. 1146.

32. Prudence Allen, *The Concept of Woman: The Aristotelian Revolution 750 BC–AD 1250* (Grand Rapids, Michigan: Eerdmans Publishing Co., 1997), p. 383.

33. Anne W. Astell, *The Song of Songs in the Middle Ages* (Ithaca: Cornell University Press, 1990), p. 13.

34. I note that Steve Clark thinks that this is a misunderstanding of the Scholastics and that Prudence Allen has misled me, but he has not provided me with any details of his disagreement.

Thomas S. Buchanan

A Cardinal Virtue Quartet

*The Four Fundamental Characteristics of a
Virtuous Person*

PRUDENCE

*The simple acquire folly, but the prudent are crowned
with knowledge. —Proverbs 14:18*

Although most people have heard of the seven deadly sins, fewer people are familiar with that other list: the seven great virtues. The virtues can be divided into two groups: the three theological virtues (faith, hope, and charity), and the four cardinal virtues (prudence, temperance, justice, and fortitude). Although the list of the seven virtues is first found among the writings of Ambrose and Augustine, the list of the cardinal virtues wasn't their creation; it was mentioned centuries before by Aristotle and Plato and represents the classical mind on what constitutes a virtuous man.

The cardinal virtues are not, I believe, what most Americans would think of if asked to define the four fundamental characteristics of a virtuous person. They are, in a sad sense, the antithesis of modern virtues. For example, consider the cardinal virtue of prudence.

Prudence is the wisdom to discern right from wrong. It is also "showing sound judgment in practical affairs" and being "sapient," according to the *Oxford English Dictionary.* One who is prudent is one who is wise and who exercises that wisdom in day-to-day issues.

Though it lies at the heart of prudence, the ability to discriminate between good and bad, or good and mediocre, or, better yet, good and very near good, is not much appreciated today as a great virtue. "Discrimination" is oftentimes condemned as a sin, even when used justly and with a noble purpose in mind. For example, the Boy Scouts have been condemned as discriminatory because they disapproved of homosexuality and upheld heterosexuality as the only acceptable norm. They thought it imprudent to allow homosexual men around young boys. Or again, many would consider it discriminatory to point out that it might be imprudent to put men and women in close quarters on naval vessels. In our backwards world, that which is consistent with the execution of wisdom on day-to-day issues is discriminatory and, hence, wrong.

We live in the age of tolerance, not prudence. These can be diametrically opposed. This is exemplified by the main character in Evelyn Waugh's short story, "Too Much Tolerance." The hero of that story thought that everyone was a "jolly good fellow," including the man who ran off with his wife, and another man who stole his inherited fortune. The hero (or more appropriately, the anti-hero) in this story had no ability to discern right from wrong, so he kindly chose to assume that everyone was good. As a result, he allowed every good thing that he had to be taken away and became a most pitiable fellow, estranged from his wife and son, reduced to selling sewing machines door-to-door in Africa. Tolerance, taken to the extreme, is a lack of the cardinal virtue of prudence.

While it is true that the lack of tolerance, taken to the extreme, is bigotry, it is often assumed by those at the left side of the forefront of the culture wars that *any* form of prudence is evil. Calling virtues "evil" is part of the double-talk common to those antagonistic to the faith. Prudence is the wisdom that allows us to discern double-talk from truth. It is that by which we avoid folly and by which we are crowned with knowledge, according to Solomon. It is a virtue sorely needed today.

TEMPERANCE

But the fruit of the Spirit is love, joy, peace, longsuffering, gentleness, goodness, faith, meekness, temperance: against such there is no law. —Galatians 5:22–23

Many years ago, I lived in Evanston, Illinois, home of the Women's Christian Temperance Union. It was the early 1980s, and the strong but waning power of that organization was evident in that this college town was still dry. One could walk past the Union's headquarters and see the ladies in long dresses at their social events.

At the time, I found it surprising that any form of the temperance movement was still alive after the 1960s, but there they were, in their splendid Victorian manor.

Those in the twentieth century's temperance movement were modern Gnostics. They believed that the world was intrinsically evil and that the things of the world were to be avoided. In this belief, they mistook the cardinal virtue of temperance for abstinence.

The virtue of temperance assumes that the world is good. It is God's creation, and it is he who said that "it is good" (Gen. 1:31). However, anything in the world can be over-consumed and perverted into a bad thing. Too much drink leads to drunkenness; too much food leads to gluttony. God gave us a day of rest, but too much rest leads to idleness. Conversely, too much work can distract us from enjoying the beauty of creation. Anything good can be twisted (as every good heretic knows).

The desert fathers teach us that even too much prayer can be a bad thing. It is written that John the Vertically Challenged Person (as he is referred to in modern lexicons, John the Dwarf in older texts) once decided to spend his life entirely in prayer. So he left his brother monks and his labors and went to live in the wilderness, where he could devote himself entirely to contemplating the mysteries of God and praying ceaselessly. One evening a few days later, a voice was heard outside the locked door of the monks' residence. "It's John; let me in. I'm hungry." His brothers pretended not to recognize his voice and replied, "John? John's not here. He went to live with the angels." They made him sleep outside until he was humbled and willing to join them in the necessary work of the monastery. By this example we learn that temperance is even required in prayer.

The Apostle Paul described temperance as one of the fruits of the Spirit. Compared to love, joy, peace, longsuffering, gentleness, goodness, faith, and meekness, the fruit of temperance may sound out of place. But it is a virtue often mentioned by Paul. In his Epistle to Titus, he wrote that a bishop must be "blameless, as the steward of God; not self-willed, not soon angry, not given to wine, no striker, not given to filthy lucre; but a lover of hospitality, a lover of good men, sober, just, holy, temperate" (1:7–8), and that aged men should be "sober, grave, temperate, sound in faith, in charity, in patience" (2:2).

Being temperate in character (as Luke described Paul when he spoke to

Felix in Acts 24:25) is one of the four cardinal virtues. It is to do nothing in excess, neither speaking, nor eating, nor drinking, nor playing, nor working. It requires watchfulness of how we carry ourselves, how we spend our time, how we meet the needs of our body—in short, how we live in this world. We should be temperate in all things except our faith, our hope, and our love.

JUSTICE

To do justice and judgment is more acceptable to the Lord
than sacrifice. —Proverbs 21:3

Justice is often listed as the first of the four cardinal virtues. It has been called the mother of all virtues by Lactantius and Leo XIII, but that title is also claimed for gratitude (Cicero), humility (Augustine and Cassian), charity (Jerome), prayer (Isaac the Syrian), discretion (Abba Moses and Benedict), obedience (Augustine—yes, again), sobriety (Origen), good will in the soul (Albert the Great), reverence (von Hildebrand), courage (Winston Churchill), patience (Hindu tradition), appreciation (Chinese tradition), jihad [struggle]-patience-sacrifice (Islamic tradition), and frugality (inscription on the State National Bank Building in Houston, Texas).

Despite this disagreement over which is the greatest of the virtues, it is clear that justice holds civilized societies together. As Augustine said in *City of God,* "A republic cannot be administered without justice." Nevertheless, justice is a very elusive thing. Justice is, in every country, more difficult to obtain if one is very poor and weak than if one is very rich and powerful. Presidents, kings, and rich young rulers can get away with scandalous things that peasants and paupers cannot. Hence, although it is our duty to live justly, we recognize that true justice for us will only be obtained in the kingdom of heaven.

This view of justice is markedly different from that of contemporary society. However, the church fathers are even more radical than this in their understanding of the meaning of justice. For they contend that real justice cannot even be practiced by one who does not know God. To quote Augustine in *City of God,* "When a man does not serve God, what justice can we ascribe to him, since in this case his soul cannot exercise a just control over the body, nor his reason over his vices?" The late third to early fourth-century church father Lactantius put it perhaps more clearly in his *Institutes,* "For what is humanity itself, but justice? What is justice, but piety? And piety is nothing else than the recognition of God as a parent."

Lactantius admitted that a pagan could do good deeds, such as giving alms to the needy, entertaining the poor, and clothing the naked, but he argued that

> all those good acts are empty and vain, so that he labored in vain in performing them. All his justice will be like a human body not having a head; for although all the limbs are in it and in their plac- es, and have beauty and shapeliness, because that is lacking which is the principle of all, it lacks both life and sensation. So those limbs have only the shape of limbs, not their use. (*Institutes* 6:9)

Likewise, he said that having knowledge of God while living unjustly is like having a head without having any limbs. Although a man might manage to live this way, he would be weak and pitiable, like a soul with little virtue.

In his *Epitome*, Lactantius wrote, "Now the first duty of justice is to acknowledge God as a parent, and to fear him as a master, to love him as a father." If the Christian story is true, this description of justice makes perfect sense. It is only on this basis that we can begin to understand right from wrong, truth from falsehood, and fairness from prejudice. Hence, true justice is only practiced by those who carry out the will of God.

FORTITUDE

And he said unto me, "It is done. I am Alpha and Omega, the begin-
ning and the end. I will give unto him that is athirst of the fountain of
the water of life freely. He that overcometh shall inherit all things; and I
will be his God, and he shall be my son." —Revelation 21:6–7

We live in a culture that embraces perpetual adolescence. Expressions of manliness in the traditional sense are seen as often as chest hair on a male model. Hence, it should be no surprise that the very idea of being virtu- ous is met with derision. After all, the word *virtue* comes from the Latin word *vir*, meaning "man." Hence, virtuousness is meant to be equated with manliness, in that a man who is fully mature in a moral sense is virtuous.

Significantly, the cardinal virtue of fortitude is historically symbolized not by the figure of a man, but by that of a woman. The ancient Greeks personified fortitude as a woman wearing a helmet and carrying a sword and shield. They often showed her accompanied by a lion, the traditional symbol of strength.

Of course, neither of these words (*virtue* and *fortitude*) maintains these sexual differences today and, in a sense, perhaps they never did. Women have always been recognized as capable of being virtuous (as exemplified by Fortitude herself) and men, one hopes, are capable of possessing fortitude.

The *Oxford English Dictionary* defines fortitude as "moral strength or courage" and as "unyielding courage in the endurance of pain or adversity." The fathers of the Church sometimes exchanged the word *fortitude* with *courage* when listing the four cardinal virtues.

This combination of moral strength, courage, and endurance is what makes this virtue so important. Fortitude goes beyond having the strength and courage to take up one's cross. It is taking up one's cross *daily*. It contains within it a requirement of endurance.

Winston "never-give-up" Churchill once gave an address at a boys' school with the words: "Never, never, never, in nothing great or small, large or petty, never give in except to convictions of honour and good sense. Never yield to force; never yield to the apparently overwhelming might of the enemy." Churchill is perhaps the twentieth century's poster child for fortitude, and rightly so, for in this virtue he excelled (at least in the secular sense). He once said, "Success is never final. Failure is never fatal. It is courage that counts."

To us Christians, this courage that counts is the courage to overcome all things, as the Apostle John recorded in the last chapter of the Bible. It is the absence of timidity and weakness. It is the sweating of blood at Gethsemane. It is not yielding to sin and desires of the flesh. It is the perseverance of the saints. It is the opposite of "just do it" and "looking out for number one." It is the blood of the martyrs. It is the virtue of fortitude.

Fortitude is an important part of the Christian response to temptation. As John Cassian wrote in the fifth century, "For the fortitude of any good man would not, as we said, be worthy of praise, if his victory was gained without his being tempted, as most certainly there is no room for victory where there is no struggle and conflict" (*Conferences*, 18:13). To the extent that there are conflict and struggle in our lives, we need to pray for fortitude. To the extent that there is no conflict or struggle, we need to pray to become Christian.

Reprinted from Touchstone: A Journal of Mere Christianity, *September, October, November, and December 2001, Volume 14, Numbers 7, 8, 9, and 10.*

WILFRED M. MCCLAY

Mastery's Shadow

Modern Medicine & the Human Soul

The modern world prides itself on its freedom from the past's unreflective orthodoxies. But of course it has accumulated quite an impressive stock of its own. None is more settled than our unquestioned belief in the rightness and efficacy of using modern science and medicine to prolong human life—so long, of course, as the life in question is deemed to be of the requisite "quality."

A SETTLED MATTER

One could almost hear the machinery of this sturdy piece of orthodoxy clanking into place during the recent debate over federal funding for embryonic stem-cell research. Only let an accredited research scientist stand before us and float the proposition that a procedure, however morally troubling, might hold some promise for the cure of diabetes, cancer, Parkinson's disease, dementia, herpes, or the common cold, and the matter is settled. The American public wants it.

They are only too happy to roll over and give the man in the lab coat whatever he wants, especially if it is no skin off their own blastocysts. The thought that such scientists, like other human beings, might have a limited perspective on the matter, and might occasionally act in self-interest, seems never to occur to our famously skeptical journalists.

There is, of course, real force behind the scientists' appeals. No one who suffers from an incurable condition, or has seen a loved one suffer and die from one, can be immune to them. It is in our nature to cherish life. Even those of us who are convinced that a better existence awaits us beyond the grave nevertheless cling to earthly existence. Those who hold no such belief, or hold it only tenuously, are sure to cling to life all the more intensely. And it is an undeniable fact that remarkable medical break-throughs occur all the time, so the hope for cures cannot be dismissed as a vain one.

Nor does it help matters that we live in an era in which shameless appeals to sentimentality and emotionalism have become the principal means by which public opinion is molded. And yet it would be cruel, even inhuman, not to be at least slightly moved by the pleas of celebrity sufferers such as Christopher Reeve and Michael J. Fox. There go I—so we think to ourselves—or someone I know, or might have known. Who could be so heartless as to deny them hope?

Let it be stipulated, then, that modern medicine's achievements have been remarkable and promise to become even more so in the years to come. Yet it takes no prophetic genius to see that medicine can have no cure for the unintended moral and spiritual consequences its progress will surely engender. In the wake of the stem-cell controversy, much thought is being given to the moral trade-offs between the promise of medical progress and the multifaceted cannibalization and degradation of existing life. This is surely the bioethical question of the hour.

But consider for a moment a different concern, one that even the most implacable opponents of embryonic stem-cell research did not express. Let us suppose that even the cannibalization issues can be solved—that, for example, stem cells can be extracted from adults, placental tissues, umbili-cal cords, and such, without recourse to the destruction of embryos—and that all other related issues can be satisfactorily resolved.

Would the progress of modern medicine be thereby rendered entirely unproblematic? Might it not rather be the case that the very meaning of suffering and death, and their place in the economy of the human soul, are in the process of being cancelled, in ways that may be hugely consequential to us?

I am not suggesting that we all should want to rush back to a world without anesthesia. And I have no idea what it would mean to be an "enemy of the future," unless one first posits that the future is foreordained. No, I am merely pointing to an inescapable irony at work in the progress of modern medicine, and to the fact that the high cost of medical care may be the least of the prices we are going to be paying for it.

THE CONVERSATION

What recently presented the issue to me in especially compelling form was an old friend's death from cancer. He was a very intelligent and convinced atheist, who had over the years been coming, little by little, to take the claims of Christianity more and more seriously and to entertain the thought that all the things he valued in life might well be meaningless without the support of some transcendental ground. He had watched my own development as a Christian with wary curiosity, and notwithstanding his deep-seated aversion to "Christers," our friendship seemed to deepen with passing years.

I thought it likely that someday we would have a serious conversation about it all. I believed he would listen to me, and I wanted to be ready for his questions when the time came. When he was diagnosed with the cancer, and it was clear that he might not have long to live, I thought "the conversation" would be coming soon, and so consciously began to prepare for it. I visited him repeatedly in his last days, each time hoping that this would turn out to be the moment when we would talk about God. But we never did. I gently sought openings, was gently rebuffed, and that was that.

Maybe, in the end, he just didn't want to have "the conversation." Not that he was especially reticent in speaking about death. On the contrary. But perhaps it would have seemed too much a confession of weakness to him to allow the mere fact that he was dying to be the cause of his reopening a lifetime's settled opinions. In any event, there was another reason why he would not have "the conversation" with me. And that was because he was too preoccupied with other matters—in particular, with an exhaustive search for a possible cure for his affliction.

All over the country and the world, there are countless clinical trials going on, drugs being tested, therapies being experimented with, miracle cures being explored and touted. It is a full-time job just to research them all and sort through the conflicting claims to decide which one to try, and then to get oneself admitted for participation. He was understandably preoccupied with this search each time I saw him, and remained so until very near the end. As it was, he died in his bed at a prestigious hospital, of an infection contracted there while awaiting his treatment for the cancer. A particularly hard irony.

Thankfully, he died in the presence of his wonderful family. And at the end he spoke to them of an inner serenity, once all the pondering and choosing was past. That thought is some comfort to me. One wants to hope for the best, particularly of one's friends. God alone knows for sure what transactions take place in a man's final moments. Still, I was left wondering whether he had really even had time to come to terms with his death. And if he hadn't, didn't "the miracle of modern medicine" have something to do with it?

Here is an instance in which the very possibility of a cure—a possibility that, to repeat, was entirely reasonable to hope for and that it would have been unthinkable not to pursue—may have robbed his death of its full meaning and distracted him from a frank consideration of his ultimate condition. How different would it have been had he been faced with the inevitability of his death some days and weeks before, as a terminal barrier looming before him like an insurmountable mountain? Would he have been led to give more serious thought to it all? Might we even have had "the conversation"?

THE SHADOW SIDE

The problem has already been with us for a long time. It is a variation on the theme that Aldous Huxley famously sounded. It is the shadow side of our growing mastery of the physical terms of our existence, a shadow that grows in ominous symbiosis with the mastery. Aleksandr Solzhenitsyn limned it memorably in his famous 1978 Harvard Commencement Address (a document whose greatness is even more evident today), when he pointed to the "weakening of human personality in the West."

One sees the same thing in a more banal, but for that very reason more sobering, phenomenon reported in the *Chronicle of Higher Education*. Two Vermont psychologists relate therein that "a steadily growing number of students who are struggling with depression, anxiety, sleep disorders, and other problems visit campus health-care services . . . for the sole purpose of refilling prescriptions . . . [They] tell us they are not interested in working toward an understanding of their lives [but] ask only that their regimens of psychotropic medications—antidepressants, Ritalin, tranquilizers, and others—be continued or adjusted."

Unfortunately, one sees it too in the psychologists' less-than-resounding arguments against such behavior (e.g., that the use of such drugs might interfere with "late-adolescent development" and might be mixed inappropriately with alcohol) and their openly self-interested arguments for "greater attention to the intrapsychic world" (which of course means we need to spend more money to hire more people like them). The pill-popping kids may be misguided, but they are right to sense that there is not much of substance behind the psychotherapeutic curtain.

Indeed, what these kids are doing increasingly mimics the modus operandi of the adult world. We now can comfortably forestall and evade confronting the cosmic questions until the very last moment, if then. Evasion, rather than belief or unbelief, is the eschatological watchword of our day. ("I'm not afraid to die," said postmodernity's windsock, Woody Allen, "I just don't want to be there when it happens.")

But this task of evasion will become more complex in the years to come. How will we make sense of death if it comes to be viewed as something with no intrinsic meaning, but chiefly as a piece of bad luck, a matter of bad timing—the misfortune, for example, of contracting the disease before the march of inevitable medical progress has caught up with it? Or worse yet, how can we ever be reconciled to death when it becomes understood as something almost entirely accidental, and largely preventable?

There will be surprisingly little room for joy or exuberance or adventure in such a world. It will be a tightly wound world, permeated with bitterness and anxiety and mutual suspicion, in which human life will be at one and the same time deeply devalued and fiercely guarded. With growing mastery comes growing responsibility—and the need to assign accountability. In a world without God and without contingency there will always be someone or something at the bottom of everything bad that happens.

The moral economy of a controlled world will demand that a villain be produced. Someone must be to blame. It will always be the twitch of the surgeon's hand or the slip of the obstetrician's forceps (or a slip-up by the managers of some future human hatchery), rather than the will of God or the finger of fate, or simply the imperfections of a fallen world, that explains deformity or death. Paranoia will flourish, and so will the trial lawyers, who may even become for a time the high priests of such a civilization—at least until they themselves become objects of litigious ire.

ONLY OURSELVES TO BLAME

But much of the burden of blame will devolve upon ourselves, since in being set free to choose so much about our lives, we will almost certainly find ourselves more and more anxious about, and dissatisfied with, the choices we make. It need hardly be pointed out that the expansion of choice does not always make for the expansion of happiness. Everyone knows the sense of inexplicable relief that comes when a hard decision is taken out of one's hands by the flow of events. That relief will become rarer. Everyone knows the aching hollowness of "buyer's regret." That ache will become more familiar. It will all be our own fault.

The more our lives are prolonged, and the more death becomes seen as an avoidable evil whose precise moment should be "chosen," rather than an inherent feature of human life, the more we will come to live imprisoned by a compulsive and narcissistic dread of all risk, since the possible consequences of such risk—the gulf between life and death, which will yawn before us like a chasm between eternity and extinction—will be too vast, too horrible, and too fully avoidable to be contemplated. The price of living life to the fullest will be deemed too high.

The typical man of the medical-miracle future will not be an *Übermensch*. He will be more like an obsessive-compulsive hand-washer who lives in constant dread of other people's germs. He might even choose to wait out the next century in the form of a frozen embryo, in anticipation of the day when the final triumph of science has been secured, and a grand and immortal entrance into life could be assured. (Assuming, of course, that he is foolish enough to believe that his "potential" life would not have long since been cannibalized by the march of progress.)

That such a world would drain human life of the very possibility of dignity and vigor is not hard to imagine. Just as the treatment of the soul as a mere congeries of manipulable psychological states renders inner life meaningless, so the infinite extension of life will render life infinitely trivial. "Death is the mother of beauty," intoned the great post-Christian poet Wallace Stevens, "hence from her, / Alone, shall come fulfillment to our dreams / And our desires."

Such words must sound strange, even pathological, to the modern ear. And yet everyone who has ever read the *Iliad* knows that the gods of Homer's epic are rendered less admirable, less noble, and less beautiful than the human warriors, precisely because these gods cannot die, cannot suffer, and therefore cannot live lives of consequence. All they can do is meddle in the lives of mortals, who have to play the game of life for keeps.

ONLY A PRELUDE

Death also is the indispensable prelude to newness of life, which is why the water of Christian baptism carries both meanings—death to old self, risen life in Christ. Without death, there is no new birth. Death is the profoundest way we know of symbolizing our need not only to put off the old self, but to be constrained and molded by a power greater than ourselves, a power in whose service is found the only enduring joy we can have as human beings.

The crass psychological models that dominate our era's self-conception emphasize autonomy, independence, control, and—of course—choice. But these are illusions to which we cling, no more real in the end than the fantastical women's bodies one sees in slick skin magazines. Illusory not only because they represent unachievable goals. Illusory because they represent unworthy goals. We will become miserable and hopeless beyond our wildest dreams once we become the masters of our fate and captains of our souls—familiar words penned by W. E. Henley, a suicide, and most recently given public utterance by Timothy McVeigh, a mass murderer.

The real beauty of human character is something different. It is something like the beauty of weathered wood, a beauty grained and deepened by its graceful and dignified incorporation of the elements within which it exists. Our dignity exists not only in our drive for mastery (and that is surely a part of it) but also in our acceptance of the limits on our will—in how we come to terms with our defeats, our failures, our decay, and our yielded territory, and nevertheless trudge ahead to a destination we could never have chosen at the outset, because we could never have had the wit to imagine it.

That is the deeper meaning of the famed "school of hard knocks." It is a school in which much is left to chance, but is also the school in which God operates most powerfully, and surprisingly. It is the arena in which our lives are transformed. It is the only real school of the soul there ever was, or ever will be.

Reprinted from Touchstone: A Journal of Mere Christianity, *March 2002, Volume 15, Number 2.*

JAMES HITCHCOCK

Things Hidden Since the Beginning of the World

The Shape of Divine Providence & Human History

As with so many aspects of Christian higher education, the disappearance of "Christian history" in the past thirty years, while justified as a sign of a new intellectual maturity, was in fact the opposite—a panicky impulse motivated by insecurity before the larger secular culture.

The ideal of historical "objectivity," first formulated by the "scientific" historians of the nineteenth century, was always misleading, in that such objectivity, implying the complete absence of personal feeling on the part of the scholar, would be possible only with respect to subjects that the scholar found uninteresting, even perhaps trivial. Almost by definition, an interesting and important subject calls forth a personal response from anyone who approaches it.

More realistically, many scholars now believe that their ideal ought to be honesty, a personal response that nonetheless strives to use evidence with scrupulous fairness and to reach conclusions based on the evidence, even though those conclusions might make the scholar uncomfortable.

POINTS OF VIEW

In fact, almost all great historical scholarship has been biased in certain respects, that is, based on the historian's point of view, although often (as,

for example, with the "Whig" interpretation of English history) not recognized as such by the historian himself. As Herbert Butterfield, one of
the most astute historians of historiography, has put it, even an overtly
polemical approach to history sometimes reveals aspects of the subject
neglected by others. Even someone who is regarded as a crank may, by
his very single-mindedness, focus attention on things no one else has
noticed.

Even as Christians were surrendering the right to have their own
history, that is, a history overtly informed by a Christian viewpoint, the
legitimacy, indeed the inevitability, of this kind of scholarship was being
urged as normative in the secular academy. Black history, women's history, homosexual history, and numerous other kinds are now enshrined,
each resting on the privileged assertion that only persons who belong to a
particular social group can adequately understand that group's history and
that scholars outside the group are irredeemably insensitive or prejudiced.
The claim of women's history, for example, is that all of history needs to be
interpreted from a feminist perspective and that those who do not do so
are morally irresponsible and intellectually deficient.

Ironically, the intellectual deficiencies of Christian colleges and universities are revealed in the fact that, almost without exception, they have
embraced this approach to scholarship even as they have systematically
expunged all evidence of a "ghetto mentality" with respect to their own
religious past.

Liberalism defines itself in terms of intellectual "openness" and thus
is required to give evidence of its sincerity through repeated public acts of
self-criticism. Perhaps the first great modern Catholic historian was Lord
John Acton, who was also one of the fathers of modern liberal Catholicism, and Butterfield noted how Acton's bias in his scholarship was against
Ultramontanism, the Catholic historian distorting historical truth in the
very act of demonstrating his "objective" detachment from credal loyalty.
(Liberal Protestant scholarship of the nineteenth century, of course, did
the same thing.)

CHRISTIAN HISTORY FROM WITHIN

On one level, "Christian history" proceeds from what Jacques Maritain
called *connatural knowledge*—the understanding of his subject that a scholar possesses by virtue of its being in some sense a part of himself. Maritain

noted that, whereas a scientist is wholly detached from the physical world that he studies, a historian approaches his human subject in terms of his entire personal disposition. Great works on religious history have been written by nonbelievers, but they are required to make a prodigious imaginative leap in order to do justice to their subjects, whereas for the believer, there is an immediate sympathetic comprehension of even the subtlest dimensions of religious history.

Thus, all things being equal, the believing historian should be a better student of religious phenomena, able to penetrate its inner meaning more profoundly. But of course, things are not always equal, and the believer may be deficient in intellect, ambition, or diligence. A peculiar temptation for believing scholars (Hilaire Belloc, for example) is to deduce reality from their principles instead of studying the empirical evidence, a habit that more than once has embarrassed Christians when a secular scholar discovers inconvenient information that the believer had neglected.

Curiously, what is still often called "the new social history," although it is now four decades old, has had immense effect in revealing the pervasive influence of religion on history, despite the fact that almost all its practitioners have been secular-minded, since it strives to map nothing less than the entire fabric of a given society, and thereby comes face to face with the ubiquitous role of religion. At the same time, such discoveries are problematical for the believer, in that they often show that there was apparently a wide gap between official teaching and actual popular practice, a gap that a theologically and spiritually sophisticated scholar might be able to close on a deeper level.

Virtually all of Christopher Dawson's works were a meditation, by a believing Catholic, on the meaning of history. Yet few of them actually required the reader himself to be a believer. Dawson's faith made him extraordinarily sensitive to the powerful influence of religion in history, and he was able to reveal its workings in such a way that all but the most biased readers had to acknowledge it. Towards the end of his life Dawson had a plan for a comprehensive educational program based on the study of "Christian culture," which was merely a plea for what is sometimes now called religious literacy—that students at least be made aware of the influence of Christianity on history, even if they reject that faith in their own lives. It was a program, Dawson noted, that would not necessarily require believing professors.

Once again, the failure of the Christian universities even to attempt an approximation of this is a sign of their intellectual deficiency, their failure to achieve a consistent and settled identity. This too may be endemic to a certain kind of Christian liberalism—Butterfield noted that Lord Acton tended to treat religion almost exclusively in institutional terms, especially the involvement of the Church in politics, which Acton deplored. The founders of the Catholic University of America, such as its first rector, Bishop John J. Keane, deliberately excluded "medievalism" from its curriculum; thus, an area where Catholics were potentially well equipped to exercise scholarly leadership was left to be developed by secular scholars like Charles Homer Haskins at Harvard.

THE HERESY OF IDEALIZATION

At the same time, Christian historians ought to avoid the trap of nostalgia, whereby the Middle Ages or the Reformation is presented as the high point of history, from which everything since has been a decline. To idealize a past historical age is itself heretical, the unrecognized assumption that orthodox belief is a guarantee against sin. Christian historians should not leave to their enemies the discovery of how often good has been perverted by self-righteous men, and the believer's very understanding of his faith ought to make him especially sensitive to this inevitability. The idealization of a particular era is also heretical in that it fails to recognize that the work of redemption continues throughout history.

The refusal to idealize any past age also serves the Christian by precluding the use of the present to judge the past. One of the central insights of the man often considered the father of modern historiography, Leopold von Ranke (a devout Lutheran), was that "each age stands by itself in the sight of God," that is, no age should be treated merely as a preliminary to what follows. Butterfield, unlike most liberal Christian historians, approached the history of Christianity itself in those terms, insisting that the greatest Christian contribution to history was its witnessing to the primacy of the spiritual and the imperative of charity. In contrast to the current practice of "politically correct" history, he insisted, for example, that the saints retain their significance despite perhaps having been wrong about certain historical questions, such as the rise of democracy. Here again, the wisdom of the historian and the wisdom of the believer, both recognizing the singularity of history, coincide.

Since history is an empirical discipline, in principle there ought not to be disagreements over facts between believing and nonbelieving scholars. The same criteria for establishing the credibility of historical sources ought to be employed identically by both. Inevitably, bias might affect the way they evaluate the evidence, but believing historians have a special obligation not to suppress or underestimate sordid chapters of church history.

Butterfield observed that, like the physical sciences, the study of history began to make "progress" when historians ceased to look for ultimate explanations and concentrated on secondary causes, which led to an increasingly detailed study of those causes. Both the scientific method and the historical method arose out of Western Christian culture. Men of faith have no shortcuts open to them to attain knowledge.

Practically speaking, a Christian historian will manifest his personal faith, at least minimally, in his recognition that the role of religion in history is often slighted, that even those who acknowledge it often do not adequately understand it as a spiritual phenomenon, and that the decline of religious belief has empirically verifiable effects on a culture, many of which are measurably debilitating. (American history, for example, is often written as though Christianity never existed, except in instances, like Puritanism, where it is unavoidable.)

EVIL IN HISTORY

In a famous remark, John Henry Newman said that experience seems to force the conclusion that mankind was implicated in some "primordial catastrophe," and this awareness, too, is one of the believer's special qualifications for the understanding of history. Specifically as a historian, the believer has no special knowledge of the exact nature of that catastrophe, but his faith allows him to understand that it did occur.

Butterfield proposed that the sense of sin is one of the believer's crucial contributions to the understanding of history. The Christian understands evil best, because he is part of it (Maritain's connatural knowledge). Historical evidence alone cannot unlock the mystery of human nature, and without this knowledge of sin, history finally remains a mystery. Butterfield noted that the historian and the Christian both begin by assuming the greatness of humanity, then proceed to offer negative accounts of human behavior. The historian's negative view of humanity is demanded by the innumerable crimes of history, while that of the believer is reinforced by his faith.

R. G. Collingwood, a secular scholar who was the rare combination of a historian and a philosopher of history, went so far as to say that the Christian doctrine of the Fall, by asserting that man is not sovereign over history, broadened that study beyond what the Greeks knew and thereby rendered it open to an awareness of impersonal forces. The Jesuit theologian Jean Daniélou argued that history simply cannot be understood apart from the fact of sin, in the form of universal selfishness, and this seems undeniable. Many secular-minded people employ the concept of sin, if not the word.

However, those who deny that a tendency towards evil is basic to human nature simply cannot make sense of history, which then becomes endless, incomprehensible tragedy, since the story of mankind is to so great an extent the story of benign dreams somehow treacherously betrayed and turned into evil. A sinless view of history could only be Sisyphean, the historian chronicling the endlessly repeated process whereby mankind approaches fulfillment of its exalted plans, only to see them destroyed in the end. Any doctrine of inherent human goodness must confront the massive and continuing evidence of James Joyce's remark that "history is a nightmare from which I am trying to awake."

MORAL JUDGMENTS

This daunting reality inspires an approach to history that is a perennial temptation for Christians, albeit by no means exclusively for them—history as moral judgment. Butterfield, who was a Methodist lay preacher as well as a distinguished historian, argued strongly against this, noting that few things foreclose historical understanding more quickly than the pronouncement of moral judgment.

Acton, he noted, was especially prone to this, and it is by no means merely the temptation of the orthodox. Indeed, contemporary historiography is awash with this kind of moralism, where the past is endlessly ransacked for examples of alleged injustice to designated groups, and appropriate condemnation then pronounced (the dominant approach at the time of the Columbus quincentenary in 1992, for example).

Butterfield offered a theological reason for refraining from such judgments—the fact that all men are sinners and thus dare not set themselves up to judge others. Acton had a famous exchange with the Anglican Bishop Mandell Creighton, himself an important historian, over the latter's refusal to condemn Pope Alexander VI, whom Acton thought a wicked man representing a wicked ecclesiastical system. Butterfield observed that, apart from the question whether the contemporary accusations against Alexander were accurate, Acton lacked sufficient knowledge of the pope's soul to condemn him, while for the same reason Creighton could not acquit him. (In fact he did not; he merely refrained from condemning.)

Acton came to believe that all the great men of history were wicked, in that virtually all of them used force and treachery to achieve their goals, and Butterfield responded that this may be true but is also unhelpful in understanding the past. (Acton's curious myopia led him to concentrate his attentions almost exclusively on men of affairs and not, for example on the great saints of history.)

THE MYTH OF PROGRESS

Such moralism is perhaps inevitable in a certain kind of liberalism, which tends to assume human goodness and is endlessly sympathetic with what it deems to be the "progressive" movements of history, and can then only attempt to salvage meaning from the wreckage by pronouncing condemnation on those who appear responsible.

The historian's task, according to Butterfield, is to record and describe the deeds of past men, deeds that may be deemed wicked by those who read of them, although it is not the historian's task to force this conclusion. In Butterfield's words,

> The whole process of emptying oneself in order to reach the thoughts and feelings of men not like-minded with oneself is an activity that ought to commend itself to the Christian. In this sense the whole range of history is a boundless field for the constant exercise of Christian charity.

An obvious argument for Butterfield's counsel of perfection is the fact that condemning the deeds of men who are long dead can have no effect whatever; they have passed into God's hands. But the danger of this, as

Acton saw, is the blunting of contemporary moral sensitivity—if the wicked deeds of past men cannot be condemned, how can modern men be held to account and their own wickedness thwarted?

The Christian historian must live with this tension, but in exactly the way that every Christian must, enjoined not to judge his fellow men but without falling into moral agnosticism. The Christian belief in human freedom proves to be one way out of this dilemma—since men can and do make responsible decisions, to understand all is not to forgive all. Historians can press to the limit their powers of empathy, without thereby becoming apologists for past wickedness.

NO MORAL VINDICATION

Moral judgment is at the origin of Western historical consciousness, which grew not only out of the Greek but also from the Hebrew sense of history, as the Hebrews were driven by an urgent need to find some comprehensible purpose in the repeated catastrophes that they suffered. As has often been pointed out, they were forced to reject the seductive, even irresistible, hypothesis that suffering was simply God's punishment for sin, since they could see quite obviously that their faithless enemies repeatedly triumphed over God's people and that Israel's own infidelities could not adequately explain this. Making moral sense of history has preoccupied human beings ever since.

The study of history immediately confirms that evil men often flourish and the good are often defeated, with no reversal or vindication in this life. Indeed, this reality is almost knowable a priori, in that the selfishly wicked, who are usually calculating and clever, would obviously not embrace wickedness if experience showed that they would inevitably suffer punishment. The dichotomy of time and eternity is nowhere more evident than in the fact that justice often does not triumph in this world. Thus, calculating people can choose to ignore the justice that may be visited on them in the next life, in order to prosper in this one.

Calvinism offers a logical explanation of this in insisting that all men deserve damnation and God cannot be blamed for bestowing free gifts on some. But this view of history also tends to foster moral agnosticism, in that the seemingly innocent are revealed as being as wicked as the obviously guilty, no final distinction to be made, presumably, between Adolf Hitler and his victims.

Liberalism, including liberal Christianity, finds the triumph of evil particularly in need of urgent explanation, although, as noted, liberalism's view of history inevitably dooms it to continuous disappointment and frustration. Butterfield pointed out that Acton originally viewed providence in the orthodox Christian sense of God bringing good out of evil, but then moved on to what is essentially a secular view that "progress" itself is the chief manifestation of divine providence in history.

The fatal flaw in the liberal idea of progress is its unavoidable short-sightedness. Thus, the evolution of the Greek polis might be celebrated as progress, but that achievement flourished for only about two centuries and was then crushed by new forms of despotism. Most liberals see the history of the past two centuries in terms of self-evident progress, yet no one would be so foolish as to deny the fragility of that achievement, vulnerable to being snuffed out by both physical and political disorders.

The liberal view of progress offers no explanation for the movement of history over the centuries, and in fact either forces the condemnation or ignoring of whole periods of history that were not "progressive," or else settles for the trivial task of scanning bleak periods of history for small signs that the light of progress was dimly shining even then.

Hidden from Our Eyes

Butterfield believed that Christianity alone provides a resolution of this dilemma, through its doctrine of vicarious suffering, Christ himself the victim through whom the sufferings of other innocent people can have meaning.

In this as in other respects, however, the believing scholar's personal faith cannot successfully be made an explicit part of his teaching and scholarship, except insofar as he explicitly makes himself into a kind of theologian. History does not prove beyond all doubt the value of vicarious suffering, and offers innumerable examples to the contrary. The triumph of Christianity can be seen as vindicating the sufferings of Christ, but the nonbeliever will persist in finding other explanations for this triumph.

Rather, faith allows the historian to approach his subject with a certain serenity, as capable as any nonbeliever of being shocked and appalled at "man's inhumanity to man" but ultimately hopeful nonetheless. As Butterfield said, history is indeed the war of good against evil, but the exact progress of that war is hidden from human eyes.

From earliest times, one of the great temptations of Christian historiography has been to deduce, from a general belief in divine providence, its specific manifestations in history. Whole theologies of history have been based on this, and each one has finally failed as a comprehensive explanation of historical events.

The belief that specific catastrophes are direct divine punishment for sin dies hard, for obvious reasons—the laudable desire to make sense of events but also the less than laudable desire to see one's enemies punished. For every wicked man who finally suffers his deserved fate, there are perhaps ten who die in prosperity, honored in their communities. Edifying stories of devout people saved from danger by divine intervention (a city spared the plague, an angelic visitor steering a child away from a precipice) fail to explain why countless other people, even more pious and innocent, have been allowed to perish.

Contours of Providence

Christianity can understand this quite easily on the individual level—suffering itself is redemptive and God takes his servants when he wants them. It is, however, far more difficult to explain events in terms of whole societies, the very mystery with which Israel was forced to wrestle obsessively.

The ultimate Christian explanation is again in terms of providence, meaning that God finally brings good from evil. Without such a belief there could be no such thing as redemption, since even Christ's redemptive act would be repeatedly and successfully thwarted.

The temptation for Christians to discern the exact contours of providence in history is even more compelling than the tendency to explain evil merely as punishment, since it speaks to the basic question whether history makes any sense at all, whether God's goodness can be vindicated within the confines of his creation. It is, however, a temptation that believers, and historians in particular, must resist. It is bad theology and even worse history. At best, its validity is limited to edifying speculation, which believers might engage in as a pious exercise but which can never be assumed as true.

The fundamental barrier to a knowledge of providential history is the simple fact of human fallibility; genuine understanding of providence would require omniscience; the pattern of history could be fully seen only by someone above history.

The most obvious obstacle is limited temporal horizons. If, as some early Christians believed, the Roman Empire came into being in order to prepare the way for the birth of the Savior, this was not at all evident to pious Jews longing for the messiah. They experienced the Roman incursion as merely another of those periodic mysterious catastrophes which fell upon them. But hindsight also does not suffice. An argument can be made for the providential role of the empire in preparing the way for Christ, but in other respects the empire was a formidable obstacle to the spread of the gospel, mainly through persecution, which had the effect of strengthening the faith of many but of intimidating many others.

Once again, this desire to discern the hand of providence is an especially strong temptation for liberal Christians, as exemplified in Acton's facile, even perversely false, view that modern "progress" is equitable with divine providence.

Maritain was not a theological liberal, but he was a political liberal, and he tended to trivialize his own philosophy of history by making a similar suggestion—that modern democracy is somehow the fulfillment of providence and vindicates the actions of God in history, a judgment that precisely illustrates the fallacy of providential history. When Maritain formulated it, shortly after World War II, it was possible to see the American experiment in those terms, because Christianity was flourishing in ways it had never flourished anywhere else, at any other time in history, and this was attributable in part to the democratic conditions that gave religion the fullest possible freedom. Maritain did not foresee that democracy might finally reveal itself as hostile to all claims of spiritual authority and thus become a force for undermining the very possibility of genuine religion. (He also proposed the evolution of moral conscience as the greatest of all historical laws, without foreseeing how that conscience, on abortion and other matters, is now being systematically repealed.)

SLOW REDEMPTION

If evil produces good, although such production is often hidden from human eyes, the ironic view of history that Christians must espouse shows also that good produces evil. To deny this is not to defend the orthodox doctrine of providence but the reverse—a heterodox denial of the reality of human sinfulness, which is able to pervert the most sublime truths into pernicious errors. Drawing on the parable of the wheat and the tares, Maritain recalled, as all historically minded Christians must, that good and evil exist together in the world, and there is a constant double movement, both upwards and downwards. The work of redemption proceeds only slowly, against the inertia of human affairs.

Belief in human freedom finally provides as satisfactory an explanation of evil as men will ever achieve. Most of the moral evil in history can be explained in those terms, in God's mysterious willingness to grant this freedom and permit its full exercise, even when it is used to thwart the divine plan. As Maritain said, God's eternal plan operates in such a way as to anticipate these human failings. Butterfield saw the action of God in history as like a composer masterfully revising his music to overcome the inadequacies of the orchestra that plays it.

The relation of freedom to providence remains finally one of the most tenaciously impenetrable of all theological mysteries, and thus, for the Christian, there can be no final understanding of history in all its fullness. Maritain asked whether Brutus was free not to assassinate Caesar, and the obvious answer is that indeed he was. But if that is true, in what sense did God will the death of Caesar at that time and under those particular circumstances? Caesar's death, like most events of human history, was the result of the freedom that God gave to man, not of some preordained script that had to be played out.

Thus, the believing historian must rely on the theologian and the preacher to remind people of the reality of divine providence, whose workings remain hidden. Not being above the historical process, the historian cannot claim to discern this through empirical investigation. In dialogue with his unbelieving colleagues, he has the advantage of knowing that all things human eventually end badly but that this is never the last word of the story. He is permanently inoculated against unrealistic expectations of progress but also against the concomitant despair that follows each disappointment. In purely worldly terms, he has achieved a ripe wisdom that is partly given to him by his faith.

THE DILEMMA OF MIRACLES

A particular category of uncertainty concerning the discernment of the workings of providence are alleged acts of direct divine intervention, much more commonly believed by Catholics than by Protestants—Constantine's vision at the Milvian Bridge, the Virgin Mary's appearances at Lourdes and Fatima. Believers are, of course, free to reject these as pious fictions or delusions and indeed the Catholic Church itself has throughout its history instinctively followed a policy of scholarly skepticism, placing the burden of proof on those who claim a miracle and warning the faithful against credulity.

Yet some miraculous events, above all, Christ's resurrection from the dead, are undeniable truths of faith, and the believing historian must judge how to include them in his work. Maritain thought that the historian is obligated to take into account all relevant information, including the supernatural, and should not bracket such events or treat them as having a natural explanation.

The Jesuit theologian Martin Cyril D'Arcy pointed to the encounter of the disciples with Jesus on the road to Emmaus as an instance of this dilemma—secular history has no way of dealing with such an occurrence, except perhaps by dismissing it as mere fiction, which is itself a dogmatically naturalistic assumption closed even to the possibility of the supernatural. D'Arcy's solution was to point out that history is not "noumenal," in the Kantian sense—what is known today is not the past as such but the past as it presents itself to the present mind. Hence, in a way, all historical events remain mysterious. He also pointed out the improbability, in purely human terms, that great men who recorded profound religious experiences, such as Paul on the road to Damascus, were simply the victims of delusion.

This hardly seems an adequate explanation for all that has followed from such events. Marc Bloch, the great medievalist who was a secular-minded Jew (he perished in a German prison camp), observed that the real question concerning the history of Christianity is why so many people fervently believed that Jesus rose from the dead, a belief of such power and duration as to be hardly explicable in purely reductionist terms.

Once again, however, the historian must separate his faith from his scholarship, for the simple reason that historical scholarship is an instrument completely unsuitable for discovering the supernatural. There is no historical argument that could convince skeptics that Jesus indeed rose from the dead and appeared to his disciples. The cliché question as to what Christians would think if his body were discovered still buried in Palestine overlooks the fact that, from a historical standpoint, such a thing could never happen. History and archaeology would have no conclusive way of proving whether such remains were really those of Jesus.

Thus, the Christian historian ought not to become involved in fruitless discussions about the reality of the supernatural in history but should simply treat such beliefs as themselves historical events—the powerful conviction that the early Christians had that Jesus had indeed risen, and the immense consequences that belief had for the future history of the world.

THE CHRISTIAN CLAIM ON HISTORY

However, Christianity is a historical religion, which is a cliché only in proportion to one's ignorance of other religions that are decidedly not historical. Emanating from a Judaism that was itself a historical religion, Christianity stakes its claim to truth on certain historical events, notably the claim that at a precise moment in history the Son of God did indeed come to earth. Thus, Christians can never be indifferent to the reliability of historical claims.

But the thrust of modern biblical scholarship has been steadily to diminish the historical reliability of the Bible, and even though there are some signs of a reversal, it is a process that seems fated to play itself out (as in the Jesus Seminar) to the point where the Scriptures are thought to provide no reliable basis for any kind of faith.

The discipline of history as such has relatively little to contribute to this discussion, which proceeds from related disciplines like philology, archaeology, and papyrology. But the whole subject is a vivid illustration of the point made by Butterfield and others—the greatest challenge to the credibility of faith comes not from the physical sciences but from the historical disciplines, which are able to discredit Christianity precisely because it is a faith based on historical claims.

The believing historian's role here is secondary but not unimportant. He can, for example, trace the pedigree of modern biblical scholarship itself, showing its presuppositions, how it has deliberately adapted itself to a "culture of suspicion." Beginning with the liberal attitude of agonized self-criticism, biblical scholarship has by now advanced to the point where many of its practitioners have a vested interest in discrediting as much of the Bible as they can. Modern biblical scholarship is one of the intellectual trends that have a history of their own and cannot be accepted merely on their own terms.

Historians can, in effect, "demythologize" claims of biblical criticism, instructing believers in the ways of modern scholarship. Phrases like "scripture scholars tell us" are almost meaningless in view of the fact that there are very sharp contradictions among such scholars. Finally, the mainstream of modern biblical scholarship tends to take a far more suspicious view of Christian origins than most historians would take towards other aspects of ancient history.

What is not open to the believer is the rejection of the "Jesus of history" and a flight to "the Christ of faith." To do so precisely denies Christianity's historical character and is a thinly veiled attempt to turn it into a myth. Thus, however troubling the theories of biblical scholars may be, the believing historian must continue to dwell on the level of historical inquiry.

The problem has relevance to the entire history of Christianity, since for over a century there has been a parallel, less-well-publicized debate over the reliability of Christian traditions (stories of saints, for example). Bloch pointed out that, parallel with the emergence of the modern scientific method, the method of modern historiography also emerged in the seventeenth century, and that Catholics (notably the Benedictine scholar Jean Mabillon) were among its pioneers. The historical method grows out of Christianity by a natural process, and Christians can never reject it.

CHRISTIANITY & THE LINES OF HISTORY

It has long been recognized that, not only is Christianity a historical religion, but it has also played a crucial role in the development of the understanding of history itself, replacing the cyclical theories common to the ancients with the "linear" view now taken for granted by almost everyone. The cyclical view was really a kind of despair, an expression of the sense that men were trapped in a process that they could not control and that would be endlessly repeated, albeit with variations.

Christianity, on the other hand, gave history a goal, an eschaton, towards which it relentlessly moves, so that repetition is more apparent than real. Thus, for the first time, the actual movement of history could have meaning. (To a lesser extent, Judaism had done the same, by pointing history towards the coming of the messiah.)

Linear time is the same both for believers and for modern historians because it is genuinely open to the future. Among the many ways in which history falls short of being a science is that it does not lead to prediction, at least not to prediction of a very high order of probability. The theologian Hans Urs von Balthasar pointed out that the Incarnation is the one absolutely unique event in all of human history, and in taking that as his starting point, the Christian historian must see history as completely open to God's free action, thus as beyond both human control and final human understanding.

The historicity of Christianity also makes it a very concrete religion, in both respects the exact opposite of a myth. As Dawson said, in understanding Christianity, it is necessary to ask why great deeds, central to all of history, occurred among an obscure Near Eastern people, why an obscure peasant in that same part of the world was hailed as the world's savior. This specificity has sometimes been an embarrassment to Christians, as well as a stumbling block to nonbelievers, and the gnostic temptation (alive again in modern times) has always been to fly to the realm of atemporal myth, which seeks to obliterate all specificity. The traditionalism of Christianity stems in part from the fact that, while God is present in all of history, Christians are also specially bound to a particular line of history, apart from any others, and are called to be faithful to that line.

THE LORD OF HISTORY

But if Christianity is by far the most historical of all religions, that should not obscure the fact that, from another point of view, it is problematical why Christians should respect history at all. The problem is obvious—Christianity points to the termination of history, which is precisely that—a termination. History will end. Christians are taught to live with the knowledge that "all this will pass away" and they will be gathered into eternity.

If one is a mere pilgrim in this life, how is it possible to regard what happens in this life as finally significant? It is a question, of course, with which Christians have wrestled since the beginning, and they will continue to do so until the end of time, when it will become meaningless.

Belief in providence is once again crucial. History has meaning because Christians know that God chose to reveal himself through history and that his providence works through history. Thus, even though believers cannot understand exactly how this occurs, they cannot dismiss history as unimportant. As Daniélou pointed out, divine revelation reveals little about the inner nature of God; it mainly reveals his actions in history.

The Incarnation itself validates history, as the eternal descends into the temporal, and men have no way of working out their salvation except in this life. If history were solely the story of the saints, it would already be infinitely valuable. But its value lies also in the story it tells of sinners, of the entire great drama of human life.

But if the cyclical view of history expressed the pagans' sense that they were at the mercy of the historical process, Christianity by no means offers the prospect of the reverse. One of the deepest insights available to the Christian is that he cannot hope to dominate history, and Butterfield judged (perhaps too simplistically) that history bestows its hardest rebuffs on those who arrogantly try. Christians "escape" from history not by mastering it but through faith in the benign Lord of History.

As Maritain observed, once this lordship was denied, it became necessary for secularists to seek for final meaning within history itself, thus giving rise to the various great "systems" of interpretation beginning with Hegel, of which Marxism was the most ambitious and influential. But the search for a supra-historical vantage point from which to see all of history is obviously futile. The end of history is beyond history, and history cannot reveal its own inner meaning.

HISTORY AS FREEDOM

The great pioneer historians of the nineteenth century self-consciously spoke of history as "science" and tailored their research to subjects that lent themselves to such precision. They were thus forced to ignore vast areas of history, and as those neglected fields (religion among them) more and more came to be rediscovered, it became less and less feasible to think of history as a science, and today practically no one does. Here human experience merely confirms the wisdom of faith, for history could be a science only if human beings were not free. But, as Balthasar said, history is that space in his universe where God has created freedom. As Maritain said, there can be no "necessary" laws in history, only "general" laws that are mere approximations.

For Balthasar, the search for a final "system" of history is itself a significant manifestation of the reality of sin. Christ, he pointed out, did not anticipate the Father's will but allowed it to unfold in time, and the desire to break out of the constraints of time is a fundamental expression of sinfulness.

Christ renounced sovereignty over his own life, as human beings must also do because they are historical beings. All things happen in the "fullness of time," which cannot be known until it has already occurred. (As D'Arcy pointed out already in 1957, the once-fashionable theories of the Jesuit theologian Pierre Teilhard de Chardin were in principle beyond the possibility of historical evidence, although they posited the end of history, allegedly on the basis of such evidence.)

Christ the Center

Just as the Christian "linear" view of history is now universally accepted, so also the fallacy of great historical systems is now all but universally conceded. Historians are content to cultivate their particular gardens, to offer their produce for whatever finite value it may have, a task with which the Christian historian should also be content, although this does not, of course, preclude him from acting in other capacities at other times.

The fact that history is problematical for Christians is also seen in the fact that, as Daniélou pointed out, there can be no "progress" beyond Christ. If Christ were merely a historical figure, he would then bring history to an end. However, he is also an eternal being whose reality permeates time, giving profound meaning to history, but a meaning that is hidden from the eyes of the historian. To D'Arcy, therefore, history is actually a kind of continuous present, although it does not seem that way to human experience.

As Dawson observed, the Christian approach to history is also perplexing to the secular mind because it is not completely linear, as all history is now assumed to be, but focuses around a central date—the coming of Christ—from which time is reckoned both forwards and backwards. (The present Western dating system, which is under some attack, is more than a pious commemoration of Christ's birth. It expresses the fundamental Christian view of history. For this reason, it is almost bound to be repealed once cultural leaders have determined how to overcome the practical problems involved.)

Dawson also observed that secular-minded people do not accept a view of history that has a beginning and an end, a view that seems to depend on belief in an all-powerful God. Debates about the origins of the universe are now among the most significant in Western culture, but the historian as such has nothing to say on that subject. Similarly, by definition, the historian cannot even guess when time will end, and the believer is enjoined by Christ to refrain from such speculation.

Although the stretch of human history seems immensely long to the finite mind, in reality history has to be viewed, according to Dawson, as a "small" space surrounded by the infinity of eternity. If the human race survives another million years, its view of history will change profoundly, as all the carefully delineated eras that are now part of the historical record will recede into a very remote past, to be disposed of by future historians in the twinkling of an eye.

Reprinted from Touchstone: A Journal of Mere Christianity, *July/August 2002, Volume 15, Number 6.*

Select Bibliography:
Acton, John, *Lectures on Modern History* (New York, 1965)
Balthasar, Hans Urs von, *A Theology of History* (New York, 1963)
Bloch, Marc, *The Historian's Craft* (New York, 1964)
Butterfield, Herbert, *Christianity and History* (New York, 1949)
____, *History and Human Relations* (New York, 1952)
____, *Man on His Past* (Boston, 1960)
Collingwood, R. G., *The Idea of History* (New York, 1956)
Daniélou, Jean, *The Lord of History* (New York, 1958)
D'arcy, M. C., *The Meaning and Matter of History* (Later edition titled *The Sense of History,* Secular and Sacred) (London, 1959)
Practically all the extensive works of Christopher Dawson either deal explicitly with the religious meaning of history or show a believing historian at work in an exemplary way.

Rod Dreher

The Godless Party

Media Bias & Blindness—And the Big Story They Missed

As a practicing Christian, a political conservative and a professional journalist, I often find myself explaining how newsrooms work to my fellow believers, and trying to disabuse them of the notion that reporters and editors begin their days thinking, "How can we trash Christianity and/or conservatism today?" Even at this late date, over a year into the Catholic sex-abuse scandal, it is possible to find stalwart Roman Catholics—not only bishops, believe it or not—who are convinced that the whole thing is a put-up job by the Godless Liberal Media. Look, I say, of course the media are prejudiced against political and religious conservatives, but it's not as simple and clear-cut as you might think. There will always be diehard conspiracy theorists who cannot be reasoned with, but I find most conservatives are open to a more nuanced, accurate view of the media-bias phenomenon.

I wish I could say the same for most of my former newsroom colleagues. I have long been amazed at how ignorant and uncurious even intelligent and urbane journalists I've worked with are about conservatives, especially religious conservatives. They are, if anything, stauncher believers in the monolithic and uncomplicated evil of religious conservatives than vice-versa. Many erstwhile colleagues have looked at me—their friend, despite my Catholicism and Republican Party registration—with the same slack-jawed incomprehension as elderly Southerners when they step off the tour bus in London and hear a black man speaking with a crisp British accent (I've seen this, and it's a hoot).

IGNORANT OF RELIGION

People like me and thee—religious conservatives who are reasonably intelligent and sociable—aren't supposed to exist. You may recall the furor a decade ago when a *Washington Post* story described Christian conservatives as "largely poor, uneducated and easy to command." It's bad enough that a reporter for one of the top newspapers in the country made an error like that; it's staggering to think that it got through several layers of copyediting. They didn't know any better. For all the caterwauling about "diversity" among media executives desperate to conjure up newsrooms that "look like America," you will be hard-pressed to find in any Catholic parish on Sunday morning the same uniformity of thinking as you find in most American newsrooms on any day of the week. Try telling that to an editor or news director, though, and he'll have no idea what you're talking about. Believe me, I've tried.

True story: I once proposed a column on some now-forgotten religious theme to the man who was at the time the city editor of the *New York Post*. He looked at me like I'd lost my mind. "This is not a religious city," he said, with a straight face. As it happened, the man lived in my neighborhood. To walk to the subway every morning, he had to pass in front of or close to two Catholic churches, an Episcopal church, a synagogue, a mosque, an Assemblies of God Hispanic parish, and an *Iglesia Bautista Hispana*. Yet this man did not see those places because he does not know anyone who attends them. It's not that this editor despises religion; it's that he's too parochial (pardon the pun) to see what's right in front of him. There's a lot of truth in that old line attributed to the *New Yorker's* Pauline Kael, who supposedly remarked, in all sincerity, "I don't understand how Nixon won; I don't know a soul who voted for him."

In the main—and I've had this confirmed to me by Christian friends who labor elsewhere in the secular media—the men and women who bring America its news don't necessarily hate religion; in most cases, they just believe it's unimportant at best, menacing at worst. Because they don't know any religious people, they think of American religion in categories that have long been outdated. For example, to hear journalists talk, Catholics are berated from the pulpit every Sunday about abortion and birth control; reporters think I'm putting them on when I tell them that I've been a practicing Catholic for 10 years and I've only heard one sermon about abortion and none about contraception. For another, outside the

Jewish community, there are no stronger supporters of Israel than among American Evangelicals, and that's been true for at least a generation. The news has yet to reach American newsrooms, where I've been startled to discover a general assumption among Jews and non-Jews alike that these "fundamentalists" (i.e., any Christian more conservative than a Spong-ite Episcopalian) are naturally anti-Semitic.

In a further comment, that *New York Post* city editor inadvertently revealed something else important to me about the way media people see religion: As far as he was concerned, Catholics and Jews were the only religious people who counted in New York City (he himself is a non-practicing Jew), because they were the only ones who had any political pull. Because journalists tend not to know religiously observant people, they see religious activity in the only way they know how—in terms of secular politics. Thus, when your average journalist hears "Southern Baptist," she immediately thinks of an alien sect whose rustic adherents lurk in the shadows thinking of cunning ways to manipulate Republican politicians into taking away a woman's right to choose. The trouble is, she doesn't think much further, *and it is unlikely that anyone in her professional and social circles will challenge her to do so.*

THE SECULAR PARTY EMERGES

So what? The bias of the news media against religious conservatives is by this point a dog-bites-man story of the first degree. Everybody knows that pro-life marchers and churches who resist gay "marriage" aren't going to get a fair shake from the newspaper, and we've gotten used to that. But the importance of this phenomenon is both broader and deeper than individual stories. In a media-driven society, the press sets the terms of public debate, and in so doing establishes the narrative that will inescapably influence the way society thinks about and acts on issues and challenges.

Anti-religious media bias has profound implications for the future of American politics, or so say social scientists Louis Bolce and Gerald De Maio in "Our Secularist Democratic Party," an important article published in a recent issue of *The Public Interest.* The Baruch College researchers say that the parochialism of journalists is blinding them to one of the biggest stories in American politics: how the Democratic Party has become a stronghold of fervent secularists, and how secularism "is just as powerful a determinant of social attitudes and voting behavior as is a religiously traditional outlook."

Among political journalists, the dominant paradigm—what you might call the "official story"—holds that religious conservatives bullied their way onto the American political scene with the election of Ronald Reagan, and rudely brought into the political arena the culture war that had been raging since the 1960s. That's exactly wrong, say the authors, who attribute the "true origins of this conflict" to "the increased prominence of secularists within the Democratic Party, and the party's resulting antagonism toward traditional values."

Until relatively recently, both major parties were of similar mind on issues of personal morality. Then came the 1972 Democratic Convention, at which secularists—defined as agnostics, atheists, and those who seldom or never attend religious services—seized control of the party and nominated George McGovern. Prior to that year, neither party had many secularists among its delegates. According to a comprehensive study of survey data from the Democratic delegates, the party was badly split between religious and moral traditionalists on one side, and secularists on the other. They fought over moral issues: abortion, women's rights, homosexuality, the traditional family. What the authors call a "secularist putsch" triumphed, giving us what Richard Nixon mocked as the party of "acid, amnesty, and abortion," and instigating—with help from the Supreme Court on January 22, 1973—the long march of religious and moral conservatives to the GOP, which became the party of traditionalists by default. "What was first an intra-party culture war among Democratic elites became by the 1980s an inter-party culture war."

Survey data from the 1992 national conventions show how thoroughly polarized the parties had by that time become around religious orientation. Only 20 percent of white Democratic delegates (N.B., this secular-religious antagonism is a white voter phenomenon, the authors say) went to religious services at least once a month, while over three times that number of white Republican delegates did. A fascinating set of statistics emerged when questioners polled each party's delegates on their views of various subgroups among the other party's activists. Both Democrats and Republicans were "significantly more negative toward groups associated with the newer religious and cultural division in the electorate than toward groups associated with older political cleavages based on class, race, ethnicity, party or ideology." That is, Republican delegates felt much warmer toward union leaders, mainline liberals, blacks, Hispanics, and Democrats than toward feminists, environmentalists, and pro-abortion activists. For their part, the Democrats were more favorably disposed to big-business types, the rich, political conservatives and Republicans than toward pro-lifers and conservative Christians. Of the 18 groups covered by the survey, Christian fundamentalists came in as the most despised, with over half the Democratic delegates giving them the absolute minimum score possible. Put another way, Republican delegates thought more highly of those who favor the legalized killing of unborn children than their Democratic counterparts thought of people who believe in a literal interpretation of Scripture.

ANTI-RELIGIOUS SECULARISTS

For their analysis, Bolce and De Maio defined secularists as "those who rejected scriptural authority, had no religious affiliation, never attended religious services or prayed, and indicated that religion provided no guidance in their day-to-day lives." Traditionalists were "those who prayed and attended religious services regularly, accepted the Bible as divinely inspired, and said that religion was important to their daily lives." Most people surveyed—two-thirds of the respondents in the American National Election Study (ANES), which polled a cross-section of the electorate—fall somewhere between these two extremes, with the remaining respondents evenly divided around the respective poles.

ANES data covering the last three presidential elections found that to be a secularist in America today is to embrace moral relativism—a position strongly rejected by traditionalists. And, say the authors, "secularism is no less powerful a determinant of attitudes on the contentious cultural issues than is religious traditionalism. In most instances, secularists consistently and lopsidedly embraced culturally progressivist positions"—the mirror image of traditionalists. The authors conclude that the increased polarization of cultural attitudes within the American electorate is, contrary to conventional wisdom, not because traditionalists have become more conservative, but because secularists (and to a lesser extent religious moderates) have become more liberal.

Indeed, religion has become such a galvanizing issue for both parties that, say the authors, "the religious gap among white voters in the 1992, 1996 and 2000 presidential elections was more important than other demographic and social cleavages in the electorate; it was much larger than the gender gap and more significant than any combination of differences in education, income, occupation, age, marital status and regional groupings." The media have thoroughly reported the key role religious conservatives play in Republican Party politics; what they've ignored is the equally important role militant secularists play in setting the agenda of the Democratic Party—as the late pro-life Governor Bob Casey, denied a decent podium at the 1992 Democratic convention, could have attested.

The divide has become so stark that the authors have discerned a new kind of voter: the "anti-fundamentalist." According to the 2000 ANES data, the hatred of religious conservatives long apparent among Democratic convention delegates has found a home among a disproportionate number of Democratic voters. Twenty-five percent of white respondents in the ANES survey expressed serious hostility towards religious conservatives, as opposed to only one percent who felt this strongly against Jews, and 2.5 percent who disliked blacks and Catholics to a strong degree. (Ironically, these are people who say they "'strongly agree' that one should be tolerant of persons whose moral standards are different from one's own.") Eighty percent of these voters picked Bill Clinton in 1996, with 70 percent choosing Al Gore in 2000. Conclude the authors, "One has to reach back to pre-New Deal America, when political divisions between Catholics and Protestants encapsulated local ethno-cultural cleavages over Prohibition, immigration, public education, and blue laws, to find a period when voting behavior was influenced by this degree of antipathy toward a religious group." If Al Smith were to return and run for president today, his enemies wouldn't be yesterday's rustic anti-Catholic bigots of the Bible Belt, but today's urbane anti-Christian bigots of liberal coastal cities dubbed (by the *Wall Street Journal*) the Porn Belt.

THE NEWS GAP

This could be the most important development in American party politics of the past 20 years, say Bolce and De Maio—and America's two leading newspapers, the *New York Times* and the *Washington Post,* whose influence on the reporting of other newspapers and TV networks cannot be overstated, have both completely missed it. In a search of the LexisNexis database of every domestic political news story, op-ed, and editorial published in those papers from 1990 to 2000, the authors found a grand total of 14 stories that mentioned the religious gap between the two parties.

"The minimization of the religious divide between the parties is also apparent when compared to the amount of press attention devoted to other 'gaps' in the electorate," the authors write. "During this same time span, the *Times* and *Post* published 392 articles on the gender gap. In the 1992, 1996, and 2000 presidential elections, white women on average gave Democrats 9 percent more of their vote than did white men; the average gap separating secularists and religious traditionalists in these same elections was 42 percentage points."

But their most striking finding was the near total lack of editorial and news coverage devoted to the increased importance of secularists to the Democratic Party versus the role of traditionalists in the GOP. The numbers are mind-boggling: 43 stories on secularist Democrats, 682 stories on traditionalist Republicans. In 1992, the *Times* alone published nearly twice the number of stories about Evangelicals in the GOP than both papers did about secularists among the Democrats *for the entire decade.* The bias is even worse among television journalists, who filled the airwaves with stories about the "Religious Right" and the Republican Party, but who didn't file a single story—not one—about the Secular Left's relationship to the Democrats.

Why is this important? Because studies show that news media shape the way the public views social groups. The authors found that in the *Times'* and *Post's* coverage, the connection between traditional religious belief and political conservatism was clearly drawn. The message was clear: Traditional religion makes people oppose abortion, vote Republican, and adopt intolerant attitudes. There was no similar connection between devout secularism and its link to pro-abortion fervor, Democratic loyalty, and anti-religious prejudice. "And thus it is not surprising," say the authors, "that ANES survey results indicate that the more attention a person pays to the national political news media, and especially to television news, the more likely is that individual to believe that Christian fundamentalists are ideologically extreme and politically militant."

And they're more likely to see all religious conservatives in political terms, and make political decisions based on how they feel about religious conservatives. In other words, the more a person exposes himself to the news media, the closer he comes to adopting the viewpoint common in American newsrooms, which is one of suspicion and hostility toward orthodox religious believers. It is fair to say that our news media, through heavily biased reporting and analysis, are turning significant numbers of American voters against religious conservatives and are delegitimizing the place believers have made for themselves at the table.

I suspect that most reporters, editors, and producers would be shocked by these findings, and reject this conclusion. They pride themselves on being objective, and they really do think of themselves as, to pinch a phrase, "fair and balanced." Yet there is the well-known survey Robert Lichter conducted a few years back, polling national reporters blindly about their political affiliation. Something like 90 percent answered "Democrat," and a similarly large number said they voted for Clinton. Bolce and De Maio cite that Lichter study's numbers on religious affiliation among the media elite, which reveal that half the journalists surveyed claimed no religion at all, and 80 percent said they seldom or rarely attend religious services.

THE GODLESS PARTY

The authors also cite a poll showing that a majority of TV news directors and newspaper editors felt that Evangelical and fundamentalist Christians "have too much power," and fully one-third of those surveyed considered these believers to be "a threat to democracy." The same survey found that only four percent thought secularists and nonbelievers had too much influence over public life, and the number of media professionals who perceived secularists as a threat was . . . zero. You see in these numbers why my former *New York Post* editor concluded that our city was thoroughly secular and that covering religion was unimportant: The media elite think that marginalizing religion in one's life is *normal,* and that those who are serious about faith are mad, bad, and dangerous to know.

When it comes to religion, America is a far different place from its newsrooms. Ours is still a religious nation, even if it is, in the main, a mild "church-of-your choice" civic religion of the sort President Eisenhower had in mind when he remarked, "Our government makes no sense unless it is founded on a deeply felt religious faith—I don't care what it is." Belief in God is, for most Americans, a sign of character. According to a March 2002 national survey conducted by the Pew Research Center and cited by the authors, more than half of those polled thought negatively of "nonbelievers." Only half that number had a low opinion of the "Christian conservative movement." Bolce and De Maio wonder if the media elite understand, deep down, that America has always been a country that reveres God, and consciously do the Democrats a favor by not pointing out what, for all intents and purposes, they are: the Godless Party. "Perhaps it is for this reason more than any other," they write, "that we do not hear in election-night analyses and postmortems that Democratic candidates have shorn up their base among the unchurched, atheists, and agnostics, in addition to the ritualistic accounts and warnings about how well Republicans are doing with evangelicals of the Christian Right."

Reprinted from Touchstone: A Journal of Mere Christianity, *April 2003, Volume 16, Number 3.*

WILLIAM J. TIGHE

Calculating Christmas

The Story Behind December 25

Many Christians think that Christians celebrate Christ's birth on December 25th because the church fathers appropriated the date of a pagan festival. Almost no one minds, except for a few groups on the fringes of American Evangelicalism, who seem to think that this makes Christmas itself a pagan festival. But it is perhaps interesting to know that the choice of December 25th is the result of attempts among the earliest Christians to figure out the date of Jesus' birth based on calendrical calculations that had nothing to do with pagan festivals.

Rather, the pagan festival of the "Birth of the Unconquered Sun" instituted by the Roman Emperor Aurelian on 25 December 274, was almost certainly an attempt to create a pagan alternative to a date that was already of some significance to Roman Christians. Thus the "pagan origins of Christmas" is a myth without historical substance.

A MISTAKE

The idea that the date was taken from the pagans goes back to two scholars from the late seventeenth and early eighteenth centuries. Paul Ernst Jablonski, a German Protestant, wished to show that the celebration of Christ's birth on December 25th was one of the many "paganizations" of Christianity that the Church of the fourth century embraced, as one of many "degenerations" that transformed pure apostolic Christianity into Catholicism. Dom Jean Hardouin, a Benedictine monk, tried to show that the Catholic Church adopted pagan festivals for Christian purposes without paganizing the gospel.

In the Julian calendar, created in 45 B.C. under Julius Caesar, the winter solstice fell on December 25th, and it therefore seemed obvious to Jablonski and Hardouin that the day must have had a pagan significance before it had a Christian one. But in fact, the date had no religious significance in the Roman pagan festal calendar before Aurelian's time, nor did the cult of the sun play a prominent role in Rome before him.

There were two temples of the sun in Rome, one of which (maintained by the clan into which Aurelian was born or adopted) celebrated its dedication festival on August 9th, the other of which celebrated its dedication festival on August 28th. But both of these cults fell into neglect in the second century, when eastern cults of the sun, such as Mithraism, began to win a following in Rome. And in any case, none of these cults, old or new, had festivals associated with solstices or equinoxes.

As things actually happened, Aurelian, who ruled from 270 until his assassination in 275, was hostile to Christianity and appears to have promoted the establishment of the festival of the "Birth of the Unconquered Sun" as a device to unify the various pagan cults of the Roman Empire around a commemoration of the annual "rebirth" of the sun. He led an empire that appeared to be collapsing in the face of internal unrest, rebellions in the provinces, economic decay, and repeated attacks from German tribes to the north and the Persian Empire to the east.

In creating the new feast, he intended the beginning of the lengthening of the daylight, and the arresting of the lengthening of darkness, on December 25th to be a symbol of the hoped-for "rebirth," or perpetual rejuvenation, of the Roman Empire, resulting from the maintenance of the worship of the gods whose tutelage (the Romans thought) had brought Rome to greatness and world-rule. If it co-opted the Christian celebration, so much the better.

A BY-PRODUCT

It is true that the first evidence of Christians celebrating December 25th as the date of the Lord's nativity comes from Rome some years after Aurelian, in A.D. 336, but there is evidence from both the Greek East and the Latin West that Christians attempted to figure out the date of Christ's birth long before they began to celebrate it liturgically, even in the second and third centuries. The evidence indicates, in fact, that the attribution of the date of December 25th was a by-product of attempts to determine when to celebrate his death and resurrection.

How did this happen? There is a seeming contradiction between the date of the Lord's death as given in the synoptic Gospels and in John's Gospel. The synoptics would appear to place it on Passover Day (after the Lord had celebrated the Passover Meal on the preceding evening), and John on the eve of Passover, just when the Passover lambs were being slaughtered in the Jerusalem Temple for the feast that was to ensue after sunset on that day.

Solving this problem involves answering the question of whether the Lord's Last Supper was a Passover meal, or a meal celebrated a day earlier, which we cannot enter into here. Suffice it to say that the early Church followed John rather than the synoptics, and thus believed that Christ's death would have taken place on 14 Nisan, according to the Jewish lunar calendar. (Modern scholars agree, by the way, that the death of Christ could have taken place only in A.D. 30 or 33, as those two are the only years of that time when the eve of Passover could have fallen on a Friday, the possibilities being either 7 April 30 or 3 April 33.)

However, as the early Church was forcibly separated from Judaism, it entered into a world with different calendars, and had to devise its own time to celebrate the Lord's Passion, not least so as to be independent of the rabbinic calculations of the date of Passover. Also, since the Jewish calendar was a lunar calendar consisting of twelve months of thirty days each, every few years a thirteenth month had to be added by a decree of the Sanhedrin to keep the calendar in synchronization with the equinoxes and solstices, as well as to prevent the seasons from "straying" into inappropriate months.

Apart from the difficulty Christians would have had in following—or perhaps even being accurately informed about—the dating of Passover in any given year, to follow a lunar calendar of their own devising would have set them at odds with both Jews and pagans, and very likely embroiled them in endless disputes among themselves. (The second century saw severe disputes about whether Pascha had always to fall on a Sunday or on whatever weekday followed two days after 14 Artemision/Nisan, but to have followed a lunar calendar would have made such problems much worse.)

These difficulties played out in different ways among the Greek Christians in the eastern part of the empire and the Latin Christians in the western part of it. Greek Christians seem to have wanted to find a date equivalent to 14 Nisan in their own solar calendar, and since Nisan was the month in which the spring equinox occurred, they chose the 14th day of Artemision, the month in which the spring equinox invariably fell in their own calendar. Around A.D. 300, the Greek calendar was superseded by the Roman calendar, and since the dates of the beginnings and endings of the months in these two systems did not coincide, 14 Artemision became April 6th.

In contrast, second-century Latin Christians in Rome and North Africa appear to have desired to establish the historical date on which the Lord Jesus died. By the time of Tertullian they had concluded that he died on Friday, 25 March 29. (As an aside, I will note that this is impossible: 25 March 29 was not a Friday, and Passover Eve in A.D. 29 did not fall on a Friday and was not on March 25th, or in March at all.)

INTEGRAL AGE

So in the East we have April 6th, in the West, March 25th. At this point, we have to introduce a belief that seems to have been widespread in Judaism at the time of Christ, but which, as it is nowhere taught in the Bible, has completely fallen from the awareness of Christians. The idea is that of the "integral age" of the great Jewish prophets: the idea that the prophets of Israel died on the same dates as their birth or conception.

This notion is a key factor in understanding how some early Christians came to believe that December 25th is the date of Christ's birth. The early Christians applied this idea to Jesus, so that March 25th and April 6th were not only the supposed dates of Christ's death, but of his conception or birth as well. There is some fleeting evidence that at least some first- and second-century Christians thought of March 25th or April 6th as the date of Christ's birth, but rather quickly the assignment of March 25th as the date of Christ's conception prevailed.

It is to this day, commemorated almost universally among Christians as the Feast of the Annunciation, when the Archangel Gabriel brought the good tidings of a savior to the Virgin Mary, upon whose acquiescence the Eternal Word of God ("Light of Light, True God of True God, begotten of the Father before all ages") forthwith became incarnate in her womb. What is the length of pregnancy? Nine months. Add nine months to March 25th and you get December 25th; add it to April 6th and you get January 6th. December 25th is Christmas, and January 6th is Epiphany.

Christmas (December 25th) is a feast of Western Christian origin. In Constantinople it appears to have been introduced in 379 or 380. From a sermon of St. John Chrysostom, at the time a renowned ascetic and preacher in his native Antioch, it appears that the feast was first celebrated there on 25 December 386. From these centers it spread throughout the Christian East, being adopted in Alexandria around 432 and in Jerusalem a century or more later. The Armenians, alone among ancient Christian churches, have never adopted it, and to this day celebrate Christ's birth, manifestation to the magi, and baptism on January 6th.

Western churches, in turn, gradually adopted the January 6th Epiphany feast from the East, Rome doing so sometime between 366 and 394. But in the West, the feast was generally presented as the commemoration of the visit of the magi to the infant Christ, and as such, it was an important feast, but not one of the most important ones—a striking contrast to its position in the East, where it remains the second most important festival of the church year, second only to Pascha (Easter).

In the East, Epiphany far outstrips Christmas. The reason is that the feast celebrates Christ's baptism in the Jordan and the occasion on which the Voice of the Father and the Descent of the Spirit both manifested for the first time to mortal men the divinity of the Incarnate Christ and the Trinity of the Persons in the One Godhead.

A CHRISTIAN FEAST

Thus, December 25th as the date of the Christ's birth appears to owe nothing whatsoever to pagan influences upon the practice of the Church during or after Constantine's time. It is wholly unlikely to have been the actual date of Christ's birth, but it arose entirely from the efforts of early Latin Christians to determine the historical date of Christ's death.

And the pagan feast which the Emperor Aurelian instituted on that date in the year 274 was not only an effort to use the winter solstice to make a political statement, but also almost certainly an attempt to give a pagan significance to a date already of importance to Roman Christians. The Christians, in turn, could at a later date re-appropriate the pagan "Birth of the Unconquered Sun" to refer, on the occasion of the birth of Christ, to the rising of the "Sun of Salvation" or the "Sun of Justice."

Reprinted from Touchstone: A Journal of Mere Christianity, *December 2003, Volume 16, Number 10.*

JONATHAN WITT

The Gods Must Be Tidy!

Is the Cosmos a Work of Poor Engineering or the Gift of an Artistic Designer?

When as a boy I read "The Scouring of the Shire" near the end of J. R. R. Tolkien's *The Lord of the Rings*, I could not understand why Tolkien felt the need to tack on such an anti-climactic and shabby bit of evil. Only later, as I began to notice modernity's penchant for ugliness in the world beyond Middle Earth, did I understand that the scouring of the Shire bespoke a present evil, a malevolence insidious precisely because it lacked the stark drama of the trenches or the gas chambers.

I came to understand that the demolition of the hobbits' lovely village possessed the striking lines of caricature not because it was unrealistic but rather because the depiction is so sharp and trenchant. Familiarity may breed contempt, but it can also breed cataracts, an incapacity to see a thing vividly, truly.

GOD OF THE NAZIS

The twentieth century was, in its darkest moments, an arresting illustration of the will to power, but it also exhibited a less imposing if somewhat more curious urge: what could be aptly termed the will to ugliness. The perversely drab "pre-fabs" of postwar England, the American slum projects constructed by a later generation, the willfully dissonant monstrosities of much modern high architecture, the willfully tortured, obscure, and graceless prose of the deconstructionists, even the black-eyed and anorexic grotesques of the Paris catwalks—all bespeak an age driven to throw up trappings repulsive in their embrace of detachment and death.

The cultural pedigree of this modern predilection for ugliness is old, various, and to some degree mysterious. But here I want to suggest that Darwinism—in which I include its DNA-inspired mutation, neo-Darwinism—has contributed to this will to ugliness not merely by underwriting a vision of the world as a godless accident, but also in the very way it critiques and thereby dismisses the idea of an Author and Designer of life.

What I call the a-teleological macroevolutionists—those who argue that the cosmos is the product of chance and has no intrinsic end or purpose—argue that life emerged by natural selection without design from single-celled organisms, and they claim to use strictly scientific methods to support their position. In truth, however, they often slip into what is essentially an aesthetic and theological argument against a designer.[1] Others have noted this, but what has not been fully explored is the dubious nature of the evolutionists' aesthetic argument.

Consider one especially prominent example, evolutionist Richard Dawkins's critique of the mammalian eye in his *The Blind Watchmaker: Why the Evidence of Evolution Reveals a Universe Without Design*:

> Each photocell is, in effect, wired in backwards, with its wire sticking out on the side nearest the light. . . . This means that the light, instead of being granted an unrestricted passage to the photocells, has to pass through a forest of connecting wires, presumably suffering at least some attenuation and distortion (actually probably not much but, still, it is the *principle* of the thing that would offend any tidy-minded engineer!)[2]

Never mind for the moment that it has been clearly demonstrated that the backward wiring of the mammalian eye actually confers a distinct advantage by dramatically increasing the flow of oxygen to the eye.[3] Let us ignore that brilliant bit of engineering and look at Dawkins's intriguing obsession with neatness. O brave new world whose supreme designer distinguishes himself first and foremost by his tidy-mindedness! Aldous Huxley has ably dramatized the horror of a society so engineered.

Do we really wish to substitute the exuberantly imaginative, even whimsical designer of our actual universe for a cosmic neat freak? Such a deity might serve nicely as the national God of the Nazis, matching Hitler stroke for stroke: Hitler in his disdain for humanity's sprawling diversity; the tidy cosmic engineer in his distaste for an ecosystem choked and sullied by a grotesque menagerie of strange and apparently substandard species. Out with that great big prodigal Gothic cathedral we call the world; in with a modern and minimalist blueprint for a new and neater cosmos.

BYE, PANDA

One of the first things that would have to go is the panda—if not the whole bear, then certainly his two thumbs. In Stephen Jay Gould's book *The Panda's Thumb,* the late Harvard paleontologist has this criticism for his title character:

> An engineer's best solution is debarred by history. The panda's true thumb is committed to another role, too specialized for a different function to become an opposable, manipulating digit. So the panda must use parts on hand and settle for an enlarged wrist bone and a somewhat clumsy, but quite workable, solution. The sesamoid thumb wins no prize in an engineer's derby. It is, to use Michael Ghiselin's phrase, a contraption, not a lovely contrivance.

Now one might take the usual defend-the-engineer tack here, and any design advocate trained in such matters certainly should scrutinize Gould's assumptions as to the inferiority of the panda's thumb. Gould even provides a small opening when he concedes that the sesamoid thumb is "quite workable" and "does its job." Indeed, when he finally witnessed a panda firsthand, he "was amazed by their dexterity and wondered how the scion of a stock adapted for running could use its hands so adroitly."

By Gould's account, the panda's thumb makes a fine peeler for bamboo, the panda's principal food, and investigation may demonstrate that it is actually superior to an opposable thumb for such work.[4]

However, do not hold your breath waiting for pandas to take up flyfishing or needlepoint. For versatility, the opposable thumb is the clear blue ribbon winner. Which raises the obvious question: If an intelligent designer designed the world, did he not think of the opposable thumb until after he designed the panda? And was he too tired to go back and upgrade that poor panda?

To such a question the Darwinian community collectively responds thus: "Obviously not. If there's a designer out there running the show, he's a real bumbler, a second-rate engineer who could not get a job in a third-rate Swiss watch factory. Since the idea of a second-rate designer is patently ridiculous, there is no designer."

This argument is rife with problems already underscored by design thinkers like William Dembski in his book *The Design Revolution*. The most basic failing of this line of reasoning is that even if the panda's thumb is proven to be less useful than it could be, that doesn't negate the evidence that the whole panda has the mark of design. It's a creature dependent upon an architecturally marvelous cathedral of complex, specified information, the sort we know from experience is fashioned only by intelligent agents.

Indeed, the panda would remain so even if it had no thumbs at all. The Yugo, I'm told, was a badly designed automobile, but no sane person would argue that with all its problems, it wasn't designed. The same logic applies to a panda or a duck-billed platypus or an ostrich.

But the point here is that these anti-design arguments by Dawkins, Gould, and other Darwinists are not scientific ones. They are aesthetic arguments, expressing an idea of what the universe should look like—that is, that it should satisfy the tidy-minded engineer. But who is to say that the Darwinists' taste is that of the cosmic designer, if there is one? Who is to say that the designer should value tidiness over, say, whimsy?

BAD ART

Recently, something else struck me about this effort to call attention to the apparently jury-rigged quality of certain elements of the cosmic "watch" and then declare that such things could not have been designed: Critics of intelligent design tuck some idiosyncratic and highly dubious aesthetic presuppositions into the metaphor of the cosmos as watch. These include an overemphasis on tidiness, a de-emphasis on beauty, and a dismissal of any possibility that the creator might wish to commune with his creation. Surely a perfect watchmaker would wind up his perfect (tidy, efficient, functional) watch and step away, freed by the perfection of his instrument from the need to tinker any further with it.

We can see how Enlightenment thinkers arrived at this metaphor of the watch, confronted as they were with fresh insights into the orderly, mathematically precise nature of the cosmos. And contemporary astrophysicists, even those who resist the idea of a cosmic design, now tell us that the laws and constants of the cosmos are, in fact, finely tuned to an almost unimaginable degree, such that even very small changes in a few of them would render complex life utterly impossible. So at least in one sense, the universe is watch-like.

But all metaphors break down if pressed far enough, and this one breaks down pretty quickly. Where a single metaphor crowds out all others in a matter as complex as our living world, it produces an intellectually impoverished and very misleading stick-figure rendering of the subject. Thus, the thinking person is wise to ask, to what *extent* is the universe watch-like? To what extent should it be watch-like?

To cling to the watch analogy in a critique of the notion of a wise cosmic designer fails to face an obvious (and theological) question: Is this an adequate way to speak of the hypothetical designer? Is his satisfying the aesthetic demands of the Darwinists a sufficient test of his existence? To put it another way, if there is a cosmic designer, what does he need a watch for? He doesn't. One would be hard-pressed to name a major religion that posits a transcendent god who uses the universe primarily as a tool.

Not even the god articulated by the orderly minds of Plato and Aristotle fits the bill. Whether we think of the morally compromised gods of Mount Olympus meddling in the affairs of their various mortal offspring; or of Plato's "the One" (what he also called "the Good" or "Father of that Captain and Cause"); or the holy God of the Bible, father and shepherd and husband of his people, the deity is not construed as one interested in the world primarily as a tool for himself. Indeed, whenever he is construed as a personality, and not merely as some sort of non-sentient organizing First Principle, he is depicted as one interested in the world itself, as a creator who delights in the work of his hands.

THE LOVER'S WATCH

Dare we use the word "love" in this context? Dare one suggest that the designer loves his creation in a way the watchmaker does not love the watch he makes, that the Creator would no more think of his creation as a tool than would a bridegroom his bride or a father his children? The fact that such terms as *love* and *bridegroom* strike many as inappropriate to the evolution/ design debate merely testifies to how thoroughly the utilitarian assumption behind the metaphor of the watch has permeated Western thinking.

Certainly, we could try to discuss the matter without considering the designer's attitude toward his creation (that is, whether he is a watchmaker or a bridegroom or father). But the evolutionists have already smuggled this issue into the debate by assuming that, if there were a designer, he would be some sort of disinterested and hyper-tidy watchmaker. Having smuggled in this highly questionable point, they then regard as beneath consideration any idea of a designer who (as they put it) "meddles in his creation."

Or they dismiss the notion that an omnipotent and omniscient designer might fashion a creature short of an optimal design. Here they not only make a theological claim but ignore a key question at once practical and aesthetic: How do concerns about ecological balance impinge upon a critique of animal structures?

Must the cosmic designer's primary concern for pandas be that they are the most dexterous bears divinely imaginable? From a purely practical standpoint, might opposable-thumbed über-pandas wreak havoc on their ecosystem? From a purely aesthetic standpoint, might not those charming pandas up in their bamboo trees with their unopposing but quite workable thumbs be just the sort of humorous supporting character this great cosmic drama needs to lighten things up a bit? If Shakespeare could do it in his tragedies, why not God?

Pandas as comic relief? To spurn the notion as if it were patently ridiculous and beneath consideration is merely to expose one's utilitarian presuppositions. Why, after all, should the designer's world read like a dreary high-school science textbook, its style humorless, homogenous, and suffocating under the dead weight of a supposedly detached passive voice? Why should not the designer's world entertain, amuse, and fascinate, as well as "work"?

In summary, virtually the entire bad-design versus good-design discussion is framed by an engineer's perspective, not an artist's or mystic's. When I mentioned this to the philosopher Jay W. Richards a few years ago, he responded in a letter: "After all, why do we assume that God created the universe to be a watch, in which a self-winding mechanism makes it 'better'? Maybe the universe is like a piano, or a novel with the author as a character, or a garden for other beings with whom God wants to interact. It's amazing how a simple image can highjack a discussion for a century and a half."

What is worse, Darwinists like Gould and Dawkins commit the error called atomism: the idea that, in Gould's own words, "wholes should be understood by decomposition into 'basic' units." In other words, they assume not only that nature is a kind of watch but that each individual design is its own watch—its own machine—meant to be judged in relative isolation. They evaluate the panda's thumb by how well it works as a thumb, not by how well it fits into the whole life of the panda, including its place in its own environment.

This is, at the most practical level, to misunderstand pandas. At the aesthetic level, it is to declare that an artist who might have created pandas could not have been thinking (as artists do) of the whole work.

UNAESTHETIC SHAKESPEARE

Interestingly, the god of the English canon, William Shakespeare, came in for much the same criticism by the tidier-minded among his neoclassical critics as the God of the cosmos has come in for from the tidier-minded scientists. This actor turned playwright lacked classical restraint, the argument went.

In 1726 Lewis Theobald perhaps initiated the century's-long criticism of Hamlet's coarse speech when he commented on a particularly bawdy line spoken by Hamlet to Ophelia: "If ever the Poet deserved Whipping for low and indecent Ribaldry, it was for this Passage."[5]

Another regarded Shakespeare's general habit of mingling the low with the high, the comic with the tragic as a "wholly monstrous, unnatural mixture."[6] With only a little more restraint, a third lamented the bard's tragedies: "How inattentive to propriety and order, how deficient in grouping, how fond of exposing disgusting as well as beautiful figures!", how often he compels the audience "to grovel in dirt and ordure."[7]

Happily, most neoclassical Shakespearean critics were enthusiastic, and yet, as one modern critic noted, even the admiration of the more sympathetic critics was always "modified and tempered . . . by regrets that Shakespeare had elected, either through ignorance or by design, to embrace a method that discarded all classical rules."[8]

What do we make of such criticism today? To use Freud's language, itself rude and vulgar, such criticism strikes us as anal-retentive. What emotionally whole and thoroughly sane admirer of Renaissance drama would want to substitute for the works of the "myriad minded" Shakespeare, the relatively impoverished fare left over after unsympathetic neoclassical critics tidied him up?

Perhaps the relevance of the analogy is becoming clear. The criticism of Shakespeare is akin to the evolutionists' criticisms of the cosmic designer. In each case the critic believes the respective artist in question should build all of his characters according to some rigid set of criteria that ignores broader concerns, be they ecological, aesthetic, or otherwise. Proponents of this line of argument value tidiness over other and often more vital aesthetic criteria like intricacy, harmony, variety, imaginative exuberance, freedom, even moral complexity.

A QUEER ASSUMPTION

The Darwinists' aesthetic criticism moves from the unconvincing to the positively odd in a further and even queerer assumption: the conviction that no all-knowing and all-powerful designer would restrict himself to the materials at hand, even when such designs are clearly superb. Darwinists are quite fond of this argument, apparently considering it irresistibly persuasive to all but the most irrational mind.

I saw an especially brazen instance of this strange aesthetic dogma at a debate at Texas Tech University between Darwinist James Carr and intelligent design microbiologist Michael Behe. Arguing against Behe, Carr used the similarities in the genetic code of chimps and humans as a bad-design argument. What all-powerful creator would need to recycle his materials like this, he argued. It was almost as if he considered it unmanly of the Fellow Upstairs.

Gould leveled essentially the same criticism against a would-be cosmic designer in his description of Charles Darwin's study of orchids:

> Orchids manufacture their intricate devices from the common components of ordinary flowers, parts usually fitted for very different functions. If God had designed a beautiful machine to reflect his wisdom and power, surely he would not have used a collection of parts generally fashioned for other purposes. Orchids were not made by an ideal engineer; they are jury-rigged from a limited set of available components.[9]

Or as one writer Gould quoted put it, nature is a superb tinkerer, not a divine artificer.[10]

The argument that no cosmic designer would so often recycle his creative material is a common tactic, one Darwin himself employed. In a letter to Asa Gray around 1861 Darwin wrote, "Your question what would convince me of Design is a poser. . . . If man was made of brass or iron and no way connected with any other organism which had ever lived, I should perhaps be convinced."[11]

Certainly humans made of iron or brass would create enormous difficulties for a Darwinian explanation of humankind's existence. But the tenor of this comment fits Darwin's attitude to the similarities among the species. His unstated assumption seems to be that the similarities are not merely one missed opportunity for the natural world to reveal its design and thus falsify his theory, but a positive argument against a cosmic designer.

DARWIN'S DESIGN

Most of us would respond, "But why?" The only logical way to use the similarities as an argument against a designer is to take as an aesthetic premise the assumption that no omniscient and omnipotent designer would design in such a way. In other words, one would have to assume that using the ho-hum materials at hand instead of consistently elevating higher works of art with newer and "better" materials violates some pre-established and widely accepted aesthetic principle. "Why," Darwin asked in *On the Origin of Species,* "should the sepals, petals, stamens, and pistils in any individual flower, though fitted for such widely different purposes, be all constructed on the same pattern?"[12]

Ironically, Darwin unwittingly suggested a very un-Darwinian answer in a letter to his sister. Expressing his admiration for the Duke of Northumberland's home, Darwin wrote, "His house was very grand; much more so than the other great nobility, and in much better taste." The young biologist did not attribute the house's nobility and beauty to a prodigal use of variously distinct materials or motifs—quite the contrary. "Every window in his house was full of straight lines of brilliant lights, and from their extreme regularity and number had a beautiful effect. *The paucity of invention* [emphasis mine] was very striking, crowns, anchors, and 'W.R.'s' were repeated in endless succession."[13]

So why should Darwin be surprised that an intelligent designer of the world would proceed in the same way? Conventional wisdom in the field of aesthetics all but demands such an artistic method. Pattern and variation are interdependent concepts fundamental to art. Where would Schubert's "Theme and Variations" be without the theme? The point is so basic one feels silly making it.

Should the later movements of Beethoven's Fifth Symphony be censured for continuing to build off an original motif? Do we exclaim with the woman at the first performance of *Bolero* that Ravel must be mad for building on his central motif? Do we not instead admire the way he built so exquisitely and powerfully on the central motif till the climactic grandeur of the finale? Ought we to demote Monet from the first rank of the impressionists because he had the bad taste to paint poplars and haystacks over and over again? Do we not instead marvel at the fecundity of his imagination, at the subtlety of his observation and insight?

No one, not even his harshest eighteenth-century critics, accuses Shakespeare of bad art on the grounds that *Much Ado About Nothing* and *Othello* share virtually the same plot, creatively altered to produce radically different plays. Few if any object to Shakespeare's repetition of motherless girls as heroines, or to his girls-disguised-as-boys theme, or to his repetitive use of the sonnet form for his poetry.

UNIMAGINABLE GENIUS

Where the atomist or reductionist regards elements in isolation (and properly so within certain intellectual disciplines), the artist seeks variety within unity, rhythm, and harmony, qualities fundamental to the creation of beauty. Notice I am not claiming a seat of honor for some culturally narrow artistic practice—say, the English sonnet—but rather appealing to principles broad and fundamental in the history of the world's art.

If there is an intelligent designer behind this astonishingly complex work of art we call the world, it's quite sensible to suppose he would be at least as artistically savvy as the artistically gifted among his creatures, that he would cultivate harmony and unity through the creative reuse of common materials. Now, the Darwinist might complain, "What is all this artistic, aesthetic balderdash? We are scientists, not poets or starry-eyed mystics. Leave the artists to their pattern-making and let us get back to our hard-nosed, empirical science." Fine, but if they wish to avoid an argument about aesthetic principles, they should not assume within their arguments aesthetic principles that are at best highly debatable, and at worst contrary to the canons of art.

In the meantime, those who reject such dubious reasoning, who understand that the world is the handiwork of unimaginable genius, could do worse than to follow the aesthetic lead of those humble and beautiful hobbits who returned to their desecrated Shire carrying elven soil: We can take a soil richer than the dead ground of materialism and sprinkle it wherever we can, honoring the miracle of creation's growth even as we tend to our proper role as stewards and gardeners of a world between Heaven and Hell, a place we might aptly call Middle Earth.

Reprinted from Touchstone: A Journal of Mere Christianity, *July/August 2004, Volume 17, Number 6.*

Notes:
1. See, for instance, Paul Nelson's "The Role of Theology in Current Evolutionary Reasoning," *Biology and Philosophy* 11 (1996), pp. 493–517; William Dembski's *Intelligent Design* (InterVarsity Press, 1999) and *The Design Revolution* (InterVarsity Press, 2004); and Cornelius G. Hunter's *Darwin's God* (Brazos Press, 2001).
2. W. W. Norton, 1996, p. 93.
3. Excerpts from "The Inverted Retina: Maladaptation or Pre-adaptation?" *Origins and Design* 19.2 (2000): 14 June 2000, *www.arn.org/docs/odesign/od192/invertedretina192.htm.*
4. W. W. Norton, 1980, pp. 21, 22, 24.
5. Quoted in Paul S. Conklin, *A History of Hamlet Criticism: 1601–1821* (Humanities Press, 1968), p. 53.
6. Charles Gildon, quoted in Herbert Spencer Robinson, *English Shakespearian Criticism in the Eighteenth Century* (Gordian Press, 1968), pp. 26–27.
7. Edward Taylor, "From Cursory Remarks . . .", in *Shakespeare: The Critical Heritage, 1774–1801,* edited by Brian Vickers (Routledge & Kegan Paul, 1981), pp. 130–132. This Taylor is not to be confused with the wonderful American poet Edward Taylor, the last of the metaphysical poets, who spent a great deal of time in the "dirt and ordure" exploring the mysteries of the divine and the human.
8. Robinson, *English Shakespearian Criticism,* p. xii.
9. *The Panda's Thumb,* p. 20.
10. François Jacob, quoted ibid., p. 26.
11. "To Asa Gray," 17 September 1861(?), volume 2 of *Life and Letters of Charles Darwin,* edited by Francis Darwin, *ftp://sailor.gutenberg.org/pub/gutenberg/etext00/2llcd10.txt.*
12. Sixth London Edition (1872), *ftp://sailor.gutenberg.org/pub/gutenberg/etext99/otoos610.txt.*
13. 9 September 1831, volume 1 of *Life and Letters of Charles Darwin, ftp://sailor.gutenberg.org/pub/gutenberg/etext00/1llcd10.txt.*

ANTHONY ESOLEN

A Requiem for Friendship

Why Boys Will Not Be Boys & Other Consequences of the Sexual Revolution

Sam Gamgee has been fool enough to follow his beloved master Frodo into Mordor, the realm of death. To rescue Frodo from the orcs who have taken him captive and who will slay him as soon as he ceases to be of use in finding the Ring, Sam has fought the monstrous spider Shelob, has eluded the pursuit of the orcs, and has dispatched a few of them to their merited deaths.

Finally he finds Frodo in the upper room of a small filthy cell, naked, half-conscious, lying in a heap in a corner. "Frodo! Mr. Frodo, my dear!" he cries. "It's Sam, I've come!" With a bluff tenderness he clasps him to his breast, assuring him that it is really he, Sam, in the flesh.

Still groggy, Frodo can hardly believe it, but he clutches at his friend. It seems to him all the tissue of a dream—that an orc with a whip has turned into Sam—and it is all mixed up with the sound of singing that he thought he heard and tried to answer. "That was me singing," says Sam, shaking his head and saying that he had all but given up hope of ever finding his friend again. He cradles Frodo's head, as one would comfort a troubled child.

At that a snigger rises from the audience in the theater. *"What, are they gay?"*

An ignorant but inevitable response. Shakespeare, or his narrative persona, expressed in his sonnets a passionate love for an unnamed and not too loyal young man, so Shakespeare must have been homosexual—despite the absence of evidence, and despite his persona's explicit statement in sonnet 20 that the young man's sexual accoutrements are of no interest (or use) to him whatever.

The bachelor Abe Lincoln long shared a bed with his closest friend, Joshua Speed, and later wrote letters expressing, with what seems a touch of self-deprecating irony, his fear that he would be lonely once Speed had taken a wife. Lincoln therefore must be homosexual. No matter that men (and women too) commonly shared beds, and also commonly spoke of their friendship in strong, earthy language that now embarrasses. The poet Edmund Spenser, celebrator of his own wedding in one of the most brilliant poems in English, used to share a bed with his friend and fellow scholar at Cambridge, Gabriel Harvey. There you go.

"Your love to me was finer than the love of women," laments David in a public song, when he learns of the death of his friend Jonathan. We know why. The godlike hero Gilgamesh and his friend Enkidu walk hand in hand into the dark forest of Humbaba. No wonder then that at Enkidu's death Gilgamesh will weep inconsolably, letting his hair grow long, flinging away his royal robes, and leaving the city to wander in the wilderness.

ONE TINY INSIGHT

For many years I have smiled as that ballast known as the Academic Left have taken one tiny linguistic insight, that the sounds we use to denote things are usually arbitrary, and have elevated it to the single law of the universe. It was not a terribly great insight, nor was it at all new.

Plato had broached it in the *Cratylus,* associating it tentatively with sophism, and having Socrates argue, I fear not convincingly, against it. Dante seems to have accepted it: In the *Paradiso* Adam himself states with shocking matter of fact that even the name for God had already changed before that unpleasantness at the Tower of Babel, implying that no particular human word to denote him takes precedence over any other. Man's ability to speak, says Adam, is the work of Nature, but as for the actual words we use, they lie within man's choice:

Before I went to banishment below
" Yah" was the name on earth for the high Good
that now has clothed me in the robe of joy;
And then they called it "El"—right that they should,
for mortal use is like a branch's leaves:
where one may fall, another springs to bud."

Even so, Dante does not assign language to the arbitrary human will alone, but also to Nature, the agent of God's providence. The medieval dictum *nomina sunt consequentia rerum*—names are consequent upon the things they name—does not hold true, if man expects the causal link between thing and name to be clear and determined, but does hold true, in the mysterious working out of God's order. If a leaf cannot fall without the will of God, then neither can the leaf be named; our language assumes its place in the providential chances and changes of time.

Thus Adam's discussion of linguistic change is preceded by his revelation of how long ago and how many years he lived, and then by his revelation of how long he and Eve managed to enjoy the bliss of Eden before they were cast out forever: six hours, from dawn till noon.

Six hours is not long—and that is part of Dante's point. Man's loss of Eden and his consequent aging and death may appear as senseless as the change of a word, arbitrary and fleeting. Yet neither the loss of Eden nor the fall of the word, even of the holy word *Yah,* escapes the governance of Nature and the wisdom of God.

ARBITRARY WORDS

And that order is what the linguists *a sinistra* object to. For their hearts lie not with words but with what the apparent arbitrariness of words can achieve, if that arbitrariness is assigned to everything else in human life. Again, they are partly correct. Language is a fit metaphor, or a powerful structuring concept, for our customs. As Dante saw, language is itself a custom.

Thus we have a language for the formal introduction of a stranger: the clipped "How do you do" with a nod and a firm handshake, for American men; the automatic smile, head tilt, "It's nice to meet you," and presentation of hand, for American women. We know that a certain style of sign outside of a restaurant means you had better go home and put on a tie (or take it off and leave it in the car). We know that if a grown man and woman are walking hand in hand, they are not brother and sister, though there seems nothing inherently untoward about brothers and sisters holding hands. We know what the teenage boy's modest crew cut means, when all around him are dyeing their spiked hair grape.

Thus the Left proceed syllogistically. Language is utterly arbitrary. Social customs form a kind of language, and sexual customs form a very powerful language. Therefore social customs are arbitrary, and therefore sexual customs are equally arbitrary.

There is no more reason, essentially, for a man's choosing a woman as his mate rather than a man, than there was for the Hebrews to name God *Yah* rather than *El*. The man may of course want children, and having a woman for a mate would obviously facilitate that desire, but that is as it happens. Sexual difference is no more an essential part of the relations between man and woman, and of a man's sexual being as a man, than the vowel "ah" is an essential part of the name of God.

A Faulty Premise

Well, the syllogism is faulty: Even its major premise, that language is utterly arbitrary, seems to be contradicted on the level of phonology, or sound, by the human wish to use words that correspond delightfully with the objects they denote. Thus it is hard to imagine a language in which a word like "lalala" means "repulsive" or "muscular" or "impenetrable."

Nor is language arbitrary on the level of syntax, the ordering of our thoughts by means of words. No language has as its typical sentence pattern Object-Verb-Subject; not one. The human mind does not like to work that way, probably because the human mind recognizes an order in actions, namely that some subject does some verb to some object, and likes its sentences somehow to respect the order.

Nor is it arbitrary in its semantics, the relation of words to meanings. That is because language has that annoying habit of referring to what the typical human being perceives as unitary things belonging to a recognizable kind. The typical human being, in his solid naiveté, believes that words have something or other (perhaps something mysterious or other) to do with things, with nature. No language invents a word to describe the union of the top half of your uncle in Milwaukee with the bottom half of your uncle in Baton Rouge.

But even if it were true that our spoken language were utterly arbitrary, it does not follow that the language of our customs is, or that our sense of good and evil is, or that the idea of human nature is. That is an unwarranted leap from phonology to anthropology to moral philosophy to metaphysics. It is a leap the Left makes precisely to attack the notion of order.

A strange double life they lead: professing fascination with language, yet abandoning any deep study of it; using it instead as a tool for dismantling the idea of natural order, or, since even academics abhor a vacuum, using it as a tool for establishing their own order and imposing it on everyone else. The language war of the early feminists—a war they have won resoundingly, despite the occasional embarrassing rout (anyone remember "waitron"?)—was about the ushering in of a new order, or rather a new and unnatural disorder. They were wrong who thought it was only a silly argument over words.

PANSEXUAL LANGUAGE

What does all this have to do with sex, or with friendship? A great deal, I am afraid. The pansexualists—they who believe in the libertarian dogma that what two consenting adults do with their privates in private is nobody's business—understand that the language had to be changed to assist the realization of their dream, and also that the realization of their dream would change the world, because it would change the language for everyone else.

Language is not language if it is not communal; it is a neat trick of political abracadabra to argue for an individual's right to change the very medium of our thought and our social intercourse. If clothing is optional on a beach, then that is a nude beach. It cannot be a nude beach for some and an ordinary beach for others; to wear clothes at that beach at the very least means something that it had not meant before. If you may paint your house phosphorescent orange and violet, and you persuade a couple of your neighbors to do likewise, you no longer have what anybody would call a historic neighborhood.

If all of Kate's friends leap into bed with whatever male gives them a hearty dinner at Burger King and a round of miniature golf, and Kate chooses instead to kiss her date once on the cheek and leave him on the porch, she will suggest to everybody that she is a prude. She may be, or may not be; she may be more firmly in the grip of lust than they are, for all we know, and may just detest the boy. But her actions have connotations they did not use to have.

Imagine a world wherein the taboo has been broken and incest is loudly and defiantly celebrated. Your wife's unmarried brother puts his hand on your daughter's shoulder. That gesture, once innocent, must now mean something, or at least suggest something. If the uncle were wise and considerate, he would not make it in the first place. You see a father hugging his teenage daughter as she leaves the car to go to school. The possibility flits before your mind. The language has changed, and the individual can do nothing about it.

By now the reader must see the point. I might say that of all human actions there is nothing more powerfully public than what two consenting adults do with their bodies behind (we hope) closed doors. Open homosexuality, loudly and defiantly celebrated, changes the language for everyone. If a man throws his arm around another man's waist, it is now a sign—whether he is on the political right or the left, whether he believes in biblical proscriptions of homosexuality or not.

If a man cradles the head of his weeping friend, the shadow of suspicion must cross your mind. If a teenage boy is found skinny-dipping with another boy—not five of them, but two—it is the first thing you will think, and you will think it despite the obvious fact that until swim trunks were invented this was exactly how two men or boys would go for a swim.

Because language is communal, the individual can choose to make a sign or not. He cannot determine what the sign is to mean, not to others, not to the one he signals, and not even to himself.

Friendship Without Blood

Friendship and the signs upon which it must subsist are in a bad way. I will focus on the friendships of men, since that is what I know about; many comparable things might be said about the friendships of women. We still have the word "friendship," and we still have something of the reality, but it is distant, dilute, bloodless. For modern American men, friendship is no longer forged in the heat of battle, or in the dust of the plains as they drive their herds across half a continent, or in the choking air of a coalmine, or even in the cigar smoke of a debating club.

That is partly because our lives, for better and for worse, no longer involve the risk and the sweat that was the cement of deep friendship. No man will help hew the oaks for our cabin, because we no longer live in cabins. No man will stand by as we jump overboard to set the trawling net, because we have no boat and set no net; we live too comfortably for that. Under such fortunate circumstances, we need all the more the camaraderie and intellectual risk of the club.

But gentlemen's clubs have vanished or have been sued out of existence. (The Citadel is not the Citadel, as the woman lawyer who sued it to death herself admitted, unwittingly and with amazing intellectual amnesia; on Monday arguing that her client wanted the same experience the young men then enjoyed, and after her victory on Tuesday crowing that a student's experience at the Citadel would now be forever changed.) More than ever do men need to come together to eat and drink and argue and think, because more than ever their work separates them from each other; but now they are virtually forbidden to do so.

It is but more of the devastation wrought by the sexual revolution. That we fail to see it as such is no surprise: Naturally, when we think of that recrudescence of paganism, we think first of its damage to the family and to relations between men and women. We think of divorce, pornography, unwed motherhood, abortion, and suicidally falling birthrates. But the sexual revolution has also nearly killed male friendship as devoted to anything beyond drinking and watching sports; and the homosexual movement, a logically inevitable result of forty years of heterosexual promiscuity and feminist folly, bids fair to finish it off and nail the coffin shut.

What is more, those who will suffer most from this movement are precisely those whom our society, stupidly considering them little more than pests or dolts, has ignored. I mean boys.

SAFELY SHARED BEDS

How is this so? Return to the example of Lincoln. His age was surely not more tolerant of homosexuality or of sexual deviancy generally than is ours: Accounts of the Civil War show young men brought to the brink of blackest despair by their inability to break the habit of self-abuse. How, then, if deviancy was such a reproach, could Lincoln risk sharing a bed with a man and having the fact be publicly known? But that is precisely the point. Only in such a case is the bed-sharing possible.

I am sorry to have to use strong language, but only when sodomy is treated as a matter of course for everyone (as in the institutionalized bug-gery of boys and young men in ancient Sparta) or when it is met with such opprobrium that nobody would assume that a good man would engage in it, could Lincoln and his friend share that bed without suffering ridicule. The stigma against sodomy cleared away ample space for an emotionally powerful friendship that did not involve sexual intercourse, exactly as the stigma against incest allows for the physical and emotional freedom of a family.

In Japan, families bathe together, and it is considered a mark of the highest honor—the deepest trust—to be invited, as an outsider, to join them. This custom is only made possible by the assumption that any sexual dalliance among family members, including anyone invited to "belong" to the family, is absolutely out of the question.

The converse is also true. If your society depends upon such emo-tionally powerful friendships—if the fellow feeling of comrades in arms is necessary for your survival—then you can protect the opportunity for such friendships in only two ways. You may go the route of Sparta, or you may demand on pain of expulsion from the group that such friendships will not be sexualized. Essentially you must do for all-male groups exactly what a husband and wife must do with regard to other members of the opposite sex. Adulterers and sodomites there will be—but they must be called so, that we may have chaste spouses and bosom friends.

How does this latest twist of the sexual revolution hurt boys in par-ticular? Some will say that it leaves them more vulnerable to be preyed upon by older men, and I have no doubt that this is true, given the psychological springs of male homosexuality, given the historical examples of ancient Greece and samurai Japan (among others), and given the terrible fact that many homosexual men were themselves abused as boys.

But I do not wish to overemphasize this; certainly most homosexual men abide by the law. I mean something quite different.

MEN'S SIGNS

The prominence of male homosexuality changes the language for teenage boys. It is absurd and cruel to say that the boy can ignore it. Even if he would, his classmates will not let him. All boys need to prove that they are not failures. They need to prove that they are on the way to becoming men—that they are not going to relapse into the need to be protected by, and therefore identified with, their mothers.

Societies used to provide them with clear and public ways to do this. The Plains Indians would insert hooks into the flesh of their thirteen-year-old braves and hang them in the sun by those hooks, for hours—a test of endurance and courage. At his bar-mitzvah the Jewish boy reads from the Holy Torah and announces, publicly, that on this day he has become a man.

In our carelessness we have taken such signs away from boys and left them to fend for themselves. Two choices remain: The boys must live without public recognition of their manhood and without their own certainty of it, or they must invent their own rituals and signs.

And here the sexual revolution comes to peddle its poison. The single incontrovertible sign that the boy can now seize on is that he has "done it" with a girl, and the earlier and more regularly and publicly he does it, the safer and surer he will feel. If sex is easy to find, and if (as mothers of good-looking teenage boys will testify) the girls themselves seek it out, then you must have a pressing and publicly recognized excuse for not having sex. To avoid scandal—think of it!—you must be protected by your being a linebacker on the football team, or by being too homely for any girl to be interested in you.

A boy who does not agree to a girl's demand for sex will be tagged with homosexuality. She will slander him herself. Ask teenagers; they will tell you. But even a linebacker known as a rake will not dare to venture into the dangerous territory of too-close association with the wrong sort. He, too, will avoid the close male friendship. The popular and athletic boys will thus have their tickets punched, while the others live under suspicion, alienated from the other boys, from the girls, and from one another.

This must happen. In large part, it has already happened. But we must try to remember when it was not so, if we are going to gauge what we have lost.

So far, I have lamented the attenuation of male friendships, which suffer under a terrible pincers attack: The libertinism of our day thrusts boys and girls together long before they are intellectually and emotionally ready for it, and at the same time the defiant promotion of homosexuality makes the natural and once powerful friendships among boys virtually impossible.

Anyone can count up the resulting cases of venereal disease and teen pregnancies. A few social analysts of more penetrating insight can note what is unquantifiable, the despair among our young people, the dullness in the eye, the feeling that people are never to be trusted, that to fall in love is to be a contemptible fool.

Audacious Men

Yet the most daunting task of all is to mark the good things that this sexual precocity has smothered in the very birth. It is one thing to say that it has made friendships among boys more distant and difficult, and to suppose that that is a bad thing for the emotional lives of those boys. It is quite another—and it takes someone willing to see through our jaded dalliance with androgyny—to see that the loss of such friendships stunts the boys intellectually and goes a long way towards depriving everybody of the benefits that such intellectual development used to provide.

That is, after all, one of the great things that male friendships are for. Consider how strong and audacious are the emotions of the young man. Suppose these are not directed towards sexual liaisons with young women, towards playing house. They do not therefore cease to exist; they must find some object. In the past that object would be the world and the group's conquest of it.

The boys might get together to build a car from scratch. They might set up a series of telegraph connections. They might pitch themselves into learning everything they could about aircraft carriers and bombers. They might form a club to read Nietzsche, or to read the Scriptures, or to read both—audacity at this age can be wildly inconsistent. They might attach themselves to an acknowledged teacher, as did the young men of Athens who followed the chaste Socrates, or, dare I say, the young men of Palestine who followed Jesus. They might form guilds to ensure that the men they paid to teach them actually followed through on their end of the bargain—and thus would they create the medieval university. They might invent jazz music. They might rob banks.

They might do a thousand things fascinatingly creative and dangerously destructive, but one thing they would not do. They would not, as our boys do now, stagnate. They would be alive.

Edison formed such attachments—as early as age thirteen he had sought and found the men who could teach him all they knew about the telegraph. Louis Agassiz and his comrades defied death in mapping and studying glaciers. George Gershwin one day left one group of buddies playing stickball in the streets to go to the house of the boy who would be his lifelong friend and associate, Maxie Rosenzweig (later Max Rosen), from whom he learned the wonders of music. Lewis and Tolkien and their friends formed the Inklings and set their stamp on literary Christianity for a century.

Read the correspondence of Louis Pasteur, and you will come away thinking that the entire edifice of chemical research in France and Germany was built upon male friendship, the bonds of comrades going forth to battle. The language of these letters, to and from dozens of fellow scientists, is powerful and unashamedly personal. "I am touched by your acknowledgment of my deep and sincere affection for you," writes the elder chemist Jean-Jacques Biot to Pasteur,

> and I thank you for it. But whilst keeping your attachment for me as I preserve mine for you, let me for the future rejoice in it in the secret recesses of my heart and of yours. The world is jealous of friendships however disinterested, and my affection for you is such that I wish people to feel that they honor themselves by appreciating you, rather than that they should know that you love me and that I love you.

What man has the space to feel anything comparable now, or the language to express it?

FAILED BOYS

Our boys are failing in school. Has it occurred to no one that we have checked them at every turn, perversely insisting that they must not form brotherhoods, that they must not identify their manhood with practical and intellectual skills that transform the world, and that they must not ever have the opportunity, apart from girls, to attach themselves in friendship to men who could teach them?

For good reason boys used to build tree houses and hang signs barring girls. They know, if only instinctively, that the fire of the friendship cannot subsist otherwise. If the company of girls is made possible, then the company of girls becomes a necessity, if only to avoid having to explain to others and to oneself why one would ever prefer the company of one's own sex. Thus what is perfectly natural and healthy, indeed very much needed, is cast as irrational and bigoted, or dubious and weak; and thus some boys will cobble together their own brotherhoods that eschew tenderness altogether—criminal brotherhoods that land them in prison. This is all right by us, it seems.

And what about the emotional damage? We learn from researchers who are willing to be derided by the sexual politicians that one of the causes of male homosexuality is precisely the disappointed desire, in certain boys, to form strong and physically expressed friendships with other boys. In our careless cruelty we have failed to protect all those whose feelings, as teenagers, are confused or ambiguous. If a teenage boy knows that nothing can happen between him and another boy, and if he knows that everybody else, including the other boy, knows it too, that knowledge must provide him the assurance that he can draw close to his friend.

He can "know" that it means only friendship, even if in another and fouler world it might mean more. He can rest easy with himself, because the meaning of his gestures and actions depends not on his confused and turbulent feelings, but upon an objective linguistic fact. Such a young man can thus negotiate his way through troubled times, fulfilling his need—and, if he has had a cruel father, it may be an aching need—for friendship, without corrupting his sexuality and without rejecting the possibility that he will become a true father and husband.

I do not know what agonies of loneliness and insecurity Abraham Lincoln, who did indeed have a cold father, suffered. But I assert that his lifeline for not becoming homosexual was the very same friendship that our pansexualists say was proof that he was. In the name of protecting homosexuals, we ignore the feelings of boys and snatch from them their dwindling opportunities to forge just such friendships whereof homosexual relations are a delusive mimicry.

NEITHER FRODO NOR DAVID

On three great bonds of love do all cultures depend: the love between man and woman in marriage; the love between a mother and her child; and the camaraderie among men, a bond that used to be strong enough to move mountains. The first two have suffered greatly; the third has almost ceased to exist.

Think about that friendship, the next time you see the perpetual adolescents in feather boas as they march down Main Street, making their sexual proclivities known to everybody whether everybody cares or not. With every chanted slogan and every blaring sign, they crowd out the words of friendship, they appropriate the healthy gestures of love between man and man. Confess—has it not left you uneasy even to read the words of that last sentence?

What do the paraders achieve, with their public promotion of homosexuality? They come out of the closet, and hustle a lot of good and natural feelings back in. They indulge in garrulity, and consequently tie the tongues and chill the hearts of men, who can no longer feel what they ought, or speak what they feel.

Reader, the next time you feel moved to pity the delicate man in the workstation near you, give a thought also to an adolescent somewhere, one among uncounted millions, a kid with acne maybe, a kid with an idea or a love, who needs a friend. Know then that your tolerance for the flambeau, which is little more than a self-congratulating cowardice, or your easy and poorly considered approval of the shy workmate's request that he be allowed to "marry" his partner, means that the unseen boy will not find that friend, and that the idea and the love will die.

No doubt about this: If you are a modern man, a half-man, many such ideas and loves have already died in you. For as much as you can admire them wistfully, from a half-understanding distance, you can be neither Frodo nor Sam, nor the man who created them. You dare not follow Agassiz, alone, to the Arctic. You will not weep for Jonathan. You once were acquainted with Enkidu, but that was all. Do not even mention John the Apostle.

Friendship, rest in peace.

Reprinted from Touchstone: A Journal of Mere Christianity, *September 2005, Volume 18, Number 7.*

PATRICK HENRY REARDON

The Agony of Gethsemane

On the Meaning of Christ's Prayer &
His Obedience in the Garden

Perhaps no part of the Gospel narrative of the Lord's Passion manifests more dramatically what St. Paul called "the weakness of God" (1 Cor. 1:25) than the account of Jesus' trial in the garden. Indeed, when the pagan Celsus, late in the second century, wrote the first formal treatise against the Christian faith, he cited that Gospel scene in order to assault the doctrine of Jesus' divinity: "Why does he shriek and lament and pray to escape the fear of destruction, speaking thus: 'Father, if it is possible, let this cup pass from me'?"

Celsus greatly oversimplified the story of course. Refuting him in the following century, Origen remarked that the Gospels do not claim that Jesus "lamented" (*oduretai*) his coming death and that Celsus failed to note that the foregoing prayer of Jesus was immediately followed by the words, "Nevertheless, not my will, but yours be done," a sentiment demonstrating our Lord's "piety and greatness of soul," his "firmness," and his "willingness to suffer."

Needless to say, all Christians are at one with Origen's critique of Celsus on this point, but they should also consider the force of that pagan's blasphemous attack. Although Celsus's "malice" (*kakourgon*) denied him access to the true meaning of the agony in the garden, that dolorous event at least instructed this unbeliever with respect to Jesus' full humanity. In fact, Celsus reasoned, Jesus in the garden was so utterly human that he could not possibly have been divine.

Even as we reject that heretical conclusion, we also recognize that the fullness of Jesus' humanity was most manifest in that event described by the Epistle to the Hebrews as "the days of his flesh" (5:7). In the Lord's experience in the garden, we perceive the most profound inferences of the doctrine of the Incarnation.

Indeed, this is the very reason that the early Church made no secret of the Lord's agony in the garden. In all the Gospels except John, Judas's treachery toward Jesus on "the night in which he was betrayed" (1 Cor. 11:23) is preceded by an account of our Lord's prayer in the garden, which thus becomes the opening scene of his sufferings.

In the comments that follow, it is my purpose to examine these Gospel accounts, along with the parallel narrative in the Epistle to the Hebrews, in order to reflect theologically on the significance of the trial and prayer of Jesus in the garden and the special, mysterious place that Holy Scripture recognizes in that event in the accomplishment of our redemption.

THE MYSTERY OF SADNESS

Interpreting the death and resurrection of Jesus in the light of biblical literature (cf. 1 Cor. 15:3–4), the early Christians savored the contrast between the disobedience of Adam and the obedience of Christ. They perceived that whereas the first man attempted, in rebellion, to become God's equal, the second, "being in the form of God, did not regard being equal to God a usurpation [*harpagmos*], but he emptied himself, taking the form of a slave, being made in the likeness of men, and being found in shape as a man, he humbled himself, becoming obedient unto death" (Phil. 2:6–8, *my translation*).

In the Epistle to the Romans, the Apostle Paul further elaborated the disparity between Adam and Jesus, observing that, "as by one man's disobedience many were made sinners, so also by one Man's obedience many will be made righteous" (5:19).

It is very important to bear in mind the traditional contrast of the obedient Jesus with the disobedient Adam when we come to the Gospel accounts of our Lord's struggle at Gethsemane, the place of his betrayal. The very name of this place (Mark 14:32; Matt. 26:36) means "olive garden," abbreviated to simply "a garden" by John (18:1).

This garden of Jesus' trial was, first of all, a place of sadness, the sorrow of death itself. "My soul is exceedingly sorrowful," said he, "even unto death" (Mark 14:34; Matt. 26:38). This sorrow unto death is common to the two gardens of man's trial, the garden of Adam and the garden of Jesus.

In the garden of disobedience, the Lord spoke to Adam of his coming death, whereby he would return to the dust from which he was taken. That curse introduced man's sadness unto death. Thus, in the Septuagint version of this story the Lord tells Eve, "I will greatly multiply your sorrows (*lypas*)," and "in sorrows (*en lypais*) you will bear your children." And to her husband the Lord declares, "Cursed is the ground for your sake; in sorrows (*en lypais*) you shall eat of it all the days of your life" (Gen. 3:16,17,19).

It is common to think of our Lord's prayer in the garden in reference to his fear, but it is significant that the accounts in Matthew and Mark emphasize his sadness more than his fear. Jesus said in the garden, "My soul is exceedingly sorrowful (*perilypos*), even unto death." The context of this assertion indicates that Jesus assumed the primeval curse of our sorrow unto death, in order to reverse the disobedience of Adam. In the garden, Jesus took our grief upon himself, praying "with vehement cries and tears" (Heb. 5:7). In the garden he bore our sadness unto death, becoming the "Man of sorrows, and acquainted with grief" (Is. 53:3,4).

Thus, St. Ambrose of Milan, commenting on the agony in the garden, says of Jesus: "Nowhere do I wonder more at his piety and majesty, because it would have profited me less if he had not assumed my own feelings (*nisi meum suscepisset affectum*). Therefore, the One that had no reason to sorrow for himself sorrowed for me, and leaving aside the enjoyment of his eternal divinity, he is afflicted with the weariness of my infirmity. He assumed my sadness (*suscepit tristitiam meam*), in order to confer on me his joy, and in our footsteps he descended even to the sorrow of death (*ad mortis aerumnam*), in order to recall us to life in his own footsteps."

In the garden Jesus returns to the very place of Adam's fall, taking on himself Adam's sorrow unto death. Thus, Ambrose regards Christ's assumption of man's sadness in the garden as integral to the Incarnation itself. He comments, "Therefore, I confidently use the word 'sadness,' because I preach the Cross, because he did not assume the appearance of the Incarnation, but its truth. Consequently, he had to take on grief (*dolorem suscipere*), in order to overcome sadness (*tristitiam*), not to exclude it. The praise of fortitude does not belong to those who bear the numbness, but rather the pain, of wounds."

The commiserating Christ bears in the garden, then, the very sorrow incurred by fallen mankind. In this garden scene St. Cyril of Alexandria places on the lips of Jesus the following explanation of his grief: "What vine-dresser, when his vineyard is desolate and laid waste, will feel no anguish for it? What shepherd would be so harsh and stern as to suffer nothing on account of his perishing flock? These are the causes of my grief. For these things am I sorrowful."

THE MYSTERY OF PRAYER

Besides the accounts in the Synoptic Gospels, the Epistle to the Hebrews also refers to the Lord's prayer in the garden. It is there that we read of Jesus, "who, in the days of his flesh, when he had offered up prayers and supplications, with vehement cries and tears to him who was able to save him from death, and was heard because of his godly fear, though he were a Son, yet he learned obedience by the things which he suffered" (5:7–8).

In this precious text, the reference to "vehement cries and tears" explains how the early believers knew about this event. It was among those things, as the author says, "confirmed to us by those who heard him" (2:3). The first apostles were immediate witnesses to the event, some of them only "a little farther" off (Matt. 26:39), "about a stone's throw" (Luke 22:41). These disciples could hear those "vehement cries," and they were able to see his kneeling posture (Mark 14:35).

All this happened, says Hebrews, "in the days of his flesh," an expression indicating Jesus' condition of human weakness, willingly assumed so "that through death he might destroy him who had the power of death, that is, the devil" (Heb. 2:14).

The object of Jesus' "prayers and supplications," Hebrews tells us, was deliverance from death. This feature of his prayers corresponds to the Gospel accounts in which Jesus prays that he be spared the "cup" of his coming sufferings (Matt. 26:39,42) and that "the hour might pass from him" (Mark 14:35).

It was in this hour, says Hebrews, that Jesus "learned obedience by the things which he suffered," a parallel to the Gospel accounts in which Jesus, in his agony, submits his own will obediently to that of his Father

(Matt. 26:39,42; Mark 14:36; Luke 22:42). As we have seen, the Apostle Paul preserves part of a hymn that speaks of Jesus' obedience unto death, "even the death of the cross" (Phil. 2:8).

These prayers and supplications of Jesus are themselves sacrificial, because Hebrews says that he "offered" them (*prosenegkas*). They are priestly prayers. That is to say, Jesus' sacrifice has even now begun. The Lord's Passion is a seamless whole. Already we perceive in his prayers and supplications the true essence of sacrifice, which is the inner oblation of oneself to God.

The Book of Hebrews insists, furthermore, that these "prayers and supplications" of Jesus were *heard* on high, precisely because of "his godly fear," which is to say, his godly piety and reverence (*evlabeia*; *reverentia* in the Vulgate). Jesus' obedient reverence is exactly what we find in the Gospel accounts of the agony.

In what sense, then, was Jesus "heard" when he offered these prayers and supplications? Properly to answer this question, it is useful to remember a principle of all godly petition: "Now this is the confidence that we have in him, that if we ask anything according to his will, he hears us" (1 John 5:14). Jesus prayed explicitly according to God's will; indeed, it was the very essence of his prayer. Therefore, his prayer was heard according to God's will. He was not delivered from death in the sense that he avoided it, but in the sense that he conquered it, that he was victorious over death, that in his own death he trampled down death forever.

This is to say that Jesus' resurrection and glorification were the Father's response to his prayer in his agony. It was in answer to his prayer, "Thy will be done," that Jesus, "having been perfected . . . became the author of eternal salvation to all who obey him" (Hebrews 5:9). This *was* God's will, the will that Jesus prayed would be done. He was thus "made perfect through sufferings" (2:10). It was because Jesus became obedient unto death that "God also has highly exalted him" (Phil. 2:9). The Paschal victory over death was the Father's reply to the prayers and supplications offered by the true High Priest in the days of his flesh.

PRAYER & THE WILL OF GOD

From these reflections it is clear that our Lord's prayer at Gethsemane illustrates the mystery of prayer itself. This illustration is worthy of further comment.

Times out of mind we have been told by some sincere Christians that the promise given by Jesus—the promise that his Father will grant us whatsoever we ask in his name (John 16:23–24)—is absolute and "allows of no exceptions." I have even heard some Christians, citing this text, go on to remark that even the addition of "if it is thy will" bespeaks a want of sufficient faith, inasmuch as it suggests that the person making the prayer is failing in confidence that his prayer will be answered. That is to say, a prayer containing an "if," because it is *ipso facto* hypothetical, expresses an inadequate faith. What the believer should do, I have been told, is simply "name it and claim it."

What the Bible has to say about petitionary prayer, however, is contained in *many* biblical verses, all of them worthy of careful regard. For example, should we say that the Apostle Paul, when he prayed three times that the Lord would remove from him the thorn in his flesh, the angel of Satan sent to buffet him (2 Cor. 12:8), was wanting in faith because this severe affliction was not taken away?

If this was the case—if the Apostle to the Gentiles really was so deficient in personal faith—it is no wonder that he was obliged to leave Trophimus sick at Miletus (2 Tim. 4:20). Poor ailing Trophimus, languishing there on his sickbed; he should have been prayed over by a person with a sounder, fuller, more unfailing faith, not that slacker Paul, a man apparently deficient on the subject of faith.

The truth of the subject, however, is quite different. The addition, "if it is thy will," is neither a limitation imposed on our confidence nor a restriction laid on our prayer. It expresses, rather, a constitutive feature of true prayer and an essential component of faith. The real purpose of prayer, after all, is not to inform God what we want, much less to impose our will on him, but to hand ourselves over more completely, in faith, to what God wants. The purpose of prayer, even the prayer of petition, is living communion with God. The man who tells God, then, "Thy will be done," does not thereby show himself a weaker believer but a stronger one.

After all, was Jesus, "the author and perfecter of our faith," weak in faith when he added the "Thy will be done" to the petition "Take this cup from me"? Did he not, rather, give us in this form of his petition the very essence of true prayer?

"If it is thy will," then, is not a limit on our trust, but an expansion of it. It does not denote a restriction of our confidence but an elevation of it. It is an elevation because in such a prayer—"Thy will be done"—we grow in personal trust in the One who has deigned, in his love, to become our Father. Indeed, when Jesus makes this prayer in the garden, the evangelists are careful to note exactly how he addressed God—namely, as "Father." Indeed, they even preserve the more intimate Semitic form, "Abba."

The "will of God" in which we place the trust of our petition is not a blind, arbitrary, or predetermined will. It is, rather, the will of a Father whose sole motive (if this word be allowed) in hearing our prayer is to provide loving direction and protection to his children. "According to thy will" is spoken to a Father who loves us because in Christ we have become his children.

All of this theology was contained in Jesus' prayer in the garden, by which his own human will was united with the will of God. Jesus, in praying for the doing of God's will, modeled for us the petition contained in the prayer that he gave us in the Sermon on the Mount. This prayer, which significantly begins with "Our *Father*," goes on to plead that *his will* may be done.

OBEDIENCE & AUTHORITY

We earlier reflected that in the Lord's agony, we perceive the most profound inferences of the doctrine of the Incarnation, the enfleshing of God's eternal Son.

Jesus in the garden subjected to the Father, not only the assent of his will, but also the disposition of his flesh. In this regard, the author of Hebrews places on the lips of the Son, "when he came into the world," the words of the psalmist, "Sacrifice and offering you did not desire, But a body you have prepared for me./ In burnt offerings and sacrifices for sin you had no pleasure./ Then I said, 'Behold, I have come—in the volume of the book it is written of me—to do your will, O God'" (10:5–7; Psalm 40 [39]:6–8).

"A *body* you have prepared for me," says the incarnate Word to his Father. We may contrast this to the Hebrew text of Psalm 40:6, which reads, "Sacrifice and offering you did not desire; *my ears* you have opened." Perhaps relying on the Septuagint (as reflected in its three earliest extant manuscripts), the author of Hebrews changes "ears" to "body." He thereby asserts that Jesus in his very body, and not simply in the assent of his will, accomplished our redemption.

This assertion must not be disregarded, lest we fall into serious doctrinal error. It has sometimes been alleged that our redemption was really wrought, not on Golgotha, but in Gethsemane, when Jesus explicitly submitted his will in obedience to the will of the Father. Some Eastern theologians, in particular, overreacting to a Western juridical soteriology, attempted to spiritualize redemption, even to moralize it. They advanced the theory that Jesus purchased our redemption, not by the immolation of his body on the Cross, but by his internal, spiritual sufferings in the garden.

According to this view, redemption was essentially accomplished by the obedient human will's deliberate submission to the divine will. Indeed, some have attempted to bolster this thesis through the biblical assertion that the true sacrifice acceptable to God consists in an internal immolation of the heart (Psalm 51 [50]:16–17).

This exaggerated theory, it must be said, does not correspond to biblical soteriology, according to which "we have been sanctified through the offering of the *body* of Jesus Christ" (Heb. 10:10). A full Christian view of redemption will insist that it happens *in the body*. To separate the suffering and death of Christ in the body from the internal obedience of his will to the Father does violence to the Holy Scriptures. Indeed, it does violence to the Incarnation itself, whereby "he himself likewise shared in [flesh and blood] that through death he might destroy him who had the power of death, that is, the devil" (2:14).

The submission of Jesus' will led directly to the immolation of his body and the libation of his blood. His agony in the garden pertains, thus, to a single purpose, extending from his assumption of our flesh all the way to its ascent, finally, into heaven. The Church knows of no redemption apart from what God's Son accomplished in the flesh.

THE PHYSICIAN'S PERSPECTIVE

When we speak of our Lord's "agony" (*agonia*) to describe his prayer in the garden, we are borrowing the expression from St. Luke (22:44), the only New Testament writer to use this word. There are two other distinctive features in Luke's version of this event.

First, Luke omits the threefold form of Jesus' prayer found in Mark and Matthew. His version, therefore, is shorter.

Second, the traditional form of the Lukan text contains certain details not found in the other two Synoptics. To wit, "Then *an angel* appeared to him from heaven, *strengthening him*. And being in agony, he prayed more earnestly. Then *his sweat became like great drops of blood* falling down to the ground" (Luke 22:43–44). These particulars about the bloody sweat and the comforting angel we know only from Luke.

Because the older, reputedly more reliable manuscripts of Luke do not contain these verses, some scholars argue that they were not part of the "original form" of Luke. For two reasons, nonetheless, I believe this judgment is too hasty.

First, given the considerable textual differences among the Lukan manuscript traditions (in the Last Supper story, for instance), I am not convinced there really was a single "original form" of Luke's Gospel. It seems to me not unreasonable to suspect that Luke himself may have left it to us in more than one form. (This consideration, let me add, seems applicable to other New Testament authors as well. Since many writers produce more than one version of their works, why would this be off-limits to the divinely inspired writers?)

Second, this impression of more than one original Lukan text is strengthened by the fact that the passage in question (Luke 22:43–44), though not found in the earliest manuscripts, was very well known from the earliest times. In truth, these Lukan features appear so soon after his Gospel's composition that it seems downright rash to claim they were not part of the "original" text.

For instance, about halfway through the second century, St. Justin Martyr wrote: "According to the Memoirs [*apomnemonevmata*, Justin's common expression for the Gospels], which I say were composed by the Apostles and their followers, his sweat fell down like drops of blood while he was praying."

This citation, as old as any extant manuscript of Luke, shows that Justin was familiar with the disputed verses. Shortly after Justin, moreover, St. Irenaeus of Lyons also wrote of the bloody sweat, as did Hippolytus of Rome, who mentioned, as well, the angel who strengthened Jesus. Later, Epiphanius of Cyprus and others followed suit.

BLOODY OBEDIENCE

For these reasons, and because this passage has long been received in the Church as integral to the Lukan text, my comments on these verses will presume Luke's authorship of them. Let us consider more closely, then, the Lord's bloody sweat and the angel who strengthened him.

First, there is the sweat of blood, a condition called hematidrosis, which results from an extreme dilation of the subcutaneous capillaries, causing them to burst through the sweat glands. This symptom, mentioned as early as Aristotle, is well known to the history of medicine, which sometimes associates it with intense fear. It is not without interest, surely, that only the evangelist who was also a physician mentions this phenomenon.

Unlike Mark (14:34) and Matthew (26:38), Luke does not speak of Jesus' sadness in the garden scene, but of an inner struggle, an *agonia,* in which the Lord "prayed more earnestly." The theological significance of this feature in Luke is that Jesus' internal conflict causes the first bloodshed in the Passion. His complete obedience to the Father in his prayer immediately produces this initial libation of his redemptive blood, the blood of which he had proclaimed just shortly before, "This cup is the new covenant in my blood, which is shed for you" (Luke 22:20).

Prior to the appearance of his betrayer, then, the Lord already begins the shedding of his blood. He pours it out in the struggle of obedience, before a single hand has been laid upon him. In Luke, the agony in the garden is not a prelude to the Passion, but its very commencement, because Jesus' stern determination to accomplish the Father's will causes his blood to flow for our redemption.

Second, there is the angel sent to strengthen the Lord during his trial. Luke, in his earlier temptation scene, had omitted the angelic ministry, of which Matthew (4:11) and Mark (1:13) spoke on that occasion. When Luke did describe that period of temptation, however, he remarked that the devil, having failed to bring about Jesus' downfall, "departed from him until an opportune *time*" (4:13). Now, in the garden, that *time* has come, and Jesus receives the ministry of an angel to strengthen him for the task.

This is one of those angels of which Jesus asks Peter in the Gospel of Matthew: "Or do you think that I cannot now pray to my Father, and he will provide me with more than twelve legions of angels?" (26:53) This angelic ministry was ever available to him, but now Jesus is in special need of it.

In Luke's literary structure, this ministering angel stands parallel to Gabriel at the beginning of the Gospel. In the earlier case, an angel introduces the Incarnation; in the present case, an angel introduces the Passion. Very shortly, angels will introduce the Resurrection (24:4).

Reprinted from Touchstone: A Journal of Mere Christianity, *April 2006, Volume 19, Number 3.*

The non-Scriptural references are, in order, to: Origen, Contra Celsum *2.24; Ambrose,* Homiliae in Lucam *10.56; Cyril of Alexandria,* Homiliae in Lucam *146; Justin Martyr,* Dialogue with Trypho *103.8; Irenaeus,* Adversus Haereses *3.22.2; Hippolytus,* Fragments on Psalms *1 [2.7]; Epiphanius,* Ancoratus *31:4–5; and Aristotle,* Historia Animalium *3.19.*

JAMES M. KUSHINER

Terror & the Last Enemy

A 9/11 Pilgrimage & the Way of the Cross

I will never forget the images of terror I saw on the morning of September 15, 2001.

On September 6, I had left Chicago for Scotland to join a group of Orthodox Christians from the British Isles on a pilgrimage to the island of Iona, and thus on 9/11 was living in a remote retreat center without television or radio. I heard about the terrorist attacks only by word of mouth on 9/11. I only saw newspapers the following day. It was not until the following weekend that I had access to a television, when I arrived back on the Scottish mainland and checked into a bed and breakfast in Dumbarton, my mother's hometown on the Clyde.

BURNING SYMBOLS

So, on Saturday morning, September 15, I studied the image of impressive twin symbols of commercial and political strength standing side by side, towering over a river that flows into the Atlantic Ocean nearby. Two plumes of smoke rose up following an attack by devotees of terror and destruction with no respect for the lives of the innocent. Many inhabitants died. Some survived the attack, and 200 of them were carried off into slavery.

Slavery? That morning I found myself in Dumbarton Castle, studying a modern artist's rendering of the Viking sack of Dumbarton in 870.

In my room the night before, I had seen on BBC television for the first time the images of the World Trade Center towers burning and falling to the ground—the parallels between the images were stunning.

Dumbarton Castle sits on twin plugs of volcanic basalt rising up on the Firth of Clyde where it flows out toward the Atlantic. The ninth-century fortress depicted in the painting was the capital of the kingdom of Strathclyde, and Vikings from Dublin found it an irresistible target.

The Vikings were the terrorists of their time, raiding and burning villages and killing and enslaving people all over the coasts of Europe, though they terrorized for plunder and territorial gain and not religion or ideology. No one was safe from their attacks, and no one knew when they would strike. Even the strongest could lose their families, property, and their own lives in a few hours.

Even the beaches of tiny Iona have soaked up the blood of those slain by Vikings. They first attacked Iona in 794 and badly damaged the monastery, returning seven years later to gut the abbey, and again five years after that, when they put to the sword 68 monks near what is now called Martyrs Bay.

FINDING THE CROSS

Near Martyrs Bay, in the early afternoon (about 8:00 A.M. in New York) on September 11, I and six other pilgrims boarded the ferry for the five-minute ride to the Isle of Mull. There we walked inland for a couple of miles to a silversmith's shop. I had promised my wife not to spend money on souvenirs, but I decided to buy her a silver cross anyway. This little journey was out of character for me. I really don't shop, especially if I have to go out to do it. Yet I found myself on Mull with the shoppers.

The early-afternoon autumn air was fragrant and still as we passed grazing highland cattle and picked and ate a few wild blackberries just ripened in the early September sun. At times we walked silently down the one-lane road under a sky that turned from hazy to cloudy to sunny several times during the walk. There were no cars.

Coming from the city, I felt the absence of sound; the silence of the empty countryside slowly swelled until I felt engulfed by it. In such a setting, each word of occasional conversation seems to take on dramatic importance. What word do you utter to break such breathtaking silence? Something from the morning news? Any spoken word that breaks such silence commands attention and scrutiny.

Lagging behind the others, I took a small prayer book out of the pocket of my rain jacket. I had resolved to start saying the daily office of prayer during the retreat. Christians from the beginning have observed daily offices of prayer. More than a thousand years before Mohammedans decided to pull out their prayer rugs and face Mecca five times a day, the Psalmist wrote, "Seven times a day I praise thee" (119:164).

The offices are seven in number and begin with sundown: vespers, compline, matins, first, third, sixth, and ninth hours. These are known as the canonical hours, the points of prayer by which a day is marked.

Outside of monasteries, few Christians pray any of these hours, so much has the habit of regular prayer faded from our lives. Given the things we must accomplish each day, it seems like a waste of time to say the same prayers over and over. The old notions behind some of the hours seem quaint and outdated—who, for example, really pays attention to sunrise anymore?

The full daily offices of prayer as prayed in monasteries add up to hours of prayer each day. But I had brought with me the Daily Prayer Book for Orthodox Christians, which severely abridges the daily offices for busy lay people—it's a prayer book for the handicapped, like me. I read belatedly from the midday psalms:

> Save me, O God, by thy name, and vindicate me by thy might. Hear my prayer, O God; give ear to the words of my mouth. For insolent men have risen against me, ruthless men seek my life; they do not set God before them. Behold, God is my helper; the Lord is the upholder of my life. . . .

And then the traditional prayer for noontime, the time of the Crucifixion:

> O Christ God, on the sixth day and hour, thou nailed to the Cross the sin which rebellious Adam committed in Paradise: Tear asunder the bonds of our iniquities and save us. Thou hast wrought salvation in the midst of the earth, O Christ God. Thou stretched out thine all-pure hands upon the Cross; thou gathered together all the nations that cry aloud to thee: Glory to thee.

After these brief prayers, we arrived at the shop of the silversmith, a spacious shed near her house.

We spent nearly an hour in the shop studying and fingering variations on the cross and other jewelry. I finally purchased a silver "highland cross" necklace for my wife.

The Good Death

On the walk back to the ferry, we found that a sturdy stone church that had been locked when we first passed by was now open. It was a Church of Scotland (Presbyterian) church.

A man outside said a funeral was going to be held there in a while and that the church would be overflowing with people coming from all over the islands and the mainland. There was nothing remarkable about its stone walls and simple but strong pews, but it did seem odd to be watching a little-used, remote country church on a beautiful September afternoon being set up for a funeral.

When we left the church, the road seemed quieter still. In what felt like the calmest spot on earth I walked ahead of some of my companions. It was now about 3 o'clock, and seeking the presence of Christ, I began to pray the prayers of the ninth hour, which commemorates the death of Christ on the Cross at that time:

> O Master, Lord Jesus Christ our God, thou hast led us to the present hour, in which, as thou hung upon the life-giving Tree, thou didst make a way into Paradise for the penitent thief, and by death destroyed death. . . . We implore thine unending goodness: Spare us, O Lord, according to the multitude of thy mercies, and save us for thy holy name's sake, for our days are passing away in vanity. Take us from the hand of the adversary and forgive us our sins. . . .

I couldn't help but think of the penitent thief and of the man whose funeral would shortly be held in that country church: The good thief had been presented with the Christ crucified and embraced him, petitioning him for mercy. The man who died and was to be buried that quiet afternoon, had he chosen to put his destiny in the hands of Christ? Had he been prepared for death, or did he die suddenly, without time to prepare? Was his the "good Christian end" we often pray for, or did he die in regret or fear? Did he have his heart set on paradise, or was he content with the things of this world?

Earlier that morning we had observed the commemoration of the death of John the Baptist, which falls on that date in the Julian Christian calendar that is followed by some of the Orthodox Christians in Britain. John had little time to prepare for his death because Salome demanded of Herod that his head be given her right away.

Many, young and old, strong and infirm, die, like John, sudden and unexpected deaths: in war, in floods and hurricanes and tornadoes, as the victims of accidents and crimes, from blocked hearts and burst arteries. Some of them do not fear death, for they see it as a falling asleep in Christ. Death has no sting for those, like John and the good thief, who live in Christ.

UNPLANNED MEMORIAL

I walked the last mile with the elderly wife of an elderly priest. She was the choir director for our pilgrimage group and was anxious that we make it back in time for choir practice before supper. We were going to rehearse music for a Panikhida scheduled for the next evening, September 12: It is an Orthodox memorial service for the faithful departed, and we had planned to remember our departed loved ones during the pilgrimage.

One of the doors on the ferry's loading ramp would not close, and we finally arrived back at the retreat house at nearly 5 o'clock, too late for choir rehearsal. We went to the meeting room for late tea, but everyone else had gone and the tea was lukewarm. One of our retreat leaders, a journalist, came in and asked us if we had heard the news from America (it was about noon there). I couldn't imagine what could be so pressing.

He told us that terrorists had flown two airplanes into the World Trade Center and a third into the Pentagon. Both towers were down and thousands of people had certainly been killed.

The thought of the terror inflicted upon those thousands of innocent victims compounded the anger, anxiety, and doubt I felt coursing through me. The other pilgrims—I was the only American—stunned and saddened, tried to comfort me. They were not detached from the effects of terrorism, having endured bombings in their own country. Their sympathy was real. Still, I was alone in a way, for I hadn't met any of them until the previous weekend.

After a solemn supper, it was announced that the prayer service we had scheduled for the next day—the memorial prayers—would be held in an hour, and we would pray for the victims of the attack as well as those of our own departed loved ones we wished to remember.

Before the service, most of us wrote down the names of departed loved ones on slips of paper to be given to the priest. I wrote the names of departed family members who had come from this part of the world. Fr. Columba, an Orthodox priest from Edinburgh, gave a moving and compassionate homily about how death relentlessly comes to us all. It is our true enemy and does not discriminate, but it is an enemy we need not fear if we are in Christ, for his Cross has put down death. Our sure and certain hope is in Christ, who raises the dead.

We sang the service, unrehearsed, as best we could. I remembered relatives who had fallen asleep in Christ: my grandparents, as well as my three sisters who died in their thirties and early forties, some suddenly, some after long illnesses. I thought of the thousands who faced terror and death in the towers in New York and in the Pentagon, victims of a vicious assault on innocent civilians. I remember most of all these words from the service that I read that evening: "Grant unto me the home-country of my heart's desire, making me a citizen of paradise."

After the service, the choir began to disperse. The choir director noticed the tears in my eyes and kissed me on the cheek as would a mother. Who could not but weep on that day? For all the dead, for death itself, for the terror of death that man has brought upon himself.

DEATH & SORROW

The next day, we went on the Island Walk sponsored by the Iona community. We walked past Martyrs Bay, and paused at the War Memorial commemorating locals who gave their lives in the World Wars, pausing in silent remembrance of the victims of the terrorist attack of the previous day. Some five hours later, after a trek to the beach where tradition says St. Columba first landed, we ended the pilgrimage walking on the Street of the Dead, which took us into the cemetery outside the chapel of St. Oran.

I read the stones: "In Loving Memory" of so-and-so; "Our Dear Baby"; here were the places where families laid to rest children taken by disease, young men taken by drowning, deaths expected and unexpected, sudden and lingering, by illness, war, accident, and old age. Some of the markers were no longer legible; some were barely standing; others were cracked or crumbling, on the brink of disappearing from the sight of the living.

Later that evening, we held the memorial prayer service as originally scheduled. Going in 24 hours from one memorial service to another, walking the abbey and the cemetery, I felt that death was hanging heavy on the world and that perpetual sorrow has been the lot of man from the beginning.

Jesus himself wept at Lazarus's tomb. But his was not the weeping of bereavement, but the emotion of a hero who saw his beloved lying in bondage to death. He wept for our weeping. Surely our Lord saw in this death and all deaths the devastation wrought by an enemy. Surely some who saw the dead on September 11 were moved by both sorrow and anger at the same time as they saw in the deaths of their loved ones the works of a hateful enemy.

The enemy seems to have triumphed, and like Martha we ask, Will we indeed rise again? I know that Christ rose from the dead, yet I don't see why that should mean that anyone else should rise from the dead, that God must undo what we have done to ourselves. Why should he?

I believe that we shall rise because he who did rise says that he will raise us up. If he says it, I believe it. I only know it because I know him. There is nothing otherwise that tells me that it must be so. We shall rise only because he loves us in a way we cannot fathom. St. Paul said as much when he prayed that the Christians in Ephesus would have their eyes opened to see the height and depth and breadth of the love of God for us in Christ. Our resurrection is far beyond reasonable expectations.

CROSS TRIUMPHANT

From the day I arrived in Scotland I had been most struck by my encounter with the Cross of Christ, especially in the midday and mid-afternoon prayers. The Cross reminds the human race of what we did and also of what we need. On Thursday evening, September 13, when we sang the vespers for the Feast of the Holy Cross, one of the hymns proclaimed:

"The Cross is raised on high, and urges all the creation to sing the praise of the undefiled Passion of him who was lifted high upon it. For there it was that he killed our slayer, and brought the dead to life again: and in his exceeding goodness and compassion, he made us beautiful and counted us worthy to be citizens of heaven."

In the ancient tradition of the Church, Christ is said to have trampled down death by death: His dying was the instrument by which he destroyed the power of hell. Christ entered Hades, and its gates did not prevail, as he led out from there those subject to sin and death.

In the apse of my home parish, there is a fourteen-foot icon of the Resurrection: Christ is grabbing the hands of Adam and Eve as he tramples down the gates of hell under his feet. In the background, along with other Old Testament figures, there is a young lad clothed in white, holding a shepherd's crook: He is the righteous Abel, slain by Cain, the first one to die in the pages of the Bible. I can't help but think of the grief of Adam and Eve as the first grief in the world at the death of a loved one. Yet all this is overcome by the Lord in his Cross and Resurrection.

Early the next morning, September 14, we ended our pilgrimage by praying the Divine Liturgy of the Exaltation of the Holy and Life-Giving Cross in the thousand-year-old chapel of St. Oran, surrounded by the graves of many who have fallen asleep in Christ. After receiving Holy Communion, we met the 9 o'clock ferry to Mull and began the trip home.

After a quiet bus ride across Mull, we boarded the ferry for the mainland. Everything came to a standstill as the ship's engines were cut. Everyone on board kept three long minutes of silence as a bell broadcast over BBC radio tolled through the ship's loudspeakers for the victims of September 11.

DEAR DEPARTED

After my visit to Dumbarton Castle, I walked less than a mile to visit my 86-year-old great-aunt Helen. After greeting me, she handed me a parcel, and said, "We'll be needing to go to the post office to mail this to Madame. This is heather for Donald's grave." Donald, her husband, had been killed in battle on June 26, 1944, in Caen, Normandy, twenty days after D-Day. He had been a policeman in town when he was called up.

After the war, many French volunteered to look after the graves of the slain from other countries. Since 1947, a French woman, "Madame," has been tending the grave in Normandy, and Helen has been sending her Scottish heather for the grave whenever it comes into bloom, usually in September.

Helen gave birth to a boy shortly after Donald was killed, a boy who grew up without a father. Helen had lost her own father in World War I.

He also was killed in France just before she was born.

Later that afternoon, I walked alone to Dumbarton Cemetery to look for the graves of my great-grandparents and other ancestors. One of the graves that I hoped to find was that of John Auchterlonie, my great-great-grandfather, born in 1844.

As a young man, John worked in the local shipyards. One day he and another man were working on a scaffold high above the Firth of Clyde when a rope broke and both men plunged into the cold waters below. John survived, but his friend drowned. When they recovered his friend's body, they found in his pocket a New Testament. After the sudden and tragic death of his friend, John committed his life to Christ and became a well-respected preacher. He died in 1937 at the age of 93.

Once inside the cemetery, I found myself occasionally quietly singing among the graves—most marked with a cross, many with stone crosses—the traditional Trisagion prayers, sung at Divine Liturgy but also for funerals: "Holy God, Holy Mighty, Holy Immortal, have mercy on us."

THE UNREMEMBERED

After more than an hour and a half of walking among the rows of upright monuments, many over six feet tall, I finally despaired of finding any of my ancestors' graves. In the lengthening shadows of early evening, I stopped and studied the long, crowded rows of silent cut-rock pillars and slabs, some leaning precariously. The sound of traffic from the nearby road seemed to fade and the silence deepened.

The monuments stood like mute casualties of some plague, a war, or some evil spell, all pillars like Lot's wife, frozen in time and space—yes, the great enemy of man is death, and these are its victims, the "slain that lie in the grave, whom thou rememberest no more" (Ps. 88:5). As with most of our ancestors, their names are eventually forgotten and their graves left untended.

But they are all remembered by God, I thought. In the Orthodox funeral service we sing, "memory eternal," not referring to man's failing memory—that would be a sad note to sing because as the generations pass, the dead are mostly forgotten, with rare exceptions—but appealing to God's memory, that he will not eternally forget but will remember us: The thief on the cross said to our Lord, "Remember me, O Lord, when thou comest into thy kingdom."

It is a prayer repeated in the traditional Communion service of the Church. In the face of the silent witnesses of the gravestones I can still say, "I believe in the resurrection of the dead and the life of the world to come. Amen."

As the shadows grew, I left the cemetery and pulled out the little prayer book from my pocket to pray vespers. It includes the song of the elder Simeon in the Temple: "Lord, now lettest thou thy servant depart in peace, for mine eyes have seen thy salvation, which thou hast prepared before the face of all people, a light to enlighten the Gentiles, and to be the glory of thy people, Israel."

My pilgrimage was nearly over. Early Monday morning I went to the airport, which I found clogged with passengers. I had been told to be there three hours before the flight. I went with my newly learned prayer book, knowing I could use the time there by stepping outside of it in prayer.

THE HOMELAND

Almost four years later, on September 9, 2005, I saw Ground Zero for the first time. Standing in the churchyard of St. Paul's Chapel across the way from the World Trade Center grounds, I realized that I was looking at 9/11, once again, from a graveyard.

From St. Paul's we walked to the south side of Ground Zero, where we happened upon a small press conference. My friend's press credentials got us in just in time to hear former mayor Rudy Giuliani tell the audience about the steel cross that appeared in the wreckage at Ground Zero, as he pointed to it still standing upright.

Since then the site has been a meeting place for prayers and the cross has been a sign of comfort for the many who took part in the long process of searching for bodies. Masses have been said beneath the cross. Yet there are some who do not want that cross to remain there, or as a part of any World Trade Center memorial. They find it offensive.

They might succeed in having it removed, but even if they do, the Cross will still be there. For just as I stood at the foot of the cross on Mull at the ninth hour on 9/11, remembering the penitent thief, the whole world lies in the shadow of the Cross. The Cross stands at the heart of our suffering world, mystically present at all times and in every place, the new tree of a new paradise, our new and true homeland.

I was drawn to Scotland because it is for me another homeland, the home of my forefathers, out of sight and until recently beyond my reach. But I traveled much farther than I intended: There, watching from afar my homeland's suffering, I was reminded of our true homeland, a paradise pledged to us in the Upper Room, a paradise in which the Cross has become a life-giving tree.

Paradise: that is what we have lost and what we long for. Nothing else can satisfy that longing. That is what Columba and the monks of Iona sought; that is what I and my fellow pilgrims sought.

Wherever we remember Christ's death and Resurrection, and his pledge of paradise, whether in Chicago, Dumbarton, Iona, or at the foot of the steel cross at the World Trade Center, he is there. And thus in the midst of death we can cry out, in faith and in love, "Remember me, O Lord, when thou comest into thy Kingdom." May he so remember us, and those we have lost, and those who died on September 11, and all the faithful departed, and may their memory be eternal.

Reprinted from Touchstone: A Journal of Mere Christianity, *September 2006, Volume 19, Number 7.*

ALLAN CARLSON

Children of the Reformation

A Short & Surprising History
of Protestantism & Contraception

It is a reckless analyst who risks reopening sixteenth-century disputes between Roman Catholics and the Protestant Reformers. I do so in the interest of a greater good, but my purpose is not to say who was right or who was wrong. I would simply like to explore why the Protestant churches maintained unity with the Catholic Church on the contraception question for four centuries, only to abandon this unity during the first half of the twentieth century.

I write as a historian, not an advocate. (I am a "cradle Lutheran," but one who believes Martin Luther was wrong about what he called the impossibility of lifelong celibacy; I have come to know too many faithful Catholic priests to accept that.)

ORDERS & DISORDERS

To understand the change in Protestant thought and practice, we need to understand the Protestant vision of family and fertility, particularly as expressed by Luther and Calvin, and how it has changed over the last hundred years.

Early sixteenth-century Europe was an era very different from ours. The late medieval Church claimed about one of every four adults in celibate orders, serving either as priests, nuns, or monks or in celibate military and trading groups such as the Teutonic Knights.

Over the centuries, the religious orders had, through bequests, accumulated vast landed estates and gathered in the wealth that came through this ownership of productive land. The trading orders held remarkable assets in land, goods, and gold. Many orders were nonetheless faithful to their purposes and vows and used this wealth to tend the sick, help the poor, and lift prayers to heaven.

However, in others, spiritual discipline had grown lax. Indeed, sexual scandals of a sort rocked the church of that era. I draw strictly on Catholic witnesses for this.

For example, the great Dutch theologian Desiderius Erasmus, while always loyal to Rome, complained: "Let them prate as they will of the status of monks and virgins. Those who under the pretext of celibacy live in [sexual] license might better be castrated. . . . [T]here is a horde of priests among whom chastity is rare."

Philip of Burgundy, the Catholic bishop of Utrecht, admitted that chastity was nearly impossible among clerics and monks who were "pampered with high living and tempted by indolence." This problem festered until the reform-minded Council of Trent convened in 1545.

GOD WAS NOT DRUNK

The key figure in developing a Protestant family ethic was Martin Luther. Himself an Augustinian monk and priest, Luther also served as Professor of Theology at the University of Wittenberg. The first element in Luther's Protestant family ethic was a broad celebration not simply of marriage but of procreation.

For Luther, God's words in Genesis 1:28, "Be fruitful and multiply and fill the earth," were more than a blessing, even more than a command. They were, he declared in his 1521 treatise on *The Estate of Marriage,* "a divine *ordinance* which it is not our prerogative to hinder or ignore."

Addressing the celibate Teutonic Knights, he also emphasized Genesis 2:18: "It is not good that man should be alone; I will make him a helper who shall be with him." The "true Christian," he declared, "must grant that this saying of God is true, and believe that God was not drunk when he spoke these words and instituted marriage."

Except among those rare persons—"not more than one in a thousand," Luther said at one point—who received true celibacy as a special gift from God, marriage and procreation were divinely ordained. As he wrote: "For it is *not* a matter of free choice or decision but *a natural and necessary thing,* that whatever is a man must have a woman and whatever is a woman must have a man."

John Calvin put even greater emphasis on Genesis 1:28. He argued that these words represented the *only* command of God made before the Fall that was still active after God drove Adam and Eve out of Eden. This gave them a unique power and importance.

While occasionally acknowledging in unenthusiastic fashion St. Paul's defense of the single life, the Reformers were far more comfortable with the social order described in Luther's *Exhortation to the Knights of the Teutonic Order:* "We were all created to do as our parents have done, to beget and rear children. This is a duty which God has laid upon us, commanded, and implanted in us, as is proved by our bodily members, our daily emotions, and the example of all mankind."

Marriage with the expectation of children, in this view, represented the natural, normal, and necessary form of worldly existence.

ESSENTIAL PROCREATION

Marriage with the expectation of children was also a spiritual expression. Luther saw *procreation* as the very essence of the human life in Eden before the Fall. As he wrote in his *Commentary on Genesis*:

> [T]ruly in all nature there was no activity more excellent and more admirable than procreation. After the proclamation of the name of God it is the most important activity Adam and Eve in the State of innocence could carry on—as free from sin in doing this as they were in praising God.

The fall of Adam and Eve into sin interrupted this pure, exuberant potential fertility. Even so, the German Reformer praised each conception of a new child as an act of "wonderment . . . wholly beyond our understanding," a miracle bearing the "lovely music of nature," a faint reminder of life before the Fall:

> This living together of husband and wife—that they occupy the same home, that they take care of the household, that together

they produce and bring up children—is a kind of faint image and
a remnant, as it were, of that blessed living together [in Eden].

Elsewhere, Luther called procreation "a most outstanding gift" and
"the greatest work of God."

Accordingly, Luther sharply condemned the contraceptive mentality that was alive and well in his own time. He noted that this "inhuman
attitude, which is worse than barbarous," was found chiefly among the
wellborn, "the nobility and princes." Elsewhere, he linked both contraception and abortion to selfishness:

How great, therefore, the wickedness of [fallen] human nature is!
How many girls there are who prevent conception and kill and
expel tender fetuses, although procreation is the work of God!
Indeed, some spouses who marry and live together . . . have various ends in mind, but rarely children.

Regarding the sin of Onan, as recorded in Genesis and involving the
form of contraception now known as "withdrawal," Luther wrote: "Onan
must have been a most malicious and incorrigible scoundrel. This is a most
disgraceful sin. It is far more atrocious than incest and adultery. We call
it unchastity, yes, a Sodomitic sin. . . . Surely at such a time the order of
nature established by God in procreation should be followed." Onan was
"that worthless fellow" who "refused to exercise love."

On this matter, Luther was again joined by Calvin. In his *Commentary on Genesis*, he wrote that "the voluntary spilling of semen outside of
intercourse between man and woman is a monstrous thing. Deliberately to
withdraw from coitus in order that semen may fall on the ground is doubly
monstrous. For this is to extinguish the hope of the [human] race and to
kill before he is born the hoped-for offspring."

A few decades later, the Synod of Dordt would declare that Onan's
act "was even as much as if he had, in a manner, pulled forth the fruit out
of the mother's womb and destroyed it."

RELIGIOUSLY MARRIED

A second element in Luther's Protestant family ethic was his concept of a
divine call to the vocations of husbandry and housewifery.

Emphasizing human frailty, he argued in *The Estate of Marriage* that a successful union was exceedingly difficult to attain if ungrounded in religious faith. In such cases, the delights of marriage—"that husband and wife cherish one another, become one, serve one another"—would commonly be overshadowed by the responsibilities, duties, and attendant loss of freedom which the married state entailed.

He believed that happiness in marriage depended on recognition that the married estate, with its attendant responsibilities, was "pleasing to God and precious in his sight." Indeed, he argued that God called women—all women—to be Christian wives and mothers and called men—all men—home to serve as Christian "housefathers."

In *The Estate of Marriage,* Luther described the father who confesses to God that "I am not worthy to rock the little babe or wash its diapers, or to be entrusted with the care of the child and its mother." He responded that "when a father goes ahead and washes diapers . . . for his child, God, with all his angels and creatures, is smiling, because he is doing so in Christian faith."

In the commandment, "Honor Thy Father and Mother," he wrote to the Teutonic Knights, we see that "God has done marriage the honor of putting it . . . immediately after the honor due to himself." He concluded that "there is no higher office, estate, condition, or work . . . than the estate of marriage."

The third element of Luther's Protestant family ethic was praise for parenting as a task and responsibility. In exalting this task, he energized the Christian home as an autonomous social sphere. "There is no power on earth that is nobler or greater than that of parents," declared the Reformer in *The Estate of Marriage*. He added: "Most certainly father and mother are apostles, bishops, and priests to their children, for it is they who make them acquainted with the gospel."

One of his colleagues, Justus Menius, explained the task of parenting in more detail. "The diligent rearing of children is the greatest service to the world, both in spiritual and temporal affairs, both for the present life and for posterity," he wrote in an advice book on childrearing.

> Just as one turns young calves into strong cows and oxen, rears young colts to be brave stallions, and nurtures small tender shoots into great fruit-bearing trees, so must we bring up children to be

knowing and courageous adults, who serve both land and people and help both to prosper.

According to Harvard University historian Steven Ozment, in his book *When Fathers Ruled: Family Life in Reformation Europe:* "Never has the art of parenting been more highly praised and parental authority more wholeheartedly supported than in Reformation Europe." Child rearing, in this view, was not just "woman's work." In the Protestant home, father and mother would share the duties of child rearing to an unusual degree.

Luther saw the years from birth to age six as a time when a child's reason was "asleep." During these years, the mother took the dominant role in childcare. But at age seven, fathers should take the lead, with special responsibility for the moral and practical education of children. Inspired by Luther's message and example, publishers turned out dozens of so-called Housefather books, sixteenth-century "self-help" volumes for dads.

LUTHER'S BURDEN

How might we judge the success of the Protestant family ethic? For nearly four centuries it worked reasonably well, as judged by its understanding of the divine ordinance to be fruitful and replenish the earth.

Accordingly, the Protestant opposition to contraception remained firm. Writing in the late eighteenth century, for example, John Wesley, the founder of Methodism, also condemned the sin of Onan, adding, "The thing which he did displeased the Lord."

The nineteenth-century Reformed Pastor Johann Peter Lange, in his *Christian Dogmatics,* described contraception as "a most unnatural wickedness, and a grievous wrong. This sin . . . is [as] destructive as a pestilence that walketh in darkness, destroying directly the body and the soul of the young."

At their 1908 Lambeth Conference, the world's Anglican bishops recorded "with alarm the growing practice of artificial restriction of the family." They "earnestly call[ed] upon all Christian people to discountenance the use of all artificial means of restriction as demoralizing to character and hostile to national welfare."

As late as 1923, the Lutheran Church/Missouri Synod's official magazine *The Witness* accused the Birth Control Federation of America of spattering "this country with slime" and labeled birth-control advocate Margaret Sanger a "she devil." Pastor Walter Maier, founding preacher of the long-running *Lutheran Hour* radio program, called contraceptives "the most repugnant of modern aberrations, representing a twentieth-century renewal of pagan bankruptcy."

On doctrine, then, Protestant leaders held firm well into the twentieth century. The weakness of the Protestant position actually lay elsewhere: in the informal institution of the Pastor's Family. One possible cause of the change in Protestant teaching not often considered is the changed family life of the clergy themselves.

In rejecting lifelong celibacy, in casting marriage as the highest order and calling on earth, in elevating motherhood and homemaking, in emphasizing the spiritual authority and practical tasks of fatherhood, in refocusing adult lives around the tasks of childrearing, in celebrating procreation and large families, and in condemning contraception, Luther implicitly laid a great burden on Protestant clerics.

They had to serve as examples for their congregations, and specifically, they had to marry and bear large families themselves. Where the Catholic priest or the cloistered monk or nun faced the challenge of lifelong celibacy, the Protestant cleric faced the lifelong challenge of building a model and fruitful home.

Luther again supplied the prototype, in his marriage to Katharine von Bora. By the standards of the time, they married late, but still brought six children into the world, and their busy home served as the inspiration to generations of Protestant clerics.

This special role of the Pastor's Family was rarely codified in church doctrine, but the Protestant rejection of both celibacy and contraception created a visible expectation. Barring infertility, a faithful Protestant pastor and his wife would be parents to a brood of children.

It was a difficult expectation to satisfy, and would only become more difficult as economic and cultural changes made providing for large families more burdensome and having many children less and less socially acceptable. Not surprisingly, many seem to have turned to contraception to limit their families, and equally unsurprisingly, this affected their articulation of the church doctrine for which they were responsible.

DECLINING NUMBERS

But again, for nearly four centuries, where it held sway, the Protestant family ethic, exemplified in the Pastor's Family, worked to reshape the culture in family-affirming, child-rich ways.

Indeed, the large families of Anglican, Lutheran, and Calvinist clergy became something of a problem for relatively poor rural parishes, and something of a comic image for novelists. In Oliver Goldsmith's 1766 book *The Vicar of Wakefield,* we find a country pastor with six children who ends up (with his brood of children) in debtor's prison, only to be rescued from his misfortunes by a benefactor.

As late as 1874, the average Anglican clergyman in England still had 5.2 living children. In 1911, however, just three years after the bishops had condemned contraception, the new census of England showed that the average family size of Anglican clergy had fallen to only 2.3 children, a stunning decline of 55 percent. The British Malthusian League—a strong advocate of contraception—had a field day exposing what it called the hypocrisy of the priests.

As the league explained, the Church of England continued to view contraception as a sin, and yet its clerics and bishops were obviously engaging in the practice. Apparently only the poor and the ignorant had to obey the church.

There was not much that Anglican leaders could say in response. This propaganda continued for another two decades, and soon some Anglican theologians were arguing that Britain's poverty required the birth of fewer children.

Pressures culminated at the 1930 Lambeth Conference, where bishops heard an address by birth-control advocate Helena Wrighton on the advantages of contraception for the poor. On a vote of 193 to 67, the bishops (representing not only England but also America, Canada, and the other former colonies) approved a resolution stating that:

> In those cases where there is such a clearly felt moral obligation
> to limit or avoid parenthood, and where there is a morally sound
> reason for avoiding complete abstinence, other methods may be
> used, provided that this is done in the light of the same Christian
> principles.

This was the first official statement by a major church body in favor of contraception. Thus was Christian unity on the question broken. The decision was condemned by many religious and secular bodies, including the editors of the *Washington Post*. Pope Pius XI responded to it in his encyclical *Casti Connubii* four months later.

The same stress line emerged in America. For example, in the very conservative Lutheran Church/Missouri Synod, the average pastor in 1890 had 6.5 children. The number fell to 3.7 children in 1920, 42 percent below the 1890 number. Other churches saw a similar decline. Here, too, the Protestant clergy had ceased to be models of a fruitful home for their congregations and the broader culture.

During the 1930s, the Missouri Synod quietly dropped its campaign against the Birth Control League of America. In the 1940s, one of the church's leading theologians, Albert Rehwinkel, concluded that Luther had simply been wrong. God's words in Genesis 1:28—"Be fruitful and multiply and fill the earth"—were not a command; they were merely a blessing, and an optional one at that.

MALTHUSIAN INFECTION

A culture infected by neo-Malthusian ideas was reshaping the clerical family. Please note: As in England, so in America, the change in clerical family behavior came *before* the change in doctrine.

Meanwhile, mainstream American Protestants embraced contraception directly. In 1931, the Committee on Home and Marriage of the old Federal Council of Churches issued a statement defending family limitation and arguing for the repeal of laws prohibiting contraceptive education and sales. Some member churches—notably the Southern Methodists and the Northern Baptists—protested the action, and the Southern Presbyterians even withdrew their membership from the Federal Council for a decade, but they were the minority and even their protests did not last.

In only three decades, the Lambeth Conference's qualified approval would turn into full celebration. At the astonishing and deeply disturbing 1961 North American Conference on Church and Family, sponsored by the National Council of Churches (successor to the Federal Council), population-control advocate Lester Kirkendall argued that America had "entered a sexual economy of abundance" where contraception would allow unrestrained sexual experimentation.

Wardell Pomeroy of the Kinsey Institute for Sex Research explained how the new science of sexology required the abandonment of all old moral categories. Psychologist Evelyn Hooker celebrated the sterile lives of homosexuals. Planned Parenthood's Mary Calderone made the case for universal contraceptive use, while colleague Alan Guttmacher urged the reform of America's "mean-spirited" anti-abortion laws.

Not a single voice in the spirit of Luther or Calvin could be heard at this "Christian conference." Indeed, the conferees saw the traditional Protestant family ethic focused on exuberant marital fertility as the problem and the act that Luther, Calvin, and others had condemned as the obvious answer.

In a way, though, this celebration of such a diversity of sexual practices followed the Protestant acceptance of contraception, which followed from the defection of the Protestant clergy from the Protestant Family Ethic. Rejecting both lifelong celibacy *and* contraception, classic Protestant theology required family-centered and child-rich pastors. When those clerical leaders, in the privacy of their bedrooms, broke faith with their tradition, when pastors and their wives consciously limited their families, the Protestant opposition to contraception faced a crisis.

Typical of a less radical development was the 1981 decision of the Missouri Synod's Commission on Theology and Church Relations, which argued that although "Be fruitful" is "both a command and a mandate," "in the absence of Scriptural prohibition" contraception was acceptable "within a marital union which is, as a whole, fruitful." And if contraception is acceptable, "we will also recognize that sterilization may under some circumstances be an acceptable form of contraception."

A later, additional development only increased the appeal of contraception to the pastors of these churches. The ordination of women by a number of Protestant groups, commonly initiated in the late 1960s and 1970s, struck a nearly fatal blow to the informal Protestant institution of the Pastor's Wife.

By upending and confusing sexual differences and by granting to women the religious functions long held exclusively by men, the ordination of women marginalized the special works and responsibilities of clerical wives, including their task of being model mothers with full quivers of children. Even more than before, contraception became their answer.

The Evangelical Turn

It would be the eventual turn by Evangelical Protestants to the pro-life position on abortion that would for some also reopen the contraception question. When in 1973 the U.S. Supreme Court, in its *Roe* and *Doe* decisions, overturned the anti-abortion laws of all fifty states, relatively few Protestants voiced opposition. Indeed, some mainline denominations had already endorsed liberalized abortion.

The prominent Southern Baptist Pastor W. A. Criswell openly welcomed the decision. Representing a position many Evangelicals then took, he claimed: "I have always felt that it was only after the child was born and had life separate from its mother that it became an individual person." Others drew the line at some point before birth, but few rejected the decisions outright.

The Southern Baptist Convention (SBC) itself had in 1971 urged its members to work for legislation that will allow the possibility of abortion under such conditions as rape, incest, clear evidence of severe fetal deformity, and carefully ascertained evidence of the likelihood of damage to the emotional, mental, and physical health of the mother.

However, reflecting the movement of Evangelicalism as a whole (though not mainline Protestantism), in 2003, the SBC declared that this and the 1974 resolution "accepted unbiblical premises of the abortion rights movement, forfeiting the opportunity to advocate the protection of defenseless women and children" and that "we lament and renounce statements and actions by previous Conventions and previous denominational leadership that offered support to the abortion culture."

An early sign of this shift occurred in 1975 when a young editor at *Christianity Today,* Harold O. J. Brown, authored a short anti-abortion editorial. From his home in L'Abri, Switzerland, the neo-Calvinist Francis Schaeffer mobilized Evangelicals against abortion with books such as *How Should We Then Live?.* This campaign grew through the founding of new Evangelical organizations with pro-life orientations, including Focus on the Family, the Family Research Council, and Concerned Women for America.

At first, this pro-life Evangelicalism avoided the issue of contraception. However, over time, it has become ever more difficult for many to draw an absolute line between contraception and abortion, because—whatever theological distinctions they made between the two—the "contraceptive mentality" embraces both, and some forms of "contraception" are in practice abortifacients.

A MAJOR RETHINKING

"It is clear that there is a major rethinking going on among Evangelicals on this issue, especially among young people," R. Albert Mohler, Jr., president of the Southern Baptist Theological Seminary, recently told the *Chicago Tribune*. "There is a real push back against the contraceptive culture now."

In his last years, Francis Schaeffer seemed to be moving toward the historic Christian view of contraception. Since 1980, several resolutions adopted by the Southern Baptists at their annual meeting have criticized contraception. By the close of the twentieth century, the Family Research Council featured special reports on "The Empty Promise of Contraception" and "The Bipartisan Blunder of Title X," the latter referring to the domestic contraception program in the United States.

Conservative Calvinist publishers are producing books not only against contraception but promoting Natural Family Planning. A movement of Missouri Synod Lutherans is working to overturn their church's current teaching and return it to Luther's, and observers report a new interest in the traditional teaching among conservative movements in the mainline churches.

There have been other signs of Protestant rethinking on this question, including individual pastors and their wives who have opened their lives to bringing a full quiver of children into the world. For example, Pastor Matt Trewhella of Mercy Seat Christian Church in Milwaukee concluded that "we have no God-given right to manipulate God's design for marriage by using birth control." He had his vasectomy reversed, and he and his wife Clara have had seven more children.

While surely in the minority, the Trewhellas are not alone. In so acting, they are rediscovering their distinctive theology and their heritage, and they are accepting their special responsibility as a pastor's family to serve as witnesses to the original Protestant understanding of the divine intent for marriage. Importantly, they are also rebuilding a common Christian front on the issue of contraception, one lost in the dark days of the first half of the twentieth century.

The quotations from the Missouri Synod's Commission on Theology and Church Relations are taken from Aaron Wolf's "Hating Babies, Hating God" in the June 2003 issue of *Chronicles* (www.chronicles magazine.org). The texts of the Southern Baptist resolutions on abortion can be found at www.john stonsarchive.net/baptist/sbcabres.html.

Reprinted from Touchstone: A Journal of Mere Christianity, *May 2007, Volume 20, Number 4.*

RUSSELL D. MOORE

Above Every Name

On the Formalities That Teach Us Reverence

Both of my six-year-old sons stood a little straighter, knowing that something was seriously wrong. There wasn't any ambiguity in my furrowed brow or in my piercing look. One of them had just said something. It wasn't a profanity, and it wasn't a recitation of the Arian heresy. He said "Yeah" to a grown woman. And it was followed up with an invitation for a long discussion with Dad in the guest bedroom upstairs. To that my son responded, "Yes, sir."

I knew the discussion by heart, ahead of time, because I had received it too, from my own father and from an entire community of Southern Baptists in coastal Mississippi.

I grew up in an intentionally undignified revivalist church. Each service began with the congregation shaking hands and hugging necks as the choir sang, "I'm So Glad I'm a Part of the Family of God." Each service ended with seven or eight verses of "Just As I Am" or "The Savior Is Waiting," usually with some penitent sinner or other crying on the steps of the platform.

But all that informality ended when it came to the name of our pastor. He was "Brother Naron." If any of us had called him by his first name, we would have walked another kind of sawdust trail, right back to a familiar switch tree down the hill.

ALIEN HONOR

Most of this may be chalked up simply to southern culture, perhaps because, as Flannery O'Connor tells us, the South is "Christ-haunted" by a theological memory that lives on in revivalism and social custom. Even if the state religion of the South is not Christian at all but Stoic, as Walker Percy tells us, Stoicism was at least "Logos-haunted," recognizing an organizing structure of the universe in which it could not help but acknowledge hierarchy.

The transcendent roots of terms of honor, though, are seen less easily in their origins than in their denial. Too often, it is thought that the southern slavery and segregationist systems were based on too high a view of hierarchy, when precisely the opposite is the case. Southern society sought to tear down a biblical (or even Stoic) understanding of hierarchy based on honor, maturity, and responsibility and replace it with a pseudo-hierarchy based on a malevolently imaginary concept of white supremacy.

Will Campbell, a liberal white Baptist preacher and hero of the civil rights movement of the 1960s, writes in his memoir *Forty Acres and a Goat* of meeting an elderly black man in the heyday of the Jim Crow South. Campbell insisted on shaking hands with him and calling him "Mister," until the man pleaded with him not to do it, for fear that other whites would hear it and, after Campbell left, see to it that he was a "dead Mister."

There is something deeply and obviously perverse in a society that insisted that a young man call his father "sir" and yet expected a twenty-year-old white man to call an eighty-year-old black pastor "boy." A society that knows to say "sir" and "ma'am" ought to know (and, beneath seared consciences, did know) that the withholding of such honor where it is due is not just rude and uncultured but dehumanizing and wicked.

NAMETAG CULTURE

Giving honor where honor is due and giving a verbal recognition of age, maturity, or office are increasingly alien to American culture. MySpace, for example, like other technologies before it, allows the cultural milieu to express itself more quickly and more expansively.

Through writing notes on one another's digital "wall," the alternative cyber-communities created by social networking sites such as Facebook

153

and MySpace simulate the signing of a junior high school yearbook. In the *New York Times,* Fordham University communications specialist Lance Strate observed that such social networking sites mimic the intimacy of the face-to-face interaction of oral communication but without the "highly formalized rituals" social networks would have in a genuine community, producing a "leveling effect." "In a primary oral culture," he notes, "you would probably refer to me as 'Dr. Strate,' but on MySpace, everyone calls me 'Lance.'"

A nation birthed in revolution against the divine right of kings can be expected to emphasize a certain "Everyone calls me Lance" egalitarian ethos. But have we really progressed when the "Hi My Name Is Tina" nametag culture has developed to the point where our political signs and bumper stickers and television commercials refer to the potential leaders of the free world as "Hillary," "Barack," and "John," not to mention "Rudy" and "Mitt"?

More and more often, in my own conservative Evangelical subculture, pastors of Evangelical churches are not "Pastor Jones" or even "Pastor Sam," but "Randy" or "Tony" or "Sam." When the nametag culture has trickled down to the life of local congregations, what do we lose?

We lose something of the gospel itself. Terms of address can be overdone, of course. Jesus counsels against those who insist on elaborate recognitions in public places (Matt. 23:1–7). He insists we recognize that our ultimate "father" and "rabbi" (Matt. 23:8–11) is not human but divine (Matt. 19:17).

But the Scriptures explicitly call us to recognize authority and hierarchy as of the essence of our identity as the people of God. One of the ten foundational words given to Israel in the Torah is the command to "honor father and mother" (Ex. 20:12). In one of the more disturbing texts of the Old Testament, a group of boys are torn apart by she-bears after jeering the prophet Elisha with the words, "Go up, you baldhead!" (2 Kings 2:23–24).

Throughout the Scriptures, honor is commanded to be given to kings and those in authority. Jesus recognized authority and even hierarchy in the choosing of the foundation stones of his temple, apostles whose authority was recognized by the Church, and is still recognized when we listen to the Spirit through the Holy Scriptures they were inspired to write. This deference to authority is continued in the respect Scripture demands that we show to those who "labor in preaching and teaching" and thus are "considered worthy of double honor" (1 Tim. 5:17).

A Universal Reverence

We must respect our fathers and mothers (in the family and in the family of God), and all others worthy of our deference, because reverence and honor given to whom it is due is at the heart of the meaning of the universe itself. Redemption itself, the Apostle Paul tells us, comes through the verbal confession of Jesus as "Lord" (Rom. 10:9), a confession that points to the final day of judgment in which the very glory of God is found in how Jesus is addressed.

God has "highly exalted" Jesus, Paul writes, an exaltation that is seen in the fact that God has given our Lord "the name that is above every name" (Phil. 2:9). This glorious exaltation is heard audibly as every creature, kneeling, confesses that "Jesus Christ is Lord, to the glory of God the Father" (Phil. 2:11).

What is at stake in the inability to verbalize legitimate honor is our ability to worship. The Bible defines human sin as, ultimately, the refusal to "honor him as God or give thanks to him" (Rom 1:21).

Can there be any more horrifying example of human blindness to the glory of God than that of the soldiers at the Crucifixion dressing Jesus in purple and crowning him with thorny vines? Mark records the sarcasm: "And they began to salute him, 'Hail, King of the Jews!'" (Mark 15:16–19). These were not "just words." They reflected consciences numb to the honor due a King.

But there's a problem with teaching honor through terms of address, because many people believe the issue is personal. When I tell my boy to say hello to "Mr. Smith," Mr. Smith will often respond by saying, "Oh, it is fine for him to call me John." Well, no, it really isn't fine, because the issue is not what Mr. Smith wants.

Many unintentionally betray the reasons behind their insistence on being on a first-name basis with a six-year-old. "'Mr. Smith' is my dad," they say, or "'Mr. Smith' makes me feel old." I think, "Well, you *are* old—and that's a good thing," or "Well, congratulations, you're a grown man, so now you're 'Mr. Smith' too!" I don't say such things because that would be rude, even disrespectful.

For me, though, the issue is not so much that I want John Smith to *feel* honored and respected. I want him to *be* honored and respected. Most importantly, I want the youngsters for whom I bear responsibility to understand respect for elders and honor for authority.

I want them to do so for the same reason they call me "Dad" and not "Russell D." I want them to do so because life in these United States is a temporary thing. I want them to learn to follow a Lord and a King.

SPEAKING TO THE LORD

I realize I'm probably a bit hyper-scrupulous about this. Mississippi mores are not easily overcome. But I want to raise young men who are able to look King Jesus in the eye, and then bow before him on the Day of Judgment. I want them to understand the goodness of hierarchy when the hierarchy is God-given, and to practice giving honor to all those whom God has placed over them, so they learn to give honor to him.

I want to see our Lord Christ ask them if they wish to enter into a new creation that is not an egalitarian democracy but a glorious monarchy.

And I want to hear them say, "Yes, sir!"

Reprinted from Touchstone: A Journal of Mere Christianity, May 2008, Volume 21, Number 4.

DAVID MILLS

Bad Books for Kids

A Guide to the World of Youth Literature
& What You Can Do About It

You may be surprised, if you don't keep up on these things, and few of us have any reason to, how tawdry and sometimes depraved are the kinds of books being offered to teenagers by the major publishers and bookstores, and even the schools. This is true especially of the books supposed in some way to describe "real life."

Before I came across a short essay on what's called "young adult literature" a few years ago, I couldn't imagine that the books were more than mildly offensive, with a few news-making exceptions. (The popular *The Face on the Milk Carton* describes the main character's increasing intimacy with her boyfriend, utterly unnecessary to the story, with lines like "She could touch him in places she had never touched another human being.") I was shocked, and I think of myself as someone who is not easily shocked, by the evidence of commercial depravity.

And these books sell in huge numbers, mostly, judging from the books on the tables at our local chain bookstore, to girls. So many books read by so many will have their effect, and it is not likely to be good.

I went to Barnes & Noble one evening to look at what they offered, and particularly what they were pushing by setting out on the tables in the central aisle, tables you have to pass to get to the children's section at the back of the store. Of the fifty or sixty books on the two tables, none were overtly Christian and, as far as I could tell, none were implicitly Christian either.

There were no classics, not even modern classics like *The Diary of Anne Frank* or *Animal Farm*. The books were all fiction. There were no true-life stories, biographies, autobiographies (though most of the books I looked at were narrated as if they were autobiographies), histories, not even any sports stories.

They were mostly "problem books," the problems usually being the typical teenage struggles with boyfriends or girlfriends or the lack thereof, cruel teachers, clueless parents, vicious peers, bad skin, bad hair, fat thighs, insecurity, and fear, though they are sometimes serious problems like sexual abuse and drug addiction. A few of the books are obviously "realistic," of the sort whose cover copy emphasizes the problem it describes, and perhaps uses the words "realistic" or "gritty," the rest more obviously fictional and apparently lighter.

About one-quarter dealt with supernatural subjects, especially vampires. Of the several hundred books on the shelves, from one-third to almost one-half had supernatural subjects, vampires dominating. Only a few of these were traditional fantasy stories.

"REAL LIFE" STORIES

I picked up a representative selection of the books intended to reflect "real life" and found a chair. The twelve books were a mixed bag, morally and otherwise. You could find something to enjoy and some lesson of value in almost all of them, but also something that undermines moral clarity and promotes one or more of several popular sins. They are not all simple-minded celebrations of hedonism, because often the real "real world" intrudes.

The first I looked at was *Story of a Girl* by Sara Zarr, published last year, and a finalist for the National Book Award. It is narrated by a girl who was caught by her father at 13 having sex with an older boy and has to live with the reputation. She deals with the stupidity and viciousness of much of high-school life in a way most adults would recognize (with imbecile gym teachers, for example). Over the course of the book she comes to accept her lot, tough it out, and learn to be satisfied with her friends.

Another book, Terry Trueman's *Stuck in Neutral,* which won several awards, is narrated by a boy with cerebral palsy, who is assumed by everyone to have the mental age of a three-month-old. At the end of chapter two, he says:

There is one final bad-news punch line to my life. . . . It's that I'm pretty sure that my dad is planning to kill me. The good news is that he'd be doing this out of love for me. The bad news is that whatever the wonderfulness of his motives, I'll be dead.

It's an unexpected pro-life statement. The narrator is given every reason to want to die, yet he wants to live. A "mercy killing" would be murder. Yet even with this unexpected moral lesson, the book offers a critical and unqualified description of family life—he sees everything because no one hides anything from him—as a forced collection of confused, uncaring, destructive, and self-centered people.

Ellen Hopkins's *Crank* is narrated by a "good girl" from a broken home, whose absent father is an addict and a loser. While visiting him, she becomes a crank (or speed) addict, with all the degradation associated with that addiction.

She almost sleeps with the boy who introduced her to the drug, doesn't, and writes how much she regrets not doing so. She eventually does, gets pregnant, goes for an abortion, thinks she feels the baby move, and, upsetting her mother, goes home to have and then to keep the baby. The last lines emphasize the nature of the addiction. She's sitting with her baby but thinks: "Crank is more than a drug. / It's a way of life. You can / turn your back. But you can / never really walk away. / The monster will forever speak / to me. And today, / it's calling me out the door."

Those were typical of the books on the youth reading table. On the table with the sign "Just for Kids" I found Hailey Abbott's *The Secrets of Boys*. The front cover shows a girl in a bikini with a boy in a bathing suit pressing up against her from behind and nuzzling her neck.

The back cover describes the major characters, and includes this: "Zach: Sophisticated college boy, wise in the ways of French painting as well as other French things." This was the worst of the books I sampled. The narrator, a girl, has the usual life problems of a teenager, at least the teenagers in these stories. She loses her virginity to Zach, and this is treated as part of growing up, of becoming a better, more mature person: someone assertive, confident, and clear-headed. At the end she leaves him when she realizes that she really loves an old friend with whom she shares her innermost thoughts and feelings.

FICTIONAL ASSUMPTIONS

I have been reading such books for almost twenty years, since our eldest was a little girl, either looking for books she could read (she was a voracious reader) or vetting books she wanted to read, which had usually been recommended by her friends at the Christian school she attended. "Real life" young adult fiction—I am summarizing a huge and diverse set of books, but I think accurately, the bad books far outweighing the good—conveys several destructive assumptions to the kids who read it.

• Kids have horribly difficult lives, even if they have every comfort and pleasure in the world. Their families are dysfunctional, their parents self-absorbed or distant, their peers cruel, and their schools Darwinian. The best parents may love their child, but they just don't understand her problems (the main character is usually a girl). In some cases, though not all, added to these problems are bad skin and hair, and the like.

• Families are rarely "havens in a heartless world," but a trial that for obscure reasons must be endured, though evaded if possible, on the way to adulthood. Some siblings are kind, but most are either unconcerned (if older) or annoying (if younger) or else an ally in resisting their parents, and some are their parents' favorites. The child's real family is her set of friends. In a few stories, the main character may admire someone else's parents or family life, but almost never her own.

• No one understands them, the people in authority over them least of all. The authorities do not see what the child actually experiences, and the child has little or no hope they ever will, which makes their advice and guidance laughably useless. You will, however, find more sympathetic teachers in these stories than sympathetic parents, and many more wise teachers than wise parents.

• Kids are alone to handle their problems, though they may have friends to help, and sometimes a sympathetic but often powerless teacher. Even then, sometimes their friends and teachers fail them or turn against them. Trust is dangerous.

• Girls are strong but often cruel and manipulative; boys are soft and stupid, though they can be physically brutal. Many of the girls' books include one kind and supportive male, though he is sometimes a homosexual or at least "sensitive." Attractive boys are rarely trustworthy, though such a boy sometimes becomes devoted to the girl after he has slept with her, and she feels empowered in dropping him.

• Talking explicitly about bodily functions, especially menstruation, is a sign of maturity and realism. Doing so embarrasses parents, because they are not as open and natural, and by implication mature, as their children.

• Sexual activity is not governed by any form of morality, at least any morality that can be formulated as a rule or law. It is at best wise or unwise, not right or wrong. Social standards are irrelevant. No one saves herself for marriage, unless she will see the pointlessness of this by the end of the book.

• But giving up your virginity is still treated as somehow special, governed by feelings that giving it up to this person is, *somehow,* right and to that one wrong. Virginity is something to be treasured and given up only to someone for whom you have some kind of affectionate feelings. It's a morality of a sort, but not one that gives the child any criteria by which to measure those feelings. (Virginity is defined in the Clintonian way, with other sexual behaviors treated as if they weren't exactly sexual.)

• That said, other sexual encounters are not governed by even a vague morality, but simply by calculation of the pleasures and costs involved, if engaged in freely and at the appropriate age. Your body is to be saved or spent in much the same way you save or spend the money in your bank account. To the extent sexual activity involves an exclusive commitment to someone else, it is a tool to be used in getting or securing that commitment, though not a very good tool.

As a rule, sexual activity is mainly recreational. It ought to be "safe," though safety is almost always defined as protection from disease and conception, and sometimes from relational complications or emotional harm (always underestimated).

THEIR GOOD LIFE

That describes in outline what these books teach about the teenage life, but they also teach a lot about the world in which teenagers live.

• The good life requires having the things you want, whether you want straighter hair or a boyfriend or a car of your own or just a higher opinion of yourself. The books assume that the wealthier you are, the happier you should be, except when some sentimental lesson about the real importance of friends or self-respect is being taught. Their blissfully unquestioned materialism is astonishing.

• Politics doesn't exist, history doesn't exist, high culture doesn't exist.

The main character may have a friend who's involved in some charity or relief effort, or maybe even a political cause, or who reads a lot of difficult books, or who plays a musical instrument or writes poetry, but she (again, usually a she) is only narrative color. If a political cause is mentioned, it is almost certainly environmentalism.

• Business, if it is thought about at all, is greedy, rapacious, uncaring, and environment-destroying, and produces conformity and monotony. The main characters feel this despite their desire for luxury items. Wealth, and indeed everything needed even for the simplest life, just appears, except when the story is about a poor child or a middle-class child who became poor. Gratitude is not encouraged.

• There is no question that can be solved only by rigorous, disciplined thought. The kid who reads philosophy may be a "brain," but he is not to be imitated. All questions can be solved by a teenager thinking like a teenager.

• God doesn't exist for any practical purpose. If you believe he does, you may ask him to bail you out, but you would never think to follow his rules, because his rules are really your parents' and society's irrational standards, which will make you unhappy.

• Religion is always formal and impersonal and the parents' thing. (Although, interestingly, some stories show a sneaking respect for Catholicism and its mysteries, though that respect may be expressed through a particularly notable hatred. Just try to find a wise old priest in one of these stories.) Spirituality can be really cool, though, especially if it's Eastern or Native American.

• Nevertheless, youth should sometimes think about the ultimate questions, though no one ever seems to come to a conclusion other than high-school-level existentialism. Life is probably meaningless, but you can make your own meaning and create an authentic life by an act of will. Accept your limitations, don't look for the big answers, don't submit to tradition or authority, and do what feels most natural and right to you.

• The answer to the kids' problems is always some form of growth and reconciliation, even resignation: of learning from the experience, accepting it, and getting tough enough to get through it. The answer is rarely any kind of heroism or self-transcendence.

• The hope presented in these books is one of two kinds: In the lighter, sillier books it is merely getting what you want, particularly a new boyfriend or better skin; and in the more serious ones it is surviving until college or adulthood, when you will finally be free to live in a world you want and to make yourself what you would like to be. The hope is never external or transcendent.

MAINSTREAM MORALITY

But these books are not absolutely free of a traditionally explicit and binding morality. They carefully observe the mainstream pieties. For example, taking illegal drugs is always bad, and smoking cigarettes is always bad. They may be forgivable, however, if indulged in as an act of independence.

Racism is most definitely always bad and always unforgivable, unless the racist has a Damascus Road conversion and turns into an apostle of quotas and reparations. "Sexism," which includes recognizing any essential difference between the sexes, is not to be imagined, even though the books' plots very often hinge on the differences between boys and girls.

If a good character belongs to a political party (not that this comes up often), he is always a Democrat. Pro-lifers (not that they come up often) are always unattractive, and seriously religious people always harsh and rigid, and ignorant of the real world and its complexities and ambiguities.

Making any sort of moral judgment is always bad, unless it reflects a mainstream piety, one of which is the wickedness of moral judgments. People who make any other sort of judgment are not attractive and lead lives the hero and the reader know they do not want to lead.

SELLING VISIONS

That is, I think, the vision of life, the "realistic" vision, these books present. Children must get along as best they can, and seize whatever small pleasures life gives them. The giggly way this vision is sometimes offered does not disguise how dreary and tawdry it is.

Why, then, are these books the way they are? Because they are meant to sell to teenagers, and to the people who assign books to teenagers, which is to say, public school teachers and public librarians.

They do sell very well, even in an age in which fewer and fewer children read. The vision they present must be the vision many children want to have, and the vision that many of their teachers want them to have. (This explains, I think, why so many books include a wise and sympathetic teacher who effectively undercuts the main character's parents' authority).

It is not hard to see why. These books—with some exceptions—appeal to the worst in every teenager. The child in these stories is a victim, and one allowed a great deal of self-pity, whose parents try to control her (it's usually a her, as I said) but are out of touch and selfish to boot. She is in pain, but she knows better than anyone else what she needs, even if all she knows is that she does not need what her parents or her school are giving her. No one understands her, and her problems are almost always someone else's fault.

These books provide an alternative story to the one by which a girl (or boy) is supposed to live, and gives authoritative approval, a kind of imprimatur, to her desire to rebel and do what she pleases. In other words, they appeal to the child's vanity and pride, and except for the rare saint, even the most moral of children is vain and prideful and thus vulnerable to being twisted.

If such stories form the child's imagination and behavior, as they undoubtedly do, the average contemporary young adult "real life" book is a dangerous book. Such books must be read, if they are read at all, carefully and critically. A child can learn from *Crank* much about the seduction of drugs and the shame of drug addiction, if that is a lesson a child needs. Few, I suspect, do. The child will even learn that sexual intercourse can have consequences, like babies that change your life (if you're a girl, at least, for in the story she decides not to tell the father because he's gotten married without telling her).

But to learn these lessons, if indeed he needs to learn them, the young reader will have to slog through a great deal of degradation, and some titillating soft-core sex scenes. The degradation cannot be good for the reader, bringing into his mind images of human suffering and degeneracy that do him no good but are not easily erased or forgotten. The effect of the soft-core sex scenes is obvious, likewise bringing images into his mind that do him no good but are not easily erased or forgotten.

The lessons do not justify the exposure, not least because a child can learn about the wages of evil from other, classic sources, which can teach him without sullying his mind. I can't explain why, exactly, but the classic tales can deal with the same problems as the modern "problem books," but at a prophylactic distance that provides intimate engagement without contamination. Robert Louis Stevenson's *Kidnapped* is a story of child abuse (though much more) that doesn't leave the reader feeling that he has gotten too close, been too involved, in abusing a child, in the way the new books do.

Perhaps, and this is only a guess, because the classic works describe the events without the detail the problem books offer, the reader experiences vicariously what he ought to experience without too detailed and intimate a knowledge. When the hero in some Victorian thriller chases a criminal through a sewer, we are told enough about the dirt and stench to imagine the experience, while in a contemporary book the feces and waste would be graphically rendered.

Having said all this, there is another category of young adult books to which my criticism does not apply. I don't know what to call it. Maybe "neo-classical secular." This kind of book is morally serious and even traditional both in its morality and in its heroic ideal, in a way the average young adult book isn't. The best examples are J. K. Rowling's Harry Potter series and Philip Pullman's *His Dark Materials* trilogy, both huge bestsellers.

Rowling is a Presbyterian, and Pullman an atheist, but one who speaks a moral language much closer to the Christian language than that of the "real life" writers. His trilogy mixes some scenes of the crudest anti-Christian propaganda with some quite moving scenes of sacrificial goodness.

I think it significant that the sales of Rowling's and Pullman's books, as well as the continuing sales of C. S. Lewis's and J. R. R. Tolkien's, are so great. This suggests that not every child is satisfied with the self-centered, unheroic stories to be found in the young adult section. They are more realistic and more interested in reality—of "real reality," if you will—than the makers of the "real life" books realize.

CHILD-LIKE READING

There is a great deal more to be said about these books, but let me offer a few suggestions for parents whose children may want to read them, if for no other reason than that other children are reading them.

First, do not assume, as I once did, that the average children's or young adult book may be secular but is at least respectful of the moral law and of parental authority. It very likely is not.

Second, to the extent you can, vet your children's reading, starting as young as possible. Ban anything that is outright seditious, and be prepared to enforce the ban against howls of protest that everyone else is reading it.

If the child really, really wants to read a book that is in some lesser way objectionable, you might let him read it, but discuss your understanding with him. I am actually not sure about this, simply because a talk can never erase the effect of a bad book. The story will be more compelling, and affect his imagination more deeply and lastingly, than your moral abstractions possibly can. He may trust you, he may believe you implicitly, but the story has still buried in his mind a dangerous image of the way the world is.

Third, do not be afraid to upset your child by telling him he can't read something he really wants to. As I have told ours about movies they want to see but can't: you will never be harmed by something you didn't see. I have also told them that I have seen movies I now profoundly wish I hadn't, because some images never leave you. I can think of one to which I was taken by a Baptist minister, which gave me more exposure to real evil than I needed. The effect is like a stain that can't ever be completely cleaned.

Fourth, read to your child as much as you can. Read good books and books slightly too old for him. Use the books as a way to explore certain issues and questions with him as they come up in the books themselves. I fully realize how difficult this is, and myself have sometimes failed to do this, but reading to him is one of the very best things you can do for a child. Heaven knows the average school is not going to expose him to many of the classics, much less the great Christian works—and if they do, they'll describe them in hostile or foolish ways that will prevent the child from reading them with an open heart and mind.

Fifth, immerse your child in the worship of the Church and every other activity that can shape his imagination as Christian because he acts it out. The greatest prophylactic against cultural infection is not a shield but his love for something better and greater and more heroic.

Something like the Christian story, in fact. This is the map you want to give him, the image of reality you want most profoundly impressed upon his brain, so his thoughts will run naturally upon it.

DREARY BOOKS

The young adult books I read startled me by how dreary they were, even when they were most chipper. The world they describe is ultimately a trivial and a tawdry and a boring one. There is much evil in them, but the evil does not frighten or challenge because the authors do not see it. The good in them is usually weak, tepid, ineffective, a helping hand or a shoulder to cry on, not a gallant knight on a glorious horse. The salvation in them is equally weak, more often resignation than transformation.

There is in them nothing like the young boy Jim Hawkins defying the pirates, or Frodo and Sam carrying the Ring up Mount Doom, or Sherlock Holmes sitting in a dark room waiting for the viper that will kill him if he hears it too late, or Mowgli preparing to face Shere Khan. There is nothing like the homely but desperate struggles of the family in *Little House on the Prairie* or the hard life of the people in *Anne of Green Gables*. There is nothing like the redemption of Scrooge.

This is the one great miscalculation the publishers have made. They sell their books by appealing to a child's worst nature—his resentment, his self-pity, his anger—when they could have sold more by appealing to his desire for glory. Why read about the odious Zach, "wise in the ways of French painting as well as other French things," when you can read about Odysseus, or Aeneas, or Aragorn, or even Harry Potter?

It is easy for us parents to worry about all the ways our culture has to corrupt our children and make them in its image. The average "real life" book tries to do so. A culture forms and reforms with enormous power. But we have God on our side, and God tells a better story. Even the great pagans told a better story.

Reprinted from Touchstone: A Journal of Mere Christianity, *July/August 2009, Volume 22, Number 6.*

DOUGLAS FARROW

The Audacity
of the State

It's Bent on Bringing Down the House
on the Family & the Church

Jeremiah Wright's 1990 sermon, "The Audacity to Hope," which lent
Barack Obama the title of his electioneering book, has the story of Hannah as its text, and a painting by G. F. Watts as its foil. Whether the lecture
at which Wright first heard of the painting, or his own subsequent reading,
included a consultation of G. K. Chesterton's 1904 treatment of Watts, I
can't say. But Chesterton writes of Watts as follows:

> Those who know the man himself, the quaint and courtly old man
> who is still living down at Limnerlease, know that if he has one
> trait more arresting than another, it is his almost absurd humility.
> He even disparages his own talent that he may insist rather upon
> his aims. His speech and gesture are simple, his manner polite
> to the point of being deprecating, his soul to all appearances of
> almost confounding clarity and innocence. But although these
> appearances accurately represent the truth about him, though
> he is in reality modest and even fantastically modest, there is
> another element in him, an element which was in almost all the
> great men of his time, and it is something which many in these
> days would call a kind of splendid and inspired impudence. It is

that wonderful if simple power of preaching, of claiming to be heard, of believing in an internal message and destiny: it is the audacious faculty of mounting a pulpit. [*G. F. Watts*, 1904]

The Reverend Wright and President Obama certainly have the courage to mount a pulpit and preach. They, too, show a certain "inspired impudence," albeit not of a Victorian variety. Obama's rhetoric in particular strikes me as lacking any underlying modesty or humility. But then our present political condition is one of immodesty, not least where the state is in view, which is why I have somewhat impudently turned the title of Obama's book back upon itself.

THE SAVIOR STATE

When I speak of the audacity of the state, the kind of state I have in mind is what we may call the savior state. The main characteristic of the savior state is that it presents itself as the people's guardian, as the guarantor of the citizen's well-being. The savior state is the paternal state, which not only sees to the security of its territory and the enforcement of its laws but also promises to feed, clothe, house, educate, monitor, medicate, and in general to care for its people. Some prefer to call it the nanny state, but that label fails to reckon with its inherently religious character. The savior state does have a religious character, precisely in its paternalism, and may even be comfortable with religious rhetoric.

We are familiar with such rhetoric from ancient times. Was Caesar not *soter*? Did his coinage not mark him out as *divi filius* and *pontifex maximus*? "This, this is he," says Anchises in Virgil's *Aeneid*, the one you've been waiting for—"the man you have heard promised to you so often, Augustus Caesar, son of a god, who will once again establish the Golden Age in Latium, in the region once ruled by Saturn."

We are familiar with it from modern times too. The savior state is the kind of state that Hobbes envisioned, or that Louis Du Moulin had in mind when he said that "the Commonwealth is a visible church." It is the kind of state that emerges when it is assumed, as Herbert Thorndike pointed out in objection to both "Hobbism and Independency," that "a man may be heir to Christ's kingdom and endowed with Christ's Spirit without being, or before he be, a member of God's church." It is the kind of state that Obama had in mind when, during the presidential campaign, he invited a

Christian audience in South Carolina to see him as "an instrument of God" and to help him "create a Kingdom right here on Earth." Presumably it is the kind of state Dorothy Cotton had in mind when she penned her new gospel ditty:

> Tell me, tell me, why was Obama born?
> Tell me, tell me, why was Obama born?
> Somebody had to inspire our youth
> Somebody had to hear every voice
> Somebody had to tell the truth
> That's why Obama was born, my lordy,
> That's why Obama was born.

A single verse—there are five others—suffices, I think, to make the point.

ESCHATOLOGICAL RESERVE

It is customary these days to associate the religiously audacious state with theocratic Islamic countries such as Iran, or with Christendom, and to see them as belonging to a "medieval" mindset. The savior state should not be associated with Christendom, however, but with the demise of Christendom. It is a great achievement of the Enlightenment to have taken credit for the doctrine of the separation of church and state, when in fact it effectively abolished that doctrine.

Separation of church and state was predicated on the eschatological reserve on which Christianity insisted, a reserve that required a doctrine of "the Two" and refused to combine the kingly with the priestly in a single office or person. To combine these offices (with their respective "swords") belonged to Christ alone, and any other claimant to both was *ipso facto* a kind of Antichrist.

This same eschatological reserve, while supporting all manner of advances in civilizing social and political life, repudiated all utopianism, whether progressive or regressive. It sought no return to a Golden Age, nor did it trumpet "Change you can believe in." It knew of two loves and two cities made by those loves, and it sought only peace as far as possible between them and within them.

The disruption of that peace in the so-called Wars of Religion was what inspired a revolution under the banner of political liberalism, but the

Wars of Religion were not merely Wars of Religion, and political liberalism has morphed into a comprehensive liberalism that is itself religious in character. Comprehensive liberalism will not hear of Christian eschatology as a matter of public and political relevance. Indeed, it has as one of its fundamental premises that Western society has done away with Christian theology (I do not say, all theology) as a matter of public and political relevance. And so it has. But that has opened the field to would-be saviors and utopians of every stripe. It has made possible the return of the savior state—the audacious state that aims at building a kingdom of God right here on earth.

Re-Sacralized State

We can hardly be surprised at this. The Erastianism which (to speak anachronistically) had long been trying to get the upper hand in Christendom, managed to do so in the wake of the Lutheran Reformation, though it was in England that it first succeeded. The year 1534 brought the Act of Succession, and a mandatory oath of allegiance that included assent to everything declared by parliament about marriage in general and about Henry's in particular. Later that year, the Act of Supremacy also established the king's ecclesiastical jurisdiction, making no mention of the proviso formerly attached to it by the bishops: "as far as the law of Christ allows."

Christendom, of course, had already seen many princes who were determined to make the church do their bidding. But Henry, by writing his supremacy into the laws of the realm, inaugurated a new era. In that era, the ongoing process of subordinating religion to the demands of the state would outrun the monarchy as such, and the Church of England too. Not merely some, but *all* of the church's authority over things public would gradually be expropriated, binding even the conscience—as the Act of Succession already did—to the authority of the state.

Today we live in a society that shrinks in horror from the very idea of established religion, something the American Constitution in any case forbids. Yet we live, even if we live in America, in states increasingly ready to withdraw conscience clauses not only from public servants but also from doctors and druggists and so forth, requiring them to violate the teachings of their religion and the dictates of their consciences in order to demonstrate their allegiance to the state.

In Britain, and increasingly in North America, even churches and charitable organizations are not exempted from laws that demand conformity to state-endorsed ideologies loaded with religious implications. Penalties for violation include heavy fines or even imprisonment. Thus have we come round to accepting Erastus's invitation to the state to punish the sins of Christians, supplanting the church's sacramental discipline. We have come round, that is, to the de-sacralization of the church and the re-sacralization of the state, which is once again taking a tyrannical turn.

A MODERN-DAY SAMSON

Tyranny can nowhere succeed without pulling down the two most prominent pillars of political freedom, the pillars that have always provided for a roof or shield over the individual and his conscience. One pillar is the natural family unit; the other is the religious community. Of course, these pillars are not everywhere equally strong or upright. They may themselves be transformed into instruments of tyranny by this or that form of idolatry. But they *are* pillars for the simple reason that they do not concede to the audacious and immodest state the total authority it craves.

The natural family unit confronts the state as an entity that claims rights not granted *by* the state but brought *to* it—rights the lawful state is obliged to recognize and respect. The religious community likewise claims rights and liberties that derive from a source other than the state, a source that transcends and relativizes the state.

These two pillars are beginning to crack, however, in the grip of a modern-day Samson. I mean precisely that muscular but (if he only knew it!) blind and captive creature called "the individual." Not the individual of whom Kierkegaard spoke when he asserted, in view of the peculiar dignity bestowed on human beings by the incarnation of God, that "one is worth more than a thousand." But rather the individual fancied by the likes of Bentham, whose dignity consists merely in the freedom to pursue his own interests in his own way, whose interests must therefore be balanced against those of his neighbor under the formula, "Each to count for one and no more than one."

Even this individual comes to the state with rights of his own, rights that do not derive from the state; but the state is always the *arbiter* of his rights. Moreover, this individual is not natural (as the "state of nature" philosophers claim) but unnatural, just because he is naked and alone, brought into the world by no one, lacking kin or allegiance, unclothed by tradition—or at all events resentful of it. With such an individual the state that has tyrannical aspirations can happily do business, for he is the individual who has been taught to see himself as chained between the two great pillars of family and church, constrained and belittled by their conventions; who in his shame and fury is willing to call, not on God, but on the power of the state *as if* on God, to bring them down to the dust.

More than one modern philosopher has dallied with this Samson, betraying him into the hands of the state. John Stuart Mill comes to mind as one of the most successful. Mill's seductive side is his libertarian individualism. The sting is in the statism that ultimately overpowers it.

LIBERTY PRIOR TO TRUTH

It is not as though no one has noticed the contradiction. William Gairdner, for one, makes much of it in *The Trouble with Democracy*. He observes how the first three chapters of *On Liberty* lay the foundations of libertarianism, the cornerstone of which is the thesis that "mankind are greater gainers by suffering each other to live as seems good to themselves, than by compelling each to live as seems good to the rest." That thesis has as its corollary the so-called harm principle, which Mill puts as follows: "The only purpose for which power can be rightfully exercised over any member of a civilized community, against his will, is to prevent harm to others."

To read these first three chapters is to be led out of the cave of civil coercion and social intolerance into the broad places of spontaneous experiments in individual freedom. "The only freedom which deserves the name, is that of pursuing our own good in our own way, so long as we do not attempt to deprive others of theirs, or impede their efforts to obtain it." "No society in which these liberties are not, on the whole, respected, is free," says Mill, "whatever may be its form of government; and none is completely free in which they do not exist absolute and unqualified."

Gairdner has put his finger on the most seductive element in these chapters of *On Liberty*, which are pitched at just about the right level, intellectually and rhetorically, for crusading law clerks and higher-court justices. It lies in the notion that "liberty is prior to truth," and indeed truth's "efficient and final cause." Gairdner is exactly right to put it this way. The power of *On Liberty* to overturn social and moral and religious conventions arises from Mill's exciting and flattering suggestion that freedom will lead you into the truth. That iconoclastic gospel from the Romantic period still competes very successfully, tractable as it is to post-modern cynicism, with the older idol-smashing gospel of Jesus, that "the truth will set you free."

Mill's gospel takes no account of the creator/creature distinction, or of the fallenness of man. It takes no account of a freedom higher than freedom of choice, and gives no thought to how the truth of our own good will be recognized, or how that good will prove commensurate with the good of others. It is incurably romantic and naively optimistic. Most significantly, it fails to reckon with the fact that, in the absence of an overarching common good, based on a prior truth to which both the individual and the state are subject, the *state* must become the arbiter of all the competing goods of "free" individuals. It is not the individual who triumphs, then, in the appeal to a freedom that is prior to truth, but the state.

THE HARM PRINCIPLE

Behind Mill stands Rousseau, of course, whose rather more obvious statism Mill hoped to avoid. The basic premise of *On Liberty* is drawn from the *Declaration of the Rights of Man and of the Citizen,* that "liberty consists in being able to do anything that does not injure another." And that dictum is in turn drawn from Rousseau, who got it from the Marquis d'Argenson, to whom we actually owe the harm principle: "In the Republic each man is perfectly free in all things that do no harm to others." Rousseau's intention in popularizing it was to downplay the obligations imposed by civil society, which he regarded as a corrupting more than a civilizing influence, especially in the form of family and church.

One's primary obligations would hereafter be understood as obligations chiefly to oneself, on the one hand, and to the state on the other. That is what the harm principle is really all about—the elimination of the oppressive middle term between the individual and the state. This begs the question, however, as to what does or does not harm another, and who will decide that. Both Mill and Rousseau have ideas about that, and one gets glimpses of Mill's ideas in the final chapters of *On Liberty.* Only glimpses, mind you, because Mill's ideas aren't really very libertarian after all.

Linda Raeder has also noted the contradiction in Mill, and her take on it is more cynical. In *John Stuart Mill and the Religion of Humanity* she develops Joseph Hamburger's argument that Mill's purpose in *On Liberty* was to implement the first stage of his Comtean agenda; that is, to assist in the people's liberation from Christian religion and morals *via* individualist ideals, with a view to their eventual re-indoctrination in the atheistic Religion of Humanity, the religion of duty to the greater good of man. In other words, first you must make of the Christian an individual; then you must free him from his "miserable individuality" (Mill's expression in *Utilitarianism*) into the new community that is the society whose ideal object is not God but itself.

Here again, Mill reminds one of Rousseau. They have in common an idea of obligation to the *res publica,* religiously conceived, that is a deliberate alternative to the idea of obligation to God and to the neighbor. Like Gairdner, Raeder points to the influence of Mill's wife, the Romantic poet Harriet Taylor, on the first three chapters of *On Liberty*. But liberty was really for great souls like Harriet, not for the masses. The masses must "be indoctrinated from infancy in the values and ethics created by the best and wisest specimens of humanity." They must be domesticated, in other words, by the savior state.

State Control of Education

However one reads Mill, it is safe to say that the further we have pressed his libertarian principles, the deeper we have submerged ourselves in the statist element of his thought and compromised our freedom. The sphere of education, and the related sphere of family law, have become particularly important battlegrounds.

For Mill, as for Bentham and others of their persuasion, the lack of a properly domesticated society is due (as Jacob Talmon puts it in *The Rise of Totalitarian Democracy*) "not to man but to the failure of governments to form man with the help of education and proper laws." Working on the premise that "in an improving state of the human mind, the influences are constantly on the increase which tend to generate in each individual a feeling of unity with all the rest," Mill invites us to imagine a situation in which

> this feeling of unity [would] be taught as a religion, and the whole force of education, of institutions, and of opinion, directed, as it once was, in the case of religion, to make every person grow up from infancy surrounded on all sides both by the profession and by the practice of it.

Today that isn't at all difficult to imagine.

Take Québec, for example, where public education in North America was begun back in the 1660s by the diligent labors of the Vicar Apostolic, François de Laval, and a small band of hard-working colonists. The remarkable system they built has been almost completely colonized by the state, which has now instituted a mandatory curriculum in religion and ethics designed to instill just such a feeling in every young citizen (even those in private or religious schools, though that has been challenged in the courts).

More proximate than Mill, in the inspiration of the program, is a 1996 report by the International Commission on Education for the Twenty-first Century, titled *Learning: The Treasure Within,* which has globalized Mill's basic idea. "We must be guided," says Jacques Delors in that report, "by the Utopian aim of steering the world toward greater mutual understanding, a greater sense of responsibility and greater solidarity, through acceptance of our spiritual and cultural differences."

One should not be deceived by the reference to acceptance of differences. What this actually means in practice is increased state intervention in areas constitutionally reserved for civil society, so as to suppress or neutralize the visions children inherit from their familial and religious communities, in favor of the vision of "the best and wisest specimens of humanity" that such commissions can muster.

STATE CONTROL OF CHILDREN

The ascendancy of the state over civil society, which it ought rather to serve, is virtually guaranteed where the state exercises full control over education—particularly if the goal of education, as one professor boldly asserted in a recent McGill forum, is to release children from the control of their parents. In America, one notes, there have long been advocates of the still more radical idea that children should be regarded as the state's property, to be educated on a compulsory basis according to state needs and requirements. That is a thesis likely to be advanced with renewed urgency as the implications of our declining birthrate begin to be grasped.

Nor is it altogether lacking support from the law. In 1840 Justice Paige of Connecticut opined in *Mercein v. People* that "the moment a child is born it owes allegiance to the government of the country of its birth, and is entitled to the protection of the government." He further explained that "with the coming of civil society the father's sovereign power passed to the chief or government of the nation." While the state, for its own convenience, passes part of this power back to the parents, it maintains sovereignty over the question of what is in the best interests of the child. The Colorado Supreme Court partly endorsed that view in a 1910 child custody case:

> Though nature gives to parents the right to the custody of their own children, and such right is scarcely less sacred than the right to life and liberty, and is manifested in all animal life, yet among mankind the necessity for government has forced the recognition of the rule that the perpetuity of the state is the first consideration, and parental authority itself is subordinate to this supreme power.

The pattern we have already observed is very much in evidence here. Radical critics such as John Taylor Gatto are not mistaken in pointing out the use of (basically Christian) doctrines of individual destiny, and of subjective rights, to separate children from their natural communities and attach them to artifacts of the state. In Canada we have performed costly exercises of public penance over such strategies in connection with the native residential schools, yet we are now doing something very similar with everyone but natives. The ever more vigorous expansion of public welfare programs, which we have witnessed on both sides of the border, works on exactly the same principle, of course: Citizens are separated from both their natural family units and their religious communities by a cultivated reliance on the state.

What is more, the normalization of divorce—one of the most significant features of our contraceptive culture—has ever more deeply insinuated the state into the child-rearing process and so into the sphere of the family. The "great and pernicious error" against which Pope Leo XIII warned in *Rerum Novarum* has thus gradually become the norm; namely, "that the civil government should at its option intrude into and exercise intimate control over the family and the household."

NAKED BEFORE THE STATE

To make matters very much worse, the *parens patriae* power has recently received an enormous boost from another feature of the contraceptive society: same-sex "marriage." Though most people have not yet realized it, the advent of same-sex marriage has transformed marriage from a pre-political institution conferring "divine and human rights," as the Roman jurist Modestinus put it, into a mere legal construct at the gift and disposal of the state. The legal terrain has thus changed dramatically, along with the cultural—something I have tried to show in a little book called *Nation of Bastards*. The family is ceasing to be what the *Universal Declaration of Human Rights* confesses it to be, viz., "the natural and fundamental group unit of society."

Replaced by a kaleidoscope of transient sexual and psychological configurations, which serve chiefly to make children of adults and adults of children, the declining family is ceding enormous tracts of social and legal territory to the state. At law, parent-child relationships are losing their *a priori* status and privilege. Crafty fools ask foolish fools, "What harm does same-sex marriage do to your marriage, or to your family?" The truthful answer is: Same-sex marriage makes us all chattels of the state, because the state, in presuming to define the substance rather than the accidents of marriage, has made marriage itself a state artifact.

Those who have trouble connecting the dots here—which lamentably includes many defenders of the traditional institution—should take time to consider the fact that the new "inclusive" definition, in striking procreation from the purview of marriage, has left both parents and children without a lawful institution that respects and guarantees their natural rights to each other.

Opening up marriage in principle to non-generative unions really means closing it in principle to the inter-generational interests on which it has always been based. From now on, the handling of those interests will be entirely dependent, legally speaking, upon the good graces of the state. Every citizen will stand naked before the state, unclothed by his most fundamental community, unbuffered by any mediating institution with its own inherent rights. Nor should it be overlooked that, what the state has the power to define, it has the power to define again and again, and even to dispense with.

Admittedly, even the state has not yet fully connected the dots, but that is happening with remarkable rapidity, as concurrent moves in education demonstrate. States and international agencies are increasingly prone to argue that children have the right to a state-directed education and that this right must be protected by the *state* against the interference of *parents*. The logic is not difficult to follow: If marriage is procreative, it is also educative; but if it is not procreative, it is not educative either—educative rights and responsibilities are up for grabs, and it is the state that will do the grabbing. The pillar that is the family appears to have cracked nearly through.

Samson's Revenge, or the Ichabod Effect

In a 2008 speech at the Catholic University of America, James Cardinal Stafford—who apparently does not see in Obama the humility that Chesterton saw in Watts—deployed his meditations on St. John's Apocalypse "to strengthen the Catholic faithful . . . against the ever increasing pretensions of the state [to make] itself absolute." Cyril of Jerusalem would have thought him wise: "If thou hast a child according to the flesh," said Cyril, "admonish him now; if thou has begotten one through catechizing, put him also on his guard, lest he receive the false one as the true. For 'the mystery of iniquity doth already work.'"

Had I space, I would now try to show you the way in which that mystery has also been at work in religion, producing cracks in the other pillar that holds up the roof which shields the individual from the state. That will have to await another opportunity, however, except insofar as I can hint at it by adverting again in conclusion to the story of Hannah.

I trust you know the story. Hannah meets Eli, who, sitting by the temple gate, mistakes her fervent prayer for drunkenness and rebukes her for being a base woman, only to discover that she is quite sober after all, and that she has been praying out of "great anxiety and vexation." He blesses her. When Samuel is born as the answer to her prayers, Hannah delivers Samuel into Eli's care in fulfillment of her vow to God.

That must have been a rather frightening prospect, given what everybody knew about the goings-on at the temple in those days. Eli's sons, whom the text describes as "worthless men [who] had no regard for the Lord," were the ones who had taken charge of it, and Eli apparently hadn't the backbone necessary to bring them into line. ("They would not listen to the voice of their father," we are told, "for it was the will of the Lord to slay them.")

But Samuel is not corrupted by the sons of Eli, a fate from which God preserves him. Instead, he is given the unhappy burden of disclosing to Eli that his family line is about to be brought to a bitter end. That is just what happens during the rout of Israel by the Philistines. Blind old Eli, learning that both his sons and the ark of God have fallen to the Philistines, falls backwards from his seat at the gate, breaks his neck, and dies. His daughter-in-law, Phineas's wife—who dies in childbirth on the same day—names her son Ichabod, "the Glory is not," for the Glory, she says, "has departed from Israel."

The Reverend Wright didn't mention any of that in his sermon. I thought I would mention it, however, for the audacity of the savior state is rather like the audacity of Hophni and Phineas, who apparently believed that the house of God, and the people of God, were there merely for plunder. The savior state has its own aims and motivations, of course, motivations that may seem (despite the ever more frequent corruption scandals) much nobler than those of Eli's sons. But the process is much the same, and the final outcome will also be the same, if its advance is not checked. That the state must collapse, when the pillars of family and church are gone, is the secret that the state itself does not know. This secret I call Samson's revenge, but we may also call it the Ichabod effect.

THE HOPEFUL CHRISTIAN

Christianity is not about revenge, however, and it is certainly not about despair. It is, as Jeremiah Wright said, about *hope* (the title of Watts's painting). Christians deny that the state is savior because they believe that God is savior. Their hope is not, like Mill's, in the state; nor, like libertarians', in themselves. Their hope, like Hannah's, is in God.

So how shall they express their hope in God? What shall they do in the face of the audacious state, which threatens to bring them and their society to ruin?

Since I live in Québec, I will begin with Québec, where there is something Eli-like about many of our older clergy, and something Phineas-and Hophni-like about certain of our civil servants, who follow a line of priests that defected from the Catholic Church during the Quiet Revolution. Which is to say, the former often content themselves with a rueful, defeated glance at the latter, while the latter proceed pretty much as if they had assumed the place of the former.

The hopeful Christian—hope being something quite different from mere optimism—will not be taken in by any of this. The Ministry of Education, though it issues documents these days that read like upside-down versions of *Gravissimum educationis,* is not the new regime in the house of the Lord. Moreover, Christians have undertaken no vow to deliver their children over to it, to be shaped by the state for its own ends. Rather, they have taken vows to God to see that their children are raised according to the faith. They must therefore demand of the state respect for their right to have their children eat from their own educational table. And they must be willing, like Bishop Laval and his "handful of colonists and scanty resources," to invest what resources they have in providing such a table.

Something similar, I suspect, can be said in the land of Obama and Wright, though its history and habits are different. To be sure, there is a much stronger tradition there of resistance to the overweening state, but the forces of the state are also far greater. In America, Christians will require the courage of Dorothy Cotton's hero, Martin Luther King, Jr., if they are to repair the pillars of freedom that have sustained such damage, and to roll back the impressive gains that have lately been made by the savior state. In America, too, the churches will need to renew their pedagogical mission and to fight for freedom of education. The natural family will need somehow to reclaim, if it can, the rights it is losing.

And in both countries, men and women will need to rediscover Hannah's hunger for progeny, for the contraceptive mentality and the practice of abortion contribute very directly to the Ichabod effect.

Inspired Impudence

The hopeful Christian will not give up on any of this. But there is something else to be said. The cracks that have appeared in the pillar that is the family appeared first in the pillar that is religion. For, in Christianity, religion is still more fundamental than the family, as Jesus made clear. "He who loves father or mother more than me is not worthy of me." The Christian religion is decidedly not an individualistic religion, however. Rather, it is an *ecclesial* religion that sacramentally embraces and transcends the family. That, alas, was obscured by the sectarianism into which it degenerated in the wake of the Protestant Reformation—the very same sectarianism that revived the beast that is the audacious state.

The hopeful Christian, then, if his hope is not misplaced, will eschew both individualism and sectarianism, seeking the union and communion of the Church. Like Hannah, who gave up her only son to serve the people of God in the temple of God, he will seek always the good of the Church, the precariousness of the times notwithstanding. If he acts with "inspired impudence," it will be an inspired impudence that begins in prayer at the temple gate. That is where Hannah began, and it is where we, too, should begin. And if we, who are sober, are thought drunk and disorderly by the state and our fellow-citizens, or even by some of our priests, so be it.

Reprinted from Touchstone: A Journal of Mere Christianity, *January/February 2010, Volume 23, Number 1.*

NATHAN SCHLUETER

The Romance of Domesticity

Marriage Thrives in Reality, Not in Our Dreams

I am honored to be asked to deliver the annual Last Day Lecture here at Hillsdale College, and to be included among the distinguished faculty who have gone before me. This is a formidable subject for a lecture. It requires one to think about and imagine an unpleasant event: death. For me, however, the assignment is not as daunting as it might be for others. As my last name suggests, I have German in my blood, which means I often think about death.

I wish I could describe this as a philosophical experience, in the way that Socrates describes philosophy in *The Phaedo*, as "learning to die." Then I would deliver an impersonal lecture on some fine point of philosophy, such as the adequacy of St. Thomas Aquinas's arguments for the existence of God, or the perverse effects of Kantian deontology on contemporary ethics.

But no, this experience of mine has all the marks of a German thing, not a Greek one. It involves the silent mourning of the passing of time, of the rapidly closing circle of possible selves into a solid and fixed point. I never cease to be stunned, even scandalized, by photographs of the aged when they were young: How could that smooth flesh, straight form, and clear eyes have suffered a sea-change into this faded, wrinkled man propped up in a wheelchair? I think of the inevitable unfolding of my own future.

And yet to look on death is to look on reality. To be human, to be an embodied soul, means to suffer time, change, and death, and our responses to these experiences are determinative of how we will live, and ultimately, of our happiness. So my lecture cannot be about learning to die in the So-cratic sense. It is rather about learning to live in the Christian sense, and this means seeing reality as it is.

The (very) loose model of my reflections is *The Confessions* of St. Au-gustine, in which personal experiences of time, change, suffering, and death are illuminated by the mysteries of Creation, Incarnation, and Redemption. As with Manichaeism in the time of Augustine, so in our own time there lurks a dangerous heresy that twists both the truth and a good many lives. I call that heresy Romanticism.

By Romanticism I mean the impulse to escape, through passionate idealization and fancy, from the real world of mortal man, the world of suffering and change, the world of what it means to be in a body with concrete limits. Gustave Flaubert provides an exemplary model of the es-sential pattern of this sort of Romanticism in his novel *Madame Bovary,* especially in his depiction of the heroine, Emma Bovary. He also subjects it to a devastating, if rather hopeless, critique. That pattern has five features.

THE FIVE FEATURES OF ESCAPIST ROMANTICISM

First, Flaubert locates Romanticism in a *disordered imagination*. Like Plato, Flaubert was profoundly aware of the essential connection between the imagination and desire, and of the singular power of art to shape the imagi-nation. He describes in detail the influence of the popular romance novels of the day on Emma's conception of happiness, especially in marriage, an influence that ultimately proves her undoing.

> Before marriage she thought herself in love; but since the hap-piness that should have followed failed to come, she must, she thought, have been mistaken. And she tried to find out what one meant exactly in life by the words *bliss, passion, ecstasy,* that had seemed so beautiful to her in books.

A second feature of the Romantic imagination is *itinerancy*. Filtered through the imaginative lens of the literature she has read, Emma experi-ences as unrelieved boredom her ordinary life as the wife of a simple (and admittedly rather dull) doctor of a small town. Happiness is always else-where, there, just over the ever-receding horizon. As such, it is a flight from home, and from domesticity. Not only does Emma press her husband to move from one small town to another in the hope of finding excitement, but she spends her spare time dreaming of a happier life elsewhere:

> It seemed to her that certain places on earth must bring happiness, as a plant peculiar to the soil, and that cannot thrive elsewhere. Why could she not lean over balconies in Swiss chalets, or enshrine her melancholy in a Scotch cottage, with a husband dressed in a black velvet coat with long tails, and thin shoes, a pointed hat and frills?

Flaubert expresses his judgment of this aspect of Emma's character with consummate irony: "She wanted to die, but she also wanted to live in Paris."

The Romantic seeks flight from domesticity not only in a spatial sense, but also in an ontological sense. He refuses to be himself in his given, concrete particularity, and instead makes various attempts at self-creation. Thus, the Romantic imagination is behind the demand for autonomy. This is a desire the market is ever ready to supply. *Consumerism*, therefore, is a third feature of Romanticism.

One of the ironies of the quest for autonomy is that it inevitably results in the imitation of models provided by someone else. Advertisers and marketers elicit, feed upon, and profit from Romantic desire by providing an endless diversion of goods, and by promising ever-new identities. In *Madame Bovary* the merchant Lheureux is the pander of Emma's illicit desires, profiting handsomely at each step of her demise. "Emma lived all absorbed in her passions and worried no more about money matters than an archduchess."

The ultimate futility of the consumerist promise rests in the fact that the "home" of human nature is to be in a body with an unchangeable genetic makeup and history. The trappings of fashion cannot re-create one's identity but only change it in the most superficial way.

Emma also manifests a fourth aspect of Romantic escapism: *adultery and promiscuity*. She is only alive in the thrill of her extramarital affairs:

> She repeated 'I have a lover! A lover!' delighting at the idea as if a second puberty had come to her. So at last she was to know those joys of love, that fever of happiness of which she had despaired! She was entering upon a marvelous world where all would be passion, ecstasy, delirium. She felt herself surrounded by an endless rapture.

She also "recalled the heroines of the books that she had read . . . an actual part of these lyrical imaginings." But her affair, like her marriage, inevitably becomes ordinary, a point Flaubert again makes with laconic precision: "She was as sick of him as he was weary of her. Emma found again in adultery all the platitudes of marriage."

Finally, and at its deepest level, Romanticism is motivated by an *existential* escapism. It is a revolt against humanity itself, against one's limits as an embodied soul and creature. Autonomy leads to death, often by suicide. Like the Romantic heroines who have gone before her (Dido, Iseult, Juliet), Emma finds in her death by suicide both the liberation from and the consummation of her Romantic desire. Yet her dying words suggest that this end is anything but Romantic: "God it's horrible!"

Emma's extravagant expectation of happiness, her vagrant homelessness and boredom, her alternating states of misery and euphoria, her promiscuity, her addictive consumerism, and her suicide all follow a pattern that is familiar to careful observers of *popular modern* American life. We have become a nation populated by Madame Bovarys.

Two Partial Truths

I have called this form of Romanticism a heresy. We should consider further what this means. John Cardinal Newman described heresies the following way:

> Heresies are *partial* views of the truth, starting from some truth which they exaggerate, and disowning and protesting against other truth, which they fancy inconsistent with it. All heresies are partial views of the truth, and are wrong, not so much in what they directly say as in what they deny.

If true, Romanticism should include at least a partial truth. In fact, it includes two partial truths.

The first is that while man longs for wholeness and for happiness, he can never quite be whole or happy in this world, because his *real home* is elsewhere. We are all in some sense pilgrims in this world, wayfarers. Our citizenship is in heaven. We can never forget the haunting words of Christ in the Gospel of Luke: "If any one comes to me and does not hate his own father and mother and wife and children and brothers and sisters, yes, and even his own life, he cannot be my disciple" (14:26).

The second partial truth Romanticism captures is the proper and necessary role the imagination plays in human knowledge and action. This relationship was clear to the classical and medieval writers, a fact evident in great works stretching from Plato's *Republic* to the *Utopia* of St. Thomas More.

MACHIAVELLI'S WEDGE

It was Machiavelli who first sought to sever the link between imagination and reality in the fifteenth chapter of *The Prince*. By driving a wedge between the "effectual truth" and the "imagination thereof," Machiavelli prepared the way for the many separations that characterize the modern world, separations between facts and values, science and religion, nature and grace.

But the genius of Machiavelli rests in the fact that he knew what seems to have eluded the rest of us: that his alleged "realism" was itself a work of imagination, an abstraction from the way things really are. The result of the concealment has been a culture deeply divided between a science without poetry (i.e., Scientism) on the one hand, and a poetry without intellect (i.e., Romanticism) on the other, and nothing to bridge the gap.

It is important to see that the alternative to the Romantic imagination is not "Realism," an opposite and perhaps equally prevalent heresy exemplified in the way of life of those who hope to overcome the painful longing of Eros by directing its attention exclusively to the needs of the body, to physical security and material prosperity. This, however, only amplifies man's misery, as he feels it more acutely in his prosperity before the inevitable and yawning chasm of death. The calculating *homo economicus* of economic theory is no more likely to discover the right road to human happiness or justice than the Romantic.

Thus, both the Romantic and the Realist imaginations involve a falsification of reality. Neither can deliver what it promises, and both meet at the same dead end. What alternative remains?

THE EXTRAORDINARY ORDINARY

What is required is a truly realist imagination, one that captures and reveals the extraordinary quality of ordinary life. Such an imagination would restore the "chest," the locus of the imagination, to its rightful place as the mediator and integrating principle of intellect and appetite, soul and body, in the human person. The pressing need for such a restoration is one of the central arguments of C. S. Lewis in *The Abolition of Man*.

Such an imaginative vision rests at the heart of the Christian story: the Creator is born to a lowly virgin in a stable, and angels, shepherds, cattle, and kings all come to pay him homage. In taking on flesh, Christ raised up the most ordinary things—water, wine, bread, marriage—and made them the means of sanctification. Here is the true Romance of Domesticity in all its glory, the very revelation of the extraordinary in the ordinary.

This discovery of the extraordinary in the ordinary is part of the "romance of the faith" that G. K. Chesterton discovered in orthodoxy, a point he puts with his uncommonly common wit in his book by that name:

> A child kicks his legs rhythmically through excess, not absence, of life. Because children have abounding vitality, because they are in spirit fierce and free, therefore they want things repeated and unchanged. They always say, "Do it again"; and the grown-up person does it again until he is nearly dead. For grown-up people are not strong enough to exult in monotony. But perhaps God is strong enough to exult in monotony. It is possible that God says every morning, "Do it again" to the sun; and every evening, "Do it again" to the moon. It may not be automatic necessity that makes all daisies alike; it may be that God makes every daisy separately, but He has never got tired of making them. It may be that He has the eternal appetite of infancy; for we have sinned and grown old, and our Father is younger than we.

SPLENDOR & HUMILITY

Josef Pieper makes a similar point in *Leisure: The Basis of Culture,* where he argues that philosophy itself is rooted in the capacity to notice the extraordinary in the ordinary:

> If someone needs the "unusual" to be moved to astonishment, that person has lost the ability to respond rightly to the wondrous, the *mirandum,* of being. The hunger for the sensational, posing, as it may, in "bohemian garb," is an unmistakable sign of the loss of the true power of wonder, for a *bourgeois*-ized humanity. To find the truly unusual and extraordinary, the *real mirandum, within*

the usual and the ordinary, is the beginning of philosophy.

Notably, Pieper makes the same claim for poetry: "According to Aristotle and Thomas," he writes, "the philosophical act is related to the poetical: both the philosopher and the poet are concerned with 'astonishment,' with what causes it and what advances it."

One of my favorite expressions of this imaginative vision is a barn my wife's late grandfather, William Schickel, converted into an oratory in Loveland, Ohio. Schickel's remarkable life raising eleven children on a farm while working as an artist is captured by Gregory Wolfe in *Sacred Passion: The Art of William Schickel*. Wolfe quotes Schickel describing the idea behind the oratory this way:

> The barn is a blend of frugality, simplicity, and poverty seen as a positive force. . . . There is a wonderful deep-rooted consciousness that our Savior came to dwell among us in a building that was constructed for the shelter and care of animals. . . . The barn at its best is an integration of splendor and humility that is . . . expressive of the most foundational Christian outlook.

A BRUTAL ASSAULT

In *Moby Dick*, Herman Melville provides a dire warning that the Romantic imagination is not merely an individual affair, that its influence inevitably affects the political order as well. Captain Ahab is a quintessential Romantic, in rebellion against his own limits and the order of reality, and the *Pequod* is a haunting symbol of an America that has revolted against nature in its mad quest for unlimited commerce and empire. "Then the rushing *Pequod*, freighted with savages, and laden with fire, and burning a corpse, and plunging into the blackness of darkness, seemed the material counterpart of her monomaniac's soul."

But midway through the novel, the sometime Romantic narrator Ishmael, who cooperated in the catastrophe of the novel and barely escapes to tell of it, makes a remarkable confession:

> Now, since by many prolonged, repeated experiences, I have perceived that in all cases man must eventually lower, or at least shift, his conceit of attainable felicity; not placing it anywhere in the

intellect or the fancy; but in the wife, the heart, the bed, the table, the saddle, the fire-side, the country.

Ishmael's observation points to the intimate connection between domesticity and ordinary life (and by extension, patriotism). Given this connection, it is not surprising that no other institution has been so brutally attacked by the Romantic imagination as marriage and the family, an assault that continues unabated in popular culture today.

If there is truth in what I have said thus far, the recovery of stable marriage and family life depends upon more than preserving the correct legal arrangements, or even providing marriage instruction and moral and spiritual guidance for the young. These things are necessary and good, but without a correct formation of the imagination, they are precariously inadequate solutions. What is wanted is the kind of poetry Pieper describes, a poetry rooted in the romance of domesticity, which reveals the real beauty of ordinary life within limits and shows the dignity of what it means to be what Wendell Berry calls a "placed person."

PERSONAL REFLECTIONS

I began these remarks by pointing out that my experience of death is an existential German thing rather than a Greek philosophical one. It seems appropriate therefore that I offer a more personal reflection on the romance of domesticity.

For years, it has been my habit to write poems on special occasions (anniversaries, birthdays, etc.). Here, then, is a verse from "Clarity," a poem I wrote on the occasion of the birth of my first child, Leo, in 1999.

> How is it that from this grotesque display
> of sight and sound, smell and touch
> concrete as weary hands and tears and blood-splattered shoes
> comes beauty so ineffable that the heart stops in awe and adoration
> of the primordial breath of Spirit over the abyss?

My shoes really did have blood on them. I wore them, still dazed, to the local restaurant to pick up the steak dinner my ravenous wife requested after the delivery. (To my amazement she ate every bite, while Leo slept soundly next to her in bed). And for years I continued to wear them, bearing these ineffable marks, while working around the house and the yard.

Most times this was an unconscious thing, but once in a while, in the midst of raking leaves or taking out the trash, I would look down and notice and remember, and be stunned once again.

I don't deny that I often envy my bachelor colleagues who can retire to quiet homes after a long day at work, and spend the rest of the evening reading their favorite books or developing a talent or hobby. My latest talent is that I can get five children tucked in bed, with teeth brushed, pajamas on, and spirits more or less settled for rest, in under five minutes. And yet it has become evident to me beyond doubt, precisely in the midst of these labors, that this is my vocation. This is how I expressed it to my wife:

REAL LOVE (2006)

When I am overwhelmed by the thickness of the world
I understand why God chose this life for me
Because I don't paint pictures I write poems
Because I don't eat chocolate I drink gin
Because I don't read history I study mythology
Because I don't tell jokes I listen to music
And soon I find myself grasping, desperately.
Then I return:
to the smell of Emil's diaper,
Helen is in despair (her baby is cold),
Leo can't get his Lego car to work (the wheel keeps coming off)
And dinner isn't ready, you tell me,
All at once
I am grateful for you, beyond words,
Beyond all reckoning, for your splendor
And your solidity.
Zossima was right: Love in reality,
compared to love in dreams,
Is a harsh and terrible thing.
So be it! So be it!

TRANSFORMATIONAL MARRIAGE

I once had a disagreement with a colleague who was an economist. His daughter had recently been married, and though he liked the young man well enough, he told me that he had advised his daughter always to keep her job, "just in case." While lifelong marriage is fine when you can get it, he told me, it is foolish and naïve to trust in it overmuch.

On the contrary, I argued, a withholding of trust in the initial promise strikes at the very root of what a marriage *is*. There is a difference in kind, and not merely in degree, between a relationship rooted in an unconditional pledge of fidelity and a relationship with an exit strategy.

This is not merely a philosophical distinction; it has incredible consequences for human experience. Marriage is not a contract—or at least it is not like any other contract—for it establishes a community that, in turn, transforms the individuals that comprise it. Wendell Berry makes the point beautifully in his novella *Remembering,* when he describes the marriage between Andy and Flora Catlett:

> They were two longing to be one, or one dividing relentlessly into two. . . . It was as though grace and peace were bestowed on them out of the sanctity of marriage itself, which simply furnished them to one another, free and sufficient as rain to leaf. It was as if they were not making marriage, but being made by it, and, while it held them, time and their lives flowed over them, like swift water over stones, rubbing them together, grinding off their edges, making them fit together, fit to be together, in the only way that fragments can be rejoined.

UNIQUELY ORDINARY

The romance of domesticity must be rooted in a culture that nurtures our ability to experience wonder in the ordinary. In the end, however, this romance cannot be completely borrowed. Every *domus,* like every person, involves a singular and deeply personal encounter with the divine that must be cultivated on its own terms. Only from the heart of this encounter will come the new "epiphanies of beauty" called for by Pope John Paul II in his *Letter to Artists.* If such epiphanies cannot quite "save the world," at least they may save a few from the fate of Emma Bovary.

This article is adapted from a "Last Day Lecture" delivered at Hillsdale College on December 4, 2009. Reprinted from Touchstone: A Journal of Mere Christianity, *January/ February 2011, Volume 24, Number 1.*

ACKNOWLEDGEMENTS

First and foremost, I wish to thank Leon and Maidie Podles for their generous financial support, which, beginning in 1997, enabled *Touchstone* to become a bi-monthly and significantly grow in circulation. Their support was an answer to prayer.

I am also indebted both to those men who joined *Touchstone* prior to 1998 to form a de facto editorial board—Thomas Buchanan, James Hitchcock, S. M. Hutchens, David Mills, Leon Podles, and Fr. Patrick Henry Reardon—and to those who joined in the years following—Robert P. George, Wilfred McClay, Russell Moore, Anthony Esolen, and Allan Carlson. I have learned much from these colleagues and brothers in Christ.

I also wish to recognize my associate editor, Anita Kuhn, who joined *Touchstone* in 1998, for her editorial management and excellent editing. And also Jerry Janquart, our art director and web developer, who joined *Touchstone* in 2004. I am grateful to both for their hard work, dedication, and consistent encouragement.

Many thanks are also due to our many devoted readers, donors, and stalwart friends who have supported, encouraged, or volunteered their services to assist and sustain the ministry of *Touchstone*.

Most of all, I thank my wife, Patricia, who, in addition to copyediting, mailings, correspondence, customer service, and marketing at conferences over the past thirty years, has borne the burden of my absences when travel was particularly helpful in developing the journal and when hours of work on weekends and evenings were required. Without her support and encouragement, you would not be holding this book.

CONTRIBUTORS

THOMAS S. BUCHANAN ("A Cardinal Virtue Quartet," p. 47), senior editor. He is the George W. Laird Professor of Mechanical Engineering and Biomedical Engineering at the University of Delaware. He has served as president of the American Society of Biomechanics and editor-in-chief of the *Journal of Applied Biomechanics*. He is on the Board of Trustees of Saint Katherine College and on the Board of Directors of the Fellowship of St. James. He began writing for *Touchstone* in 1987 and wrote a regular column, "Practical Christianity," from 1993 through 2004. He is a member of the Orthodox Church and lives in Chester County, Pennsylvania, with his wife. They have three adult children.

ALLAN CARLSON ("Children of the Reformation," p. 139), senior editor. He is the President emeritus and founder of the Howard Center for Family, Religion, and Society in Rockford, Illinois, where he serves as editor of *The Natural Family: An International Journal of Research and Policy*. Among his books are *Family Cycles: Strength, Decline & Renewal in American Domestic Life, 1630–2000* and *Conjugal America: On the Public Purpose of Marriage*. He has been published in *The Washington Post, New Oxford Review, Intercollegiate Review, University Bookman, Communio, Chesterton Review,* and *Wall Street Journal*. He is a Lutheran and lives with his wife on a farm near Rockford, Illinois.

ROD DREHER ("The Godless Party," p. 79), contributing editor. He is a senior editor and blogger at the *American Conservative* and author of *How Dante Can Save Your Life: The Life-Changing Wisdom of History's Greatest Poem, The Benedict Option: A Strategy for Christians in a Post-Christian Nation,* and *Live Not by Lies: A Survival Manual for Christian Dissidents*. He has written and edited for the *New York Post, The Dallas Morning News, National Review,* the *Washington Times,* and the *Baton Rouge Advocate*. His commentary has appeared in *The Wall Street Journal, Commentary, The Weekly Standard,* among other publications. He is Eastern Orthodox and lives with his wife in Baton Rouge, Louisiana.

ANTHONY ESOLEN ("A Requiem for Friendship," p. 104), senior editor. He is a professor and writer-in-residence at Magdalen College of the Liberal Arts in

Warner, New Hampshire. His many books include *Life Under Compulsion: Ten Ways to Destroy the Humanity of Your Child, Out of the Ashes: Rebuilding American Culture, The Hundredfold: Songs for the Lord,* and *Sex in the Unreal City: The Demolition of the Western Mind.* He is a regular contributor to *Chronicles, Crisis Magazine, The Claremont Review, Inside the Vatican, The Catholic Thing,* and *American Greatness.* He has translated Dante's *Divine Comedy.* He is a Roman Catholic and lives with his wife in New Hampshire.

ROBERT P. GEORGE ("Disinheriting the Wind," p. 17), senior editor. He is the McCormick Professor of Jurisprudence at Princeton University and the director of Princeton's James Madison Program in American Ideals and Institutions. He is a senior fellow at the Witherspoon Institute. His books include *Conscience and Its Enemies: Confronting the Dogmas of Liberal Secularism, Embryo: A Defense of Human Life, The Clash of Orthodoxies: Law, Religion, and Morality in Crisis, Making Men Moral: Civil Liberties and Public Morality,* and *What is Marriage? Man and Woman: A Defense.* His writings have been widely published. He lives in Princeton, New Jersey, with his wife. They have two adult children.

JAMES HITCHCOCK ("Things Hidden Since the Beginning of the World," p. 60), senior editor. He is professor of history emeritus at St. Louis University. He is a founding board member of the Fellowship of Catholic Scholars. His books include *What is Secular Humanism?, Recovery of the Sacred, Catholicism & Modernity: Confrontation or Capitulation?, The Supreme Court and Religion in American Life* (2-vols), and *The History of the Catholic Church: From Apostolic Times to the Third Millennium.* He has written for many periodicals, including *Crisis, Catholic World Report, Human Life Review,* and *National Catholic Register.* He and the late Helen Hull Hitchcock raised four daughters; he lives in St. Louis.

S. M. HUTCHENS ("The Fairy-Tale God," p. 8), senior editor, has been writing for *Touchstone* for more than thirty years. He also has served as Chairman of the Board of the Fellowship of St. James. He received a Th.D. under the supervision of Carl E. Braaten with a dissertation on the epistemologies of Karl Barth and Carl F. H. Henry. Until his retirement in 2015, he served as a public librarian in Kenosha, Wisconsin. His writing has also appeared in *The New Oxford Review, The Congregationalist, The Southern Baptist Journal of Theology, The Religion and Society Report, The Evangelical Catholic, Sursum Corda, Books and*

Culture, and *The New Atlantis.* He and his wife Mary live in Racine, Wisconsin, and are the parents of two daughters.

JAMES M. KUSHINER ("Terror & the Last Enemy," p. 128), executive editor and executive director of the Fellowship of St. James since 1992. He is also executive editor and co-founder of *Salvo Magazine.* He co-edited *Signs of Intelligence: Understanding Intelligent Design* and edited *Creed & Culture: A* Touchstone *Reader.* He writes a weekly on-line column, "Friday Reflections," for the Fellowship of St. James. He and his wife, Patricia, are members of All Saints Antiochian Orthodox Church and live in Chicago where they raised six children. They have 16 grandchildren.

WILFRED M. MCCLAY ("Mastery's Shadow," p. 53) is Professor of History at Hillsdale College. His most recent book, *Land of Hope: An Invitation to the Great American Story,* won the 2020 Henry and Anne Paolucci Prize of the Intercollegiate Studies Institute. Among his other books are *The Masterless: Self and Society in Modern America, The Student's Guide to U.S. History, Religion Returns to the Public Square: Faith and Policy in America, Figures in the Carpet: Finding the Human Person in the American Past,* and *Why Place Matters: Geography, Identity, and Public Life in Modern America.* He is a past member of the editorial board of *Touchstone,* and worships at Holy Trinity Anglican Parish in Hillsdale, Michigan.

RUSSELL D. MOORE ("Above Every Name," p. 152) served as senior editor from 2006 until 2021 when, after serving eight years as the President of the Ethics and Religious Liberty Commission of the Southern Baptist Convention, he became director of the Christianity Today Public Theology Project. His books include *Adopted for Life: The Priority of Adoption for Christian Families and Churches, The Storm-Tossed Family: How the Cross Reshapes the Home, Onward: Engaging the Culture Without Losing the Gospel,* and *The Courage to Stand: Facing Your Fear Without Losing Your Soul.* His numerous articles have been published widely. He lives with his wife and their five children in Nashville, Tennessee.

DAVID MILLS ("Bad Books for Kids," p. 157) served as senior editor until 2003 and editor from 2003–2008. He was also editor of the *Evangelical Catholic, Mission & Ministry,* and executive editor of *First Things.* He is a senior editor of The Stream, editorial director for Ethika Politika, and columnist for Aleteia, the *New*

Oxford Review, and several other Catholic publications, including *Crisis.* His books include *The Pilgrim's Guide: C. S. Lewis and the Art of Witness, The Saints' Guide to Knowing the Real Jesus,* and *Discovering Mary: Answers to Questions About the Mother of God.* He and his wife are members of the Roman Catholic Church, have four children, and live in Pennsylvania.

DOUGLAS FARROW ("The Audacity of the State," p. 168) is Professor of Christian Thought at McGill University in Montreal, Québec. His books include *1 & 2 Thessalonians: Brazos Theological Commentary on the Bible, Theological Negotiations: Proposals in Soteriology and Anthropology, Desiring a Better Country: Forays in Political Theology, Ascension Theology,* and *Nation of Bastards: Essays on the End of Marriage.* His reviews and articles have appeared in *Pro Ecclesia, First Things, Nova et Vetera, The Tablet, Theology Today, Communio,* and the *International Journal of Systematic Theology.* He and his wife are Roman Catholics, have five children, and live in Montreal.

LEON J. PODLES ("Missing Fathers of the Church," p. 32), senior editor. He holds a Ph.D. in Old English and Old Icelandic from the University of Virginia and worked for many years as a federal investigator. He is the author of *The Church Impotent: The Feminization of Christianity, Sacrilege: Sexual Abuse in the Catholic Church,* and *Losing the Good Portion: Why Men Are Alienated from Christianity.* In addition to his *Touchstone* column ("The Matter at Hand") and articles, he has written for *America, The American Spectator, Crisis,* and *The Antioch Review.* He lives with his wife in Baltimore, Maryland, where they attend an Anglican Rite Catholic Church. They have six children and four grandchildren.

NATHAN SCHLUETER ("The Romance of Domesticity," p. 183) is Professor of Philosophy and Religion at Hillsdale College. Nathan has been a fellow of the National Endowment for the Humanities and Princeton's James Madison Program. He is the author of *One Dream or Two? Justice in America and in the Thought of Martin Luther King, Jr.,* co-editor of *The Humane Vision of Wendell Berry,* and co-author of *Selfish Libertarians and Socialist Conservatives: The Foundations of the Libertarian-Conservative Debate.* His articles have appeared in *First Things, Logos, Communio, Public Discourse* and *Perspectives in Political Science.* He and his wife live in Hillsdale with their eight children.

PATRICK HENRY REARDON ("The Agony of Gethsemane," p. 117), senior editor. He is pastor emeritus of All Saints Orthodox Church in Chicago, Illinois. His "As It Is Written" column has appeared in *Touchstone* since 2001. His biblical commentaries include *Christ and the Psalms, Christ in His Saints, Creation & the Patriarchal Histories* (Genesis), *Out of Step with God* (Numbers), *The Trial of Job, Chronicles of History and Worship* (Chronicles), *Wise Lives* (The Wisdom of Sirach), *Romans,* and *Revelation: A Liturgical Prophecy.* His theological work has been published widely and includes the first volume of a trilogy, *Reclaiming the Atonement: The Incarnation.* He lives in Chicago with his wife, Denise.

WILLIAM J. TIGHE ("Calculating Christmas," p. 88), senior editor. He is Professor of History at Muhlenberg College in Allentown, Pennsylvania, where he has taught since 1986. His academic specialization is in 15th to 17th Century British History. He began writing for *Touchstone* in 1998 and is also a contributing editor for the journal *New Oxford Review.* He is a member of the St. Josaphat Ukrainian Catholic Church in Bethlehem, Pennsylvania. He and his wife Silvija live in Allentown, Pennsylvania and are the parents of three adult children.

ROBERT LOUIS WILKEN ("Prayer & the Work of God," p. 1) is William R. Kenan, Jr., Professor of the History of Christianity Emeritus, University of Virginia, and Chairman of the Board of the Institute on Religion and Public Life, publisher of *First Things.* He is the author of many books, including *The Christians as the Romans Saw Them, Remembering the Christian Past, The Spirit of Early Christian Thought: Seeking the Face of God,* and *The First Thousand Years: A Global History of Christianity.* Periodicals in which his articles have appeared include *America, Christian Century, Christianity Today, Church History, Commonweal, New York Times Book Review,* and *Theological Studies.*

JONATHAN WITT ("The Gods Must Be Tidy!" p. 93) is a senior fellow with the Discovery Institute's Center for Science and Culture. His books include *Heretic: One Scientist's Journey from Darwin to Design,* with Matti Lesiola, *The Hobbit Party: The Vision of Freedom that Tolkien Got, and the West Forgot,* with Jay Richards, and *A Meaningful World: How Arts and Sciences Reveal the Genius of Nature,* with Benjamin Wiker. His articles have appeared in numerous venues, including *The American Spectator, Crisis, Philosophia Christi, The Flannery O'Connor Bulletin, Salvo, The Stream,* and *Literature and Theology* (Oxford). He and his wife, Amanda, live in Denton, Texas.

INDEX